Constitutional
Development
in the Commonwealth
Caribbean

Constitutional
Development
in the Commonwealth
Caribbean

Hamid A. Ghany

IAN RANDLE PUBLISHERS
Kingston • Miami

First published in Jamaica, 2018 by
Ian Randle Publishers
16 Herb McKenley Drive
Box 686
Kingston 6, Jamaica W.I.
www.ianrandlepublishers.com

ISBN: 978-976-637-959-9

National Library of Jamaica Cataloguing-In-Publication Data

Ghany, Hamid A.
  Constitutional development in the Commonwealth Caribbean /
Hamid A. Ghany.

  p. ; cm
Bibliography: p. – Includes index.
ISBN 978-976-637-959-9 (pbk)

1. Constitutional history – West Indies, British
2. Constitutional history – Caribbean, English-speaking
3. Caribbean, English-speaking – Politics and government
I. Title

342.729   dc 23

Cover and book design by Ian Randle Publishers

Printed and bound in the United States of America

Contents

Introduction

> ...(I)t is widely supposed that British policy, if it has ever had any long term aims at all, has throughout the centuries of imperial rule – "the Commonwealth experience" – been at pains to establish, even to impose, in the dependencies of the Crown, a Westminster model, irrespective of local wish or circumstance: that the Mother of Parliaments was concerned to spawn a brood of little Westminsters and to export them to the colonies. Though this is the common currency of contemporary British politicians, and of British schoolmasters, it seems on investigation to be substantially quite untrue.[1]

This quotation summarizes the essence of the creation of the constitutional systems of government in the Commonwealth Caribbean. While A.F. Madden devotes the thrust of his article to disproving the thesis that the British government ever had any intention of establishing the Westminster model overseas, he fails to address the reality of what was erected for the ex-colonies at their independence by Britain.

On closer examination, it appears that a completely unique system of government was introduced. The identification and description of that unique system of government and the legislative institutions that were created and subsequently retained disprove the theory of the transfer of the Westminster model to the Commonwealth Caribbean. Indeed, it confirms the existence of an evolved system of government whose roots can be traced to the British imperial dominance of what was once called the 'British West Indies'.

The independent territories of the Commonwealth Caribbean and their years of independence, at the time of writing, are as follows:

Jamaica (1962); Trinidad and Tobago (1962); Guyana (1966); Barbados (1966); the Bahamas (1973); Grenada (1974); Dominica (1978); St Lucia (1979); St Vincent and the Grenadines (1979); Antigua and Barbuda (1981); Belize (1981); and St Kitts and Nevis (1983).

The Whitehall Model

The Whitehall model represents the systems of government that were established in the Commonwealth Caribbean after various territories gained independence from Great Britain. While the title was given to these systems of government by Leslie Wolf-Phillips,[2] the structure was further researched by the author for his doctoral dissertation at the London School of Economics and Political Science.[3]

There are essentially five major tenets of the Whitehall model that best describe its core characteristics:

> (1) the inclusion of a Bill of Rights in the Constitution; (2) a unique bicameral system in eight of the 12 independent countries; (3) a more rigid enforcement of the separation of powers that pre-dated the Westminster alterations of 1999–2009; (4) the written interpretation of many unwritten Westminster constitutional conventions that pre-dated the reforms of 1999–2011; and (5) the entrenchment of constitutional provisions.

These characteristics have undergone some changes between 1987, when they were first articulated, and today in their revised format. The separation of powers in the United Kingdom (UK) under the Westminster model has come closer to what exists in the Commonwealth Caribbean by virtue of the reforms to the position of lord chancellor in 2005, undertaken in the Constitutional Reform Act 2005,[4] while the introduction of the UK Supreme Court in 2009, based on part 3 of the provisions of the said Constitutional Reform Act 2005, has removed from the House of Lords the dual role of being a legislative body as well as a court. The final separation of the UK Supreme Court and the House of Lords came on October 1, 2009, and ushered in a new era for the Westminster model that would make it more akin to the Whitehall model, with the separation of powers, that had existed in the Commonwealth Caribbean since the arrival of independence. The only overlap between the branches of government is now to be found in the requirement for a parliamentary system of government whereby the executive branch is drawn from the legislature.

Another area of change lies in the abolition of the power of dissolution of Parliament in the Westminster model in the UK by virtue of the provisions of the Fixed-term Parliaments Act 2011.[5] This has removed one of the more significant constitutional conventions by which the Westminster system of government in the UK had operated and placed it in the domain of statutes subject to further amendment at a future date. The correlation with the Commonwealth Caribbean lay with the issue of dual interpretations of the prior convention in the UK whereby it had been felt, on the one hand, that the dissolution of Parliament was done on a compliant basis by the monarch at the request of the prime minister, while, on the other hand, there was another school of thought that argued that the monarch had a residual power of refusal in respect of any prime ministerial request for a dissolution of Parliament.

The Westminster Model

Before embarking on any further discussion of the Whitehall model, it will be useful to establish the basic parameters of the Westminster model in order to fully appreciate the nature of the Whitehall differences which will lead us to a 'Westminster–Whitehall' classification.

The Westminster model has been described as:

> ...a constitutional system in which the head of state is not the effective head of government; in which the effective head of government is a Prime Minister presiding over a Cabinet composed of Ministers over whose appointment and removal he has at least a substantial measure of control; in which the effective executive branch of government is parliamentary in as much as Ministers must be members of the legislature; and in which Ministers are collectively and individually responsible to a freely elected and representative legislature.[6]

This definition, as S.A. de Smith rightly confesses, is a narrow one. It is narrow because it emphasizes the executive and legislative branches of government to the exclusion of the role, powers, duties, and functions of the judiciary. The definition is apt only as far as it goes, which confirms the need for a broader definition, particularly in the Commonwealth Caribbean, as well as the renaming of the model. However, it is an appropriate definition for executive–legislature relations in Commonwealth Caribbean countries that were accessing their independence in the 1960s using a model that bore striking resemblance to this definition offered by de Smith.

However, it is necessary to comment on the absence of the judiciary from the definition in the context of the emerging Commonwealth Caribbean countries whose new constitutions carved an important role for the judiciary. The presence of a Bill of Rights in the Constitution and the consequent power of redress held by the citizen against the state, coupled with other significant provisions, have made the judiciary in the Commonwealth Caribbean far too important for an exercise in redefinition and remodelling to be ignored.

Sacred Westminster doctrines such as the supremacy of Parliament are being challenged in the constitutions of the Commonwealth Caribbean because of the Bills of Rights. Furthermore, the spirit of the Westminster model cannot comfortably settle itself in the Commonwealth Caribbean because of substantial parliamentary and procedural differences in its architecture and process, more so than its symbolism. These differences have fundamentally altered the character and content of the so-called Westminster model in the Commonwealth Caribbean, to the extent that to continually refer to the model as 'the Westminster model' is a misnomer.

The idea of the Westminster model as defined by de Smith above and the export of that model as discussed by Alan Burns[7] would have suited the 1960s and early 1970s. This was an era during which many new states gained their independence from Great Britain, and the composition of the British Commonwealth assumed a greater Third World representation. It was too early to assess the impact and the significance of the constitutions that had been established in many of these new independent states, especially in the Commonwealth Caribbean whose era of independence started in 1962, with Jamaica and Trinidad and Tobago emerging out of a failed federation that was supposed to have been granted its independence on May 31, 1962, but never came to pass.

By the late 1970s, doubts about 'the Westminster model' and its export were expressed. Freddie Madden[8] rejected, in a general sense, the idea that 'the Westminster Model of Government' could be exported and established overseas. In fact, Madden argued that it was never the intention of British colonial administrators to export 'the Westminster Model' in its purest form. According to him, 'the only true Westminster model remained inevitably at home in Westminster: it was not intended for export, but was strictly 'to be consumed only on the premises'.[9]

This argument, therefore, begs the question: If the Westminster model was not exported, then what was, if anything at all? Madden does not answer this question but makes a curious assertion. According to him:

> Canadians, Australians and Indians made constitutions which they believed would last. The new generation of constitution makers in the 1950s and 1960s were not concerned with creating a permanent instrument for government so much as a device for securing independence which could be altered subsequently at will. Something akin to the British model might serve its temporary purpose in allaying fears in Britain about transferring power. But it remains to be proved that it is appropriate for the tasks of self-government anywhere else than in Britain.[10]

This assertion could be applied to the Commonwealth Caribbean where constitutions 'akin to the British model' have been established. Fifty-six years after the first territories in the English-speaking Caribbean gained their independence from Great Britain, only Guyana has actually undertaken any fundamental constitutional reform to the extent that their constitution can no longer be described as being 'akin to the British model'. All of the other countries have made changes that can only be described as cosmetic and, therefore, the identity of those constitutions has been preserved, thereby allowing them to still be classified as belonging to 'the Whitehall model'. Furthermore, the procedures of entrenchment of the provisions of these constitutions have made them secure from being 'altered subsequently at will'.

Major formal-legal initiatives for constitutional reform were undertaken in St Vincent and the Grenadines in 2009 and in Grenada in 2016, and both efforts were roundly rejected by their respective electorates in accordance with their constitutional provisions for post-parliamentary validation or rejection through the use of referenda.

This 'Whitehall model' that was named by L.A. Wolf-Phillips[11] bears no relation to the Whitehall model advocated by A. Birch,[12] which stresses the importance of the Crown in the British constitution and places less emphasis on the role and importance of Parliament. Birch's Whitehall model relates to the UK, while Wolf-Phillips's Whitehall model relates to the Commonwealth Caribbean.

Nevertheless, the argument put forward by Birch reveals a disagreement about the concept of the Westminster model in the UK itself. In these circumstances, the Whitehall model overseas reflects the input of the Colonial Office and civil servants in Whitehall (hence the name) in the drafting of independence constitutions with the input of local and other colonial precedents and also agreements brokered by Colonial Office officials at constitutional conferences. However, this exercise was not completely one-sided from the point of view of the recipients.

The acceptance of the Whitehall model in the Commonwealth Caribbean reveals a high degree of reverence for British-inspired constitutional technique. This can be accounted for in terms of the fact that the political elites of the Commonwealth Caribbean were brought up under an English-influenced educational system, while those who went abroad to study invariably went to England. Many of them became barristers-at-law of the four Inns of Court or solicitors of the Law Society.

Furthermore, the experiences of British colonialism would not have exposed these elites or the wider society to any other type of constitutional formula, apart from the British Constitution and the evolved constitutional provisions in each colony.

There is another dimension to this phenomenon, and it relates to the heritage of the Commonwealth Caribbean and its society. This society today is an essentially immigrant one and bears no relation to its indigenous inhabitants whose population size is now miniscule. Everyone in the Commonwealth Caribbean, with a few exceptions, can trace their heritage to somewhere else. This lack of an indigenous base has had an impact on an acceptance of, and reverence for, British institutions.

This phenomenon was first recognized by Major E.F.L. Wood, M.P. (later Lord Halifax) on a visit to the West Indies and British Guiana in his capacity as Parliamentary Under-Secretary of State for the Colonies in 1922. Part of Major Wood's Report read, as follows:

> The whole history of the African population of the West Indies inevitably drives them towards representative institutions fashioned after the British model. Transplanted by the slave trade or other circumstances to foreign soil, losing in the process their social system, language and traditions, and with the exception of some relics of obeah, whatever religion they may have had, they owe everything that they have now, and all that they are, to the British race that first enslaved them, and subsequently to its honour restored to them their freedom. Small wonder if they look for political growth to the only source and pattern that they know, and aspire to share in what has been the peculiarly British gift of representative institutions.[13]

The perception of Major Wood some 40 years before the first territories of the English-speaking Caribbean were granted their independence was grounded in a superiority complex that was based on the premise that slavery stripped the African population in the West Indies of their identity and connection to their own social and cultural systems and values, which were replaced by British ones. Indeed, all of the independent countries of the Commonwealth Caribbean have aspired to, and retained, the Whitehall model with the exception of Guyana. It is in this context that one can understand the constitutional thinking of one of the foremost scholars and politicians of the English-speaking Caribbean, Dr Eric Williams, who was later to become, at first, the chief minister, then the premier, and subsequently the prime minister as Trinidad and Tobago progressed towards its independence from Great Britain. In an address to a public meeting, about 14 months before he became chief minister, in Port of Spain, Trinidad, on July 19, 1955 Williams said: 'The Colonial Office does not need to examine its second hand colonial constitutions. It has a constitution at hand which it can apply immediately to Trinidad and Tobago. That is the British Constitution.'[14]

He went further in the same meeting to reinforce this point:

> Ladies and Gentlemen, I suggest to you that the time has come when the British Constitution, suitably modified, can be applied to Trinidad and

Tobago. After all, if the British Constitution is good enough for Great Britain, it should be good enough for Trinidad and Tobago.[15]

Williams's rationale reinforced the views of Major Wood, expressed in 1922, because there was clear validation for the importation of the British Constitution, suitably modified on the basis that if it was 'good enough for Great Britain, it should be good enough for Trinidad and Tobago'. At no time did Williams suggest an alternative approach to constitutional development. He was simply prepared to imitate, as far as possible, the British model.

The views Williams expressed openly contradict the intellectual line of argument that he developed in his famous work *Capitalism and Slavery* in which he challenged the foundations upon which the philosophy of British trusteeship in the West Indies had been built.

His central thesis was that the British government had not abolished slavery and the slave trade for humanitarian reasons, but rather for economic reasons because the sugar industry was no longer economically profitable in this region for them. According to him, '…the issues were not only the inhumanity of West Indian slavery, but the unprofitableness of West Indian monopoly'.[16]

The humanitarian argument had provided a view that British imperial policy could have been swayed by moral and humanitarian appeals to put an end to inequality, injustice, and exploitation that were the hallmarks of the colonial state. As a consequence, continued British trusteeship in the West Indies could, therefore, be trusted because of its genuine concern for the upliftment of the West Indian person, which was the line of argument adopted by Major Wood.

Williams's argument challenged all of that. However, his view of the British system of government can be seen as a contradiction of his views on British trusteeship and the end product of that trusteeship which was fully responsible status otherwise known as independence, with constitutional arrangements that reflected a 'suitably modified' version of the British Constitution.

Williams's advocacy of the British Constitution in a suitably modified format was his way of saying that the British constitutional formula was one that we could adopt as our own because we did not have an indigenous system of government.

Indeed, his entire stewardship as chief minister, premier and prime minister of Trinidad and Tobago represented a defence of the British Constitution suitably modified and when the greatest opportunity of all presented itself for constitution reform in 1971 when his People's National

Movement (PNM) won all of the seats in the general election, he adopted the approach of engaging in a further suitable modification of the existing constitution, which was already a suitably modified version of the British Constitution.

However, there is a clear contrast to Williams's view that was expressed by the former Jamaican premier, Norman Manley, at the time of Jamaica's deliberations on its independence.

Speaking in the Jamaican House of Representatives on the subject of a new Constitution for an independent Jamaica, Manley stated:

> Let us not make the mistake of describing as colonial, institutions which are part and parcel of the heritage of this country. If we have any confidence in our own individuality and our own personality we would absorb these things and incorporate them into our being and turn them to our own use as part of the heritage we are not ashamed of.[17]

Norman Manley was not speaking about importing the British constitution and converting it into local usage in the way that Williams had advocated, but rather he was urging that the existing institutions of the colonial era, which evolved as part of Jamaica's development, should not be regarded as colonial, but rather as indigenous.

His point of view also challenged the opinions of Major Wood insofar as he seemed to have been rejecting the notion of not having 'social system, language and traditions' of their own as expressed by Major Wood in his 1922 report. Indeed, Manley was asserting that Jamaica has a 'heritage' of which it was not 'ashamed'.

It is in this context that the Whitehall model must be viewed. That is to say, that it consists, on the one hand, of the British Constitution 'suitably modified' (according to Williams) or something 'akin to the British model' (according to Madden), while on the other hand, it consists of something that is part of 'the heritage' of the region. However viewed, there seems to be ample evidence to show that the Westminster model was not exported or transplanted to the Commonwealth Caribbean and that colonial evolution along a pathway to eventual independence is perhaps the stronger argument.

There can be no doubt that constitutions in the Commonwealth Caribbean are a blend of the pure Westminster model that was designed for 'consumption on the premises only', according to Madden, or the 'British constitution suitably modified' of which Williams spoke, together with the evolved constitutional formulae that comprised the 'heritage' of which Manley spoke.

To this end, it might be better to speak of a Westminster–Whitehall model to capture adequately this blend of narratives that comprise the essence of a model of governance that is uniquely West Indian in its composition. However, the underlying expressions of adulation for the British Crown and British honours that underpin these narratives cannot be ignored.

The knighthood is regarded as the gold standard of Commonwealth Caribbean public affairs accomplishment, while membership of Her Majesty's Privy Council and the accompanying title of 'The Right Honourable' is a cherished symbol of Commonwealth Caribbean judicial and political achievement.

When Major Wood spoke about the process of 'losing in the process their social system, language and traditions', he recognized a fundamental aspect of the psychological impact of slavery and the slave trade upon the population of the Commonwealth Caribbean today. The reverence for the British honours system can be linked directly to this phenomenon and indeed can explain the persistence of the Westminster–Whitehall model in the region.

Apart from the Eric Williams statement about suitably modifying the British Constitution for use in Trinidad and Tobago, there was also another current of thought that influenced constitution-makers in the Commonwealth Caribbean, which was copying the words of other independence constitutions created by the Colonial Office for other newly independent territories.

An example of this can be gleaned from the architect of Trinidad and Tobago's 1962 independence Constitution, Sir Ellis Clarke. In an explanatory memorandum on the draft independence constitution for Trinidad and Tobago dated April 16, 1962, Clarke had this to say about the provisions created for the tenure of office of judges:

> Perhaps the most important single feature which goes to ensure the independence of the Judiciary and the attraction to the Judiciary of the right type of Judge is the security of tenure afforded to Judges. For that reason no attempt has been made in the draft Constitution to be original. A formula, carefully devised by the Colonial Office after many years as being the most likely to be effective and acceptable and yet not to derogate from the principles of independence, has been adopted. It is word for word the formula that the Colonial Office was able to persuade Nigeria, Sierra Leone and Tanganyika to accept. There can be little doubt that it is what they would wish Trinidad and Tobago to accept.[18]

Ellis Clarke reveals that the provisions regarding the tenure of office of judges in the Trinidad and Tobago independence Constitution were lifted word-for-word from the independence constitutions of Nigeria (1960), Sierra Leone (1961), and the then state of Tanganyika (1961), which later became Tanzania. He, like Eric Williams, was confident that the population of Trinidad and Tobago would accept what the Colonial Office, he presumed, would want Trinidad and Tobago to accept.

These provisions were essentially retained in the 1976 Republican Constitution as the president has been substituted for the governor general. Their intent, as devised by the Colonial Office in the 1960s, has never been changed.

It is this line of thought that has contributed to the persistence of the Westminster model in the Commonwealth Caribbean. Indeed, at the end of the Conference on the Closer Association of the British West Indian Colonies held in Montego Bay in September 1947, the following resolution was unanimously passed:

> 16. Mr. H.A. Cuke, O.B.E. of Barbados, then asked permission, as a representative of the oldest of the British Caribbean Colonies, to move the following resolution, which was seconded by Mr. F.A. Pixley of Jamaica, as members of the Conference rising to their feet while recording their unanimous agreement:-
>
> RESOLUTION 15
>
> RESOLVED:
>
> That this Conference humbly affirms its loyalty and allegiance to the Person and Throne of His Most Gracious Majesty King George the Sixth, and that the terms of this resolution be conveyed to the Secretary of State for the Colonies for transmission to His Majesty.[19]

It was this allegiance and loyalty to the British Crown that pervaded the constitutional discussions for a Federation of the West Indies in 1947 that has persisted in many respects in the Commonwealth Caribbean for over 70 years that explains the persistence of the Westminster model and the fascination with the British honours system.

Major Wood may have been controversial in 1922, but there is much to unlock in his controversial theory which may contribute to the persistence of the Westminster model long after independence first came to the Commonwealth Caribbean in 1962.

In 2014, Trinidad and Tobago attempted to reform its Constitution by changing its electoral system from the first-past-the-post system to the second ballot runoff system. There was fierce resistance to this measure from the then opposition. The essence of the argument against the runoff system was best captured by then Opposition MP Colm Imbert when he said:

> And the countries that have it like France, they have a presidential system, Mr. Speaker, they follow the Napoleonic Code. Their laws are not based on English common law. It is a completely different system. [Interruption] Yes, the entire court system, the judicial system, the administration of justice, they are based on that Napoleonic Code, completely different to our English common law system.[20]

In 1947, there was clear evidence of loyalty to the British Crown as part of the emerging independence movement. In 2014, there is evidence of reverence for English common law as a reason not to make any amendment to the Constitution.

It is at this point that the fundamental tenets of the Westminster–Whitehall model in the Commonwealth Caribbean must be highlighted. Unlike the Westminster model in the UK, all of the constitutions in the Commonwealth Caribbean are written.

The Fundamental Tenets of the Westminster–Whitehall Model

1. The Bill of Rights

The first of the fundamental tenets of the Westminster–Whitehall model is the inclusion of a Bill of Rights in the constitutions of the independent countries of the Commonwealth Caribbean. This affords the citizen the power to seek redress for any infringement of his/her constitutional rights through the use of the court system. The inclusion of a Bill of Rights that recognizes and protects the fundamental human rights and freedoms of the individual does not exist in the constitutional formulae at Westminster in a written constitution. All of the independent territories of the Commonwealth Caribbean have Bills of Rights, which are enshrined and protected in their constitutions.

This is a major departure from Westminster tradition on two counts: firstly, the existence of a written Constitution, and, secondly, the declaration, recognition, and guaranteed protection of fundamental human rights and freedoms. Most of these independent territories have essentially followed a suitably amended format of the European Convention for the Protection of Human Rights and Fundamental Freedoms[21] for inclusion in their constitutions. This Convention was drawn up by the Council of Europe in 1950 and ratified in 1953. Trinidad and Tobago is the only exception having copied the formula of the Canadian Bill of Rights 1960[22] for inclusion in its Constitution.

Regardless of the formula used, the direct effect of the inclusion of a Bill of Rights in Commonwealth Caribbean constitutions is the diminishing of the effect of the Westminster doctrine of the supremacy of Parliament. This can be clearly seen, for example, in the Constitution of Antigua and Barbuda: 'Except as is otherwise expressly provided in this Constitution, no law may abrogate, abridge or infringe or authorize the abrogation, abridgement or infringement of any of the fundamental rights and freedoms of the individual hereinbefore recognised and declared.'[23]

Not only does the human rights chapter place limits on the Westminster doctrine of the supremacy of Parliament in the Commonwealth Caribbean, it also places constraints on executive action in the following way:

> If any person alleges that any of the provisions of section 3 to 17 (inclusive) of this Constitution has been, is being or is likely to be contravened in relation to him (or, in the case of a person who is detained, if any other person alleges such a contravention in relation to the detained person), then, without prejudice to any other action with respect to the same matter that is lawfully available, that person (or that other person) may apply to the High Court for redress.[24]

Needless to say, none of this existed at Westminster between 1962 and 1983, which covered the period of independence for the 12 independent countries of the Commonwealth Caribbean, starting with Jamaica in 1962 and ending with St Kitts and Nevis in 1983. It was not until 1998 that the Human Rights Act[25] was enacted in the UK to give effect to the declaration, recognition, and protection of fundamental human rights and freedoms of the European Convention on Human Rights to which it was a signatory on November 4, 1950.

Indeed, the whole character of the constitutions in the Commonwealth Caribbean is fundamentally altered away from the Westminster model because the supremacy of Parliament is diminished and executive as well as legislative action can be challenged. Most of the Commonwealth Caribbean constitutions have essentially similar provisions that have been quoted from the Antigua and Barbuda Constitution above.

If the doctrine of the supremacy of Parliament is diminished, then there must be some other doctrine that is supreme. The supremacy of the Constitution can be recognized as the effective doctrine in lieu of the doctrine of the supremacy of Parliament. This is reinforced by the constitutions of the Commonwealth Caribbean which have clauses similar to that of Trinidad and Tobago: 'This Constitution is the supreme law of Trinidad and Tobago, and any other law that is inconsistent with this Constitution is void to the extent of the inconsistency.'[26]

This doctrine of the supremacy of the Constitution is one that is diametrically opposed to the doctrine of the supremacy of Parliament under the Westminster model. There is no Constitution to regulate the powers of Parliament at Westminster. However, under the Westminster–Whitehall model, Parliament is not supreme in the Westminster sense, because of the Constitution. In these circumstances, the supremacy of the Constitution can be considered a Westminster–Whitehall doctrine.

Perhaps, the proof of this theory lies in the fact that the existence of Parliament in the Commonwealth Caribbean is directly dependent upon the Constitution making specific provision for the existence of Parliament and also empowering Parliament at the same time. In the absence of a written Constitution, there would not be any legal or constitutional basis for Parliament to exist. This is unlike the Westminster tradition where Parliament asserted its dominance following the Glorious Revolution of 1689.[27] This Westminster doctrine of the supremacy of Parliament has become an accepted part of British constitutional theory and practice.

2. The Unique Bicameral System

The second tenet of the Westminster–Whitehall model is the unique bicameral system that is found in eight of the 12 independent countries of the Commonwealth Caribbean. The uniqueness of the bicameral system in these eight countries (Antigua and Barbuda, the Bahamas, Barbados, Belize, Grenada, Jamaica, St Lucia, and Trinidad and Tobago) is established, firstly, on the basis that there are only 18 countries in the 52-member Commonwealth of Nations that have such systems, and, secondly, the method of appointment and composition of these senates make them unique to the Commonwealth Caribbean and nowhere else.

Of these 18 countries with bicameral systems, seven of them are federations – Australia, Canada, India, Malaysia, Nigeria, Pakistan, and South Africa. Of the remaining 11 unitary states in the Commonwealth, eight are found in the Commonwealth Caribbean (listed above) and the other non-Caribbean bicameral unitary states are Lesotho, Swaziland, and the UK. In this context, it is obvious that bicameralism is quite popular in the Commonwealth Caribbean.

The other unique aspect about Commonwealth Caribbean bicameralism is that, unlike Westminster, it is based on nomination through patronage with no security of tenure. At Westminster, there are three types of peers in the House of Lords – the hereditary peers, the life peers, and the spiritual peers. In 2009, the law lords were removed and relocated in the UK Supreme Court.

The hereditary peers were previously recruited into the House of Lords on the basis of succession to title through the principle of primogeniture. However, that changed with the enactment of the House of Lords Act 1999,[28] which excluded future hereditary peers from elevation to membership of the House of Lords and restricted to 92 the voting rights of sitting hereditary peers. The life peers are appointed on the advice of the prime minister in accordance with the provisions of the Life Peerages Act 1958[29] and hold office for the duration of their lives with no rights to succession. The spiritual peers sit in the House of Lords by virtue of their senior positions in the Church of England. The law lords were previously appointed under the provisions of the Appellate Jurisdiction Act 1876[30] and they sat both as legislators and as judges, because the House of Lords was both the final court of appeal for the UK as well as a legislative body. After October 1, 2009, the House of Lords ceased to perform this judicial function upon the creation of the UK Supreme Court.

In the Commonwealth Caribbean, there has never been any duality of functions as between the Senate and the Supreme Court. Each performs different functions. Furthermore, dissolution does not affect the tenure of all peers at Westminster, whereas it affects the tenure of all Senators in the Senates of the Commonwealth Caribbean in that they vacate their seats with no guarantee of resumption by way of re-appointment.

Bicameralism has provided a way for the elected members of the former Legislative Councils of the colonial era to be separated from the nominated members who could be placed in another chamber so as to ensure the continued representation of various interests in the legislative process.

In Jamaica, the bicameral system that was introduced in 1944 with an elected House of Representatives of 32 members and a nominated Legislative Council of 15 members all appointed by the governor in his discretion was retained at independence when it was agreed that the upper house of the new Parliament would be called a Senate with a revised composition.

According to paragraphs 11 and 12 of the Report of the Jamaica Independence Conference 1962:

> 11. The existing bi-cameral form of legislature will be retained.
>
> The Senate

12. The Upper House will consist of 21 Senators of whom 13 will be appointed by the Governor-General on the advice of the Prime Minister and 8 by the Governor-General on the advice of the Leader of the Opposition. [31]

The model of the Senate introduced by Jamaica in 1962 was not followed by Trinidad and Tobago which created two competing senatorial models. The fundamental difference between them is the absence of so-called independent senators in the Jamaican model and the presence of so-called independent senators in the Trinidad and Tobago model.

In examining these models, it is important to trace their historical antecedents as the predominant model that emerged after the first two Commonwealth Caribbean countries got their independence was the one that included independent senators.

The influence for the structure of the bicameral model in the region based on a combination of government, opposition, and independent senators may be traced back to 1918 and the Conference on the Reform of the Second Chamber in the UK under the chairmanship of Lord Bryce.[32] There is a particular pathway of evolution that bicameralism has traversed historically from the Bryce Conference of 1918 through the Government of India Act 1935,[33] the 1945 Soulbury Commission in Ceylon,[34] the 1951 Waddington Commission in British Guiana,[35] and the work of Eric Williams in Trinidad and Tobago between 1955 and 1976 that provided a blueprint for the model of bicameralism adopted in the Commonwealth Caribbean with the sole exception of Jamaica.

That this format of an elected lower house and a nominated upper house has not been altered is a reflection of the persistence of the Westminster–Whitehall model in such a way as not to part with the principle of bicameralism as first established with the concurrence of the Colonial Office for independence constitutions from 1962 onwards in the Commonwealth Caribbean.

A variation of this model was adopted in Dominica, St Vincent and the Grenadines, and St Kitts and Nevis whereby elected and nominated members sit side-by-side in a unicameral Parliament. This confirms the desire for endorsing the continuation of the principle of nomination as a method of recruitment for the post-independence legislatures of the Commonwealth Caribbean.

The principle of nomination was indeed a hallmark of the Crown Colony system of government that was introduced by the British government into most of its West Indian possessions in the nineteenth century and the old Representative System before it. Despite various reforms in the twentieth century in the region, that particular method of legislative recruitment persisted into the independence era.

The only Commonwealth Caribbean country to adopt a unicameral model without the principle of nomination being retained was Guyana, which chose instead to adopt the electoral system of proportional representation based on the Hare method for the election of its 53 legislators at the time of its independence.

There is no comparison between the unicameral legislatures of the Commonwealth Caribbean and the bicameral UK Parliament, either with the principle of nomination or with the use of proportional representation.

There have been three categories of senators since the 1962 independence model of bicameralism was confirmed in Trinidad and Tobago, namely government, opposition, and independent senators. The last category owes no allegiance to any party or anyone else for that matter and can vote without supporting a party line. Apart from Jamaica and the Bahamas, all of the other independent countries of the Commonwealth Caribbean have included these three categories of senators. Jamaica does not formally include independent senators in its Senate and only has a divide between government and opposition, while the Bahamas provides for a third category of senators that is political in nature in order to guarantee the representation of other political voices outside of the government and the Opposition as determined by the governor general in his/her own discretion.

Another reason why there have not been any changes in the bicameral arrangements in the Commonwealth Caribbean can be found in the difficult procedures to be satisfied in amending these constitutions. The majority of seats won by the parties that formed the government after general elections may vary in the elected House depending on the outcome of every general election; however, there is always a fixed arithmetic in the Senate, and this means that it is not always easy for any government to acquire a special majority in that House.

Such an arrangement constitutes a permanent check and balance against abuse of parliamentary power in small legislatures where the possibility of winning all of the seats in a general election is real. At the time of writing, such a phenomenon had happened in Trinidad and Tobago (1971), Jamaica (1983), St Vincent and the Grenadines (1989), and twice in Grenada (1999 and 2013).

3. The Separation of Powers

Having identified the evolution of the unique bicameral system in the region and its sustenance, it is necessary to place the Legislature within the context of the third fundamental tenet of the Westminster–Whitehall model. That is a more rigid separation of powers than at Westminster that persisted from the independence of the first two countries in the region in August 1962 until October 2009 when the UK Supreme Court came into existence as a consequence of constitutional reforms in 2005.

The separation of powers is a feature of the system of government at Westminster; however, there was considerable overlap between the various branches of government – the executive, the legislative and the judicial. The Westminster model recognized that the dominance of the executive is dependent upon their ability to command that support of the majority of the elected members of the Legislature and whichever member of the House of Commons is able to command the support of such a majority will be appointed prime minister.

This situation is the same in the Westminster–Whitehall model. However, that is where the similarities ended up until 2009, because there were other officers and institutions that defied the separation of powers in the Westminster model. For example, the lord chancellor is appointed on the advice of the prime minister and sits in cabinet as its principal legal adviser. Previously, by virtue of his office, he was required to preside over the House of Lords (the upper house). At the same time, the lord chancellor was the head of the Judiciary under the Westminster model. He was considered the 'Trinity' of the Constitution in that he operated in total defiance of the separation of powers by performing functions in the three branches of the state.

This diluted separation of powers was a major characteristic of the Westminster model and was further reinforced by the House of Lords performing the duty of the final court of appeal for cases in the UK until 2009. The lords of appeal who sat and heard cases also belonged to the House of Lords where they sat as legislators and thereby performed dual functions.

That was not possible in any Commonwealth Caribbean country because of a rigid separation of powers between the judiciary, the executive and legislature.

There was no institutional overlap in the Westminster–Whitehall model comparable to what existed between the House of Lords as a legislative body, on the one hand, and its other role as the final court of appeal in the Westminster model, on the other hand, up until 2009. In addition, there was no equivalent of the lord chancellor in the constitutions of the Commonwealth Caribbean, and that office was subsequently joined with the position of secretary of state for Constitutional Affairs in 2003 and then joined with the new post of secretary of state for Justice in 2007 upon the abolition of the Department of Constitutional Affairs. Quite clearly, Westminster has adopted a separation of powers that is now more akin to that of the Commonwealth Caribbean insofar as the only overlap lies now with the dual membership of the prime minister and ministers in both the executive and legislative branches of government.

4. Codified Constitutional Conventions

The performance of duty under the separation of powers of the Westminster model is based on the application of unwritten constitutional conventions to constitutional behaviour in office. Under the Westminster–Whitehall model in the Commonwealth Caribbean, there has been an attempt to have these conventions written into the various constitutions. This now introduces the fourth fundamental tenet of the Whitehall model, namely constitutional conventions that are written and not left to interpretation. As a result of being written, there is a certain degree of rigidity in the interpretation of these conventions as opposed to the Westminster model where there is a high degree of flexibility owing to the fact that the conventions are unwritten. These conventions in the Whitehall model constitutions have all been copied from Westminster; however, because of different interpretations and even competing schools of thought, it is difficult to render in writing the varying effects of any unwritten convention.

Conventions in the Westminster model are central to the operation of the British Constitution. Indeed, they have been described in the following way:

> One is that conventions are what we might call the positive morality of the Constitution - the beliefs that the major participants in the political process as a matter of fact have about what is required of them. On this view the existence of a convention is a question of historical and sociological fact. The alternative possibility is that conventions are the rules that the political actors ought to feel obliged by, if they have considered the precedents and reasons correctly. This permits us to think of conventions as the critical morality of the Constitution.[36]

While there may be two views about the purpose and existence of conventions, there are some conventions that have more than one interpretation. One such was the the power of the dissolution of Parliament that was exercisable by the monarch on the advice of the prime minister before the enactment of the Fixed-term Parliaments Act 2011.[37] At least that had been the popular view, yet there were ministers in the

Westminster system who had argued that the monarch was not bound to grant a dissolution upon request by the prime minister.

For example, in 1974, there was a minority Labour government in Britain and after a few months in office there was some discussion about another general election being held to break the deadlock that existed in the House of Commons. The then leader of the House of Commons, Edward Short, told backbenchers that: 'Constitutional lawyers of the highest authority are of the clear opinion that the sovereign is not in all circumstances bound to grant a Prime Minister's request for a dissolution.'[38]

Another ministerial view had also been expressed as far back as 1923 by H.H. Asquith in a speech to Liberal MPs in discussing the right of Ramsay MacDonald's minority Labour government to dissolve Parliament. He said:

> The notion that a Minister – a Minister who cannot command a majority in the House of Commons – is invested with the right to demand a dissolution is as subversive of constitutional usage as it would, in my opinion, be pernicious to the general and paramount interests of the nation at large.[39]

This demonstrates that there were two schools of thought in the Westminster model about dissolution; however, the Monarch was not restricted by a written and narrow constitutional interpretation of the Crown's position on an interpretation of the issue. There was apparently some flexibility enjoyed by the Crown in the exercise of this power. Either the monarch must grant a dissolution upon the request of the prime minister, or, the prime minister may seek a dissolution of Parliament and it will be considered based on the particular situation.[40]

This pre-2011 dual interpretation clearly made its way into the constitutions of the Westminster–Whitehall model between 1962 and 1983, and represents the dilemma faced by constitutional draftsmen in codifying unwritten practices in a written Constitution that can only be averted by direct political instructions to draft one way or another. For example, the power of dissolution is expressed differently in Trinidad and Tobago and in St Lucia as follows:

> Trinidad and Tobago Section 68(1)
>
> The President, acting in accordance with the advice of the Prime Minister, may at any time prorogue or dissolve Parliament.[41]
>
> St Lucia Section 55(4)
>
> In the exercise of his powers to dissolve Parliament, the Governor-General shall act in accordance with the advice of the Prime Minister:

Provided that –

(a) if the Prime Minister advises a dissolution and the Governor-General acting in his own deliberate judgment, considers that the government of St. Lucia can be carried on without a dissolution and that a dissolution would not be in the interests of St. Lucia, he may, acting in his own deliberate judgment, refuse to dissolve Parliament;....[42]

In Trinidad and Tobago, the president simply acts on the advice of the prime minister in respect of a dissolution. In St Lucia, the governor general has been accorded a right to refuse the advice of the prime minister in respect of a dissolution of Parliament. However, the governor general cannot take it upon himself/herself to dissolve Parliament on his/her own. The advice of the prime minister is necessary, and the governor general can consider the advice tendered and then agree or disagree. These St Lucian provisions are also to be to be found in Belize and in St Vincent and the Grenadines. The other Commonwealth Caribbean countries have the Trinidadian provisions, except for Guyana which has an executive president who can dissolve Parliament in his/her own deliberate judgment.

Quite clearly, the pre-2011 dual interpretation of the Westminster convention was transferred to the Commonwealth Caribbean when their independence constitutions were crafted between 1962 and 1983 because their draftsmen had to choose on the basis of political instructions in the face of two interpretations of the same convention. The same can be said for a number of other conventions where the impact of a written constitution has altered their character by making them far more rigid than their Westminster precedents, e.g., the appointment of a prime minister, motions of no confidence, ministerial responsibility, etc.

5. The Entrenchment of Constitutional Articles

While the impact of the differences between written and unwritten conventions has been emphasized here, there is another area where the Westminster–Whitehall model has features that do not even exist at Westminster, namely the entrenchment of constitutional articles.

The constitutions of the Commonwealth Caribbean are all protected from easy amendment by the entrenchment of their provisions. Essentially, the parliaments of the region cannot amend their constitutions by a simple majority in all instances, because this is one of the various checks and balances that has been placed in these constitutions to protect them from political abuse or easy amendment.

There are three main types of entrenchment employed in the constitutions of the Commonwealth Caribbean: (i) special majorities in the Parliament for bills that seek to amend the constitution; (ii) time delay procedures between first and second readings of such bills for amendment; and (iii) approval of such amendment bills by post-parliamentary referenda.

As far as (i) above is concerned, all of the constitutions of the Commonwealth Caribbean have this device which specifies that certain sections of the Constitution require special majorities in their respective parliaments for bills that seek to amend them. Unlike Westminster, the Westminster–Whitehall model dictates to its parliaments the majorities that must be obtained in order to effect constitutional amendments. At Westminster, simple majorities alone are the order of the day as there is no formally written constitution and, therefore, nothing to entrench.

Some of the constitutions of the Commonwealth Caribbean specify a period of delay between the first and second readings of a bill that will amend the Constitution as a pre-condition for the governor general or president to give assent to such a bill. Once again, this is alien to the Westminster model. In addition, the supremacy of Parliament is undermined in that Parliament cannot fix its own agenda for the consideration of an important bill, but has to be guided by the dictates of the Constitution. The effect of a delay is that Parliament cannot consider any bill to amend the Constitution hurriedly and more time is given for a deeper consideration of any proposed amendment.

Some of the constitutions of the Commonwealth Caribbean require that certain bills that seek to amend the Constitution be subjected to approval by a referendum after they have been passed in the Parliament. Again, this is alien to the Westminster model. Furthermore, the supremacy of Parliament is diminished because Parliament must subject its authority to the votes of the electorate in a post-parliamentary referendum on certain constitutional amendments.

This fifth fundamental tenet of the Whitehall model is a phenomenon that does not even exist at Westminster and, therefore, only serves to emphasise that the transfer of the Westminster model to the Commonwealth Caribbean in an exact format is indeed mythical and more likely to be a mix of local and colonial or foreign customs copied or evolved over time.

Conclusion

The idea that the Westminster model was transferred to the Commonwealth Caribbean by the British government as part of its decolonization process in the region is a myth. The constitutions of the region demonstrate that the spirit and character of Westminster are missing, despite the presence of similar titles and intended functions. Fundamental dimensions of the Westminster model are challenged under the Westminster–Whitehall model.

Sacred Westminster doctrines such as the supremacy of Parliament are fundamentally altered in their character when applied in the Commonwealth Caribbean. Constitutional conventions lose their flexibility of interpretation once they are transferred in a written form depending on which school of thought is being copied. The character of the bicameral systems is such that the Westminster and Westminster–Whitehall models are poles apart. The thought of the citizen challenging legislation or executive action on the ground that it infringes the provisions of a written constitution is alien to Westminster, yet it is a way of life in the Commonwealth Caribbean.

Perhaps Madden was right. The Westminster model is for 'consumption only on the premises'. [43] What the Commonwealth Caribbean possesses by way of constitutional design is a model that reflects its own constitutional evolution and the introduction of principles that could not be consumed at Westminster. It is this collection that must be called the Westminster–Whitehall model, because after all it was the civil servants in the Colonial Office in Whitehall who played a significant role in drafting these constitutions anyway, yet there is the reality of an evolution of uniquely West Indian processes that have a measure of indigenous identity as identified by Norman Manley.

The legislative institutions that were created are of such a nature that they embody both the principles of nomination through patronage as well as popular election. This phenomenon can also be found in three of the four unicameral legislatures of the region where elected and nominated members sit side-by-side in those parliaments.

The legacy of the Crown Colony system of government that existed in the region in the nineteenth century can be observed in these arrangements, while the evolution of bicameralism is curiously a part of British imperial experiments with colonial legislatures based on reforms that were intended for the House of Lords just after the First World War in the Bryce Report, but never implemented.

This book shows that the constitutional systems of the Commonwealth Caribbean are largely indigenous and not imported. There are clear differences and whatever similarities exist, when measured with the Westminster model, are more titular than they are structural-functional. Their survival over time is a function of being indigenous and autochthonous, for if they were imported their shelf-life would have expired quite some time ago.

My primary reason for the juxtaposition of the two views as expressed by Eric Williams and Norman Manley, who were both part of the independence movement in the early 1960s, will help the region to understand the difficulties that have been experienced with the prospect of constitution reform.

Are we reforming constitutions that have been imported into our societies, or constitutions that are indigenous to our societies? For Williams, the argument was that if it was good enough for Great Britain, it would be good enough for Trinidad and Tobago. For Manley, it was not colonial, but rather part of the heritage of Jamaica. Somehow, they both seemed to be talking about the same thing.

The only difference was that one argument advocated that what we have belongs to us by evolution and the other argument is that what we have belongs to us by importation.

The fundamental underlying question to be asked in both cases is whether there was widespread involvement of the population in the formulation of these constitutions or whether this was an arrangement that suited the West Indian political elites as opposed to the West Indian populations themselves.

In that context, the argument to be settled by latter-day constitutional reformers would be to find an answer to why would we want to change something that could be regarded as ours by evolution or that has been adapted to suit our needs after importation?

What are we searching for? Is it a desire to seek greater functional efficiency to include the mantras of today that surround the usual suspects who go by the names of 'good governance', 'transparency', and 'accountability'?

Is it that we are wedded to the Westminster–Whitehall model of governance and any alteration may only get as far as the creation of a hybrid by importing features that are genuinely alien to our heritage of the British Constitution suitably modified or our evolved colonial institutions that are supposedly part of our heritage?

Notes

1. A.F. Madden, "'Not for Export": The Westminster Model of Government and British Colonial Practice,' *Journal of Imperial and Commonwealth History* 8 (Issue 1, 1979): 10–29.
2. L.A. Wolf-Phillips, 'A Long Look at the British Constitution,' *Parliamentary Affairs* 37 (Issue 4 1984): 385–402.

3. Hamid A. Ghany, *Constitution-making in the Commonwealth Caribbean with Special Reference to Trinidad and Tobago* (Ph.D Thesis, London University, 1987).
4. Laws of the United Kingdom 2005, c. 4.
5. Laws of the United Kingdom 2011, c. 14.
6. S.A. de Smith, *The New Commonwealth and its Constitutions* (London: Stevens and Sons, 1964), 77–78.
7. Alan Burns, *Parliament as an Export* (London: George Allen and Unwin, 1966).
8. Madden, "Not for Export".
9. Ibid., 24.
10. Ibid.
11. L.A. Wolf-Phillips, 'A Long Look'
12. Anthony Birch, *The British System of Government* (4th ed. London: George Allen and Unwin, 1980), 25–26.
13. *Report by the Hon. Major E.F.L. Wood, MP (Parliamentary Under Secretary of State for the Colonies) on his Visit to the West Indies and British Guiana, December 1921– February 1922*, Cmnd. 1679/1922 (London : H.M.S.O., 1922), 6.
14. Eric Williams, *Constitution Reform in Trinidad and Tobago* (Port-of-Spain: Teachers' Educational and Cultural Association, Public Affairs Pamphlet No.2, 1955), 30.
15. Ibid.
16. Eric Williams, *Capitalism and Slavery* (London: Andre Deutsch, 1964), 188.
17. Norman Manley, *Proceedings of the Jamaican House of Representatives 1961–62*, January 24, 1962, 766.
18. *United Kingdom National Archives, CO 1031/3226*, Explanatory Memorandum by the Constitutional Adviser to the Cabinet on the Draft Independence Constitution for Trinidad and Tobago, April 16, 1962, 10.
19. *Conference On The Closer Association of the British West Indian Colonies 1947*, Cmnd. 7291/1948, Part One: Report (London, H.M.S.O., 1948), 11.
20. *Trinidad and Tobago Hansard, House of Representatives*, August 11, 2014, 336.
21. Council of Europe, *The European Convention on Human Rights* (Strasbourg: Directorate of Information, 1952).
22. *Canadian Bill of Rights* S.C. 1960, c. 44.
23. *The Antigua and Barbuda Constitution Order 1981*, S.I. 1981/No.1106, s.19.
24. Ibid., s.18 (1).
25. *Laws of the United Kingdom* 1998, c. 42.
26. *Laws of Trinidad and Tobago*, Ch. 1:01, Schedule, s.2.
27. 'Legalization of the Convention Parliament, 1 Will and Mary, Cap. I. 1689,' in *Select Statutes Cases and Documents*, ed. Sir Charles Grant Robertson, 105–106 (London: Methuen & Co. Ltd., 1935).
28. *Laws of the United Kingdom* 1999, c. 34.
29. *Laws of the United Kingdom* 6 & 7 Eliz. 2, c. 21
30. *Laws of the United Kingdom* 39 & 40 Vict., c. 59.
31. *The Report of the Jamaica Independence Conference 1962*, Cmnd. 1638/1962 (London: H.M.S.O., 1962), 7.
32. *Conference on the Reform of the Second Chamber*, Cmnd.9038/1918 (London: H.M.S.O., 1918).
33. *Laws of the United Kingdom* 25 & 26 Geo. 5, c. 42.
34 *Ceylon: Report of the Commission on Constitutional Reform*, Cmnd. 6677/1945 (London: H.M.S.O., 1945).
35. *British Guiana: Report of the Constitutional Commission 1950–51 and Dispatch from the Secretary of State for the Colonies to the Governor of British Guiana dated*

October 6, 1951, Colonial No. 280, 1951 (London : H.M.S.O., 1951).

36. Geoffrey Marshall, *Constitutional Conventions* (Oxford: Clarendon Press, 1984), 11–12.
37. *Laws of the United Kingdom* 2011, c.14.
38. *The Times*, May 11, 1974.
39. *The Times*, December 19, 1923.
40. For a fuller discussion of this debate see Hamid Ghany, 'The Evolution of the Power of Dissolution: The Ambiguity of Codifying Westminster Conventions in the Commonwealth Caribbean,' *The Journal of Legislative Studies* 5 (Issue 1 1999), 54–76.
41. Laws of the Republic of Trinidad and Tobago, c. 1:01, s. 68(1).
42. *The St Lucia Constitution Order 1978*, S.I. 1978 / No.1901, s. 55(4).
43. Madden, "Not for Export".

1.
Federation and Independence

The pursuit of individual independence by former colonies in the British West Indies must be understood in the context of the demise of the Federation of the West Indies in 1962 and the sudden decision by the British government to grant independence, on an individual basis, to Jamaica and Trinidad and Tobago, in the first instance, in 1962. The subsequent grant of independence to Barbados in 1966 came after an initial attempt had been made by both the British government and the government of Barbados to pursue a Federation of the so-called 'Little Eight' that was to be made up of the remaining eight territories of the failed Federation of the West Indies.

The full complement of territories that comprised the Federation of the West Indies that had been established in 1957 and came into being in 1958 was: (i) Antigua and Barbuda, (ii) Barbados, (iii) Dominica, (iv) Grenada, (v) Jamaica, (vi) Montserrat, (vii) St Kitts/Nevis/Anguilla, (viii) St Lucia, (ix) St Vincent and the Grenadines, and (x) Trinidad and Tobago.

The eventual desire of the government of Barbados to take the island to independence in 1966 is better understood by the revelation of the confidential and secret discussions that took place between the British and the Barbadian governments. Declassified British government documents reveal the approach of the British government to the demise of the federation and the subsequent issue of independence.

The Federal Independence Negotiations and the Referendum

Before the March 1961 Lancaster House negotiations between the British government and the Federal government of the West Indies on the subject of independence for the Federation of the West Indies, a significant challenge was mounted by Alexander Bustamante and the Jamaica Labour Party (JLP) to the idea of Jamaica becoming part of an independent Federation of the West Indies.

The Jamaican premier, Norman Manley, resolved that this matter should be settled by way of a referendum on the issue in Jamaica. According to the Report of the Jamaica Independence Conference that was also held at Lancaster House in London during the period February 1–9, 1962, the following was said about the referendum:

> 2. Jamaica had been a member of the Federation of the West Indies since its inception in 1957. Having regard however to the growth of opposition in Jamaica to its continued participation in the Federation, and its desire to seek independence on its own, the Jamaican Government announced on the 31st May, 1960, that the electorate would be given an opportunity to determine the issue by way of referendum. The Government introduced the necessary legislation and the referendum which was held on the 19th September, 1961 resulted in a majority of 35,535 votes against Jamaica remaining in the Federation.[1]

In the referendum that was held on September 19, 1961, the result was a narrow victory in favour of Jamaica's exit from the Federation.

The headline in the *Gleaner* newspaper in Jamaica on September 20, 1961 screamed 'IT'S JAMAICA – ALONE'. According to the Report of the Chief Electoral Officer [2] the total number of persons who voted was 479,220 for a turnout of 61.51 per cent of which 5,640 ballots were rejected thereby leaving 473,580 accepted ballots. The actual question on the ballot paper was 'Should Jamaica remain in the Federation of the West Indies?'

The number of persons who voted YES was 217,319 and the number of persons who voted NO was 256, 261.[3]

The actual breakdown by Parish and Constituency was as follows:

PARISH AND CONSTITUENCY	ANSWER	TOTALS	PERCENTAGE
KINGSTON EASTERN	YES	7,455	75.51
	NO	2,418	24.49
KINGSTON EAST CENTRAL	YES	5,361	58.17
	NO	3,865	41.83
KINGSTON WEST CENTRAL	YES	4,516	53.77
	NO	3,883	46.23
KINGSTON WESTERN	YES	3,820	43.02
	NO	5,055	56.98
ST ANDREW EAST RURAL	YES	9,111	63.73
	NO	5,201	36.27
ST ANDREW EAST URBAN & SUB-URBAN	YES	11,417	70.68
	NO	4,737	29.32
ST ANDREW CENTRAL	YES	8,584	55.59
	NO	6,587	44.41

PARISH AND CONSTITUENCY	ANSWER	TOTALS	PERCENTAGE
ST ANDREW WEST RURAL	YES	5,427	44.36
	NO	6,807	55.64
ST ANDREW WEST CENTRAL	YES	11,014	62.67
	NO	6,560	37.33
ST ANDREW SOUTH WESTERN	YES	6,915	39.93
	NO	10,404	60.07
ST THOMAS WESTERN	YES	4,255	63.90
	NO	7,532	36.10
ST THOMAS EASTERN	YES	3,641	31.46
	NO	7,932	68.54
PORTLAND EASTERN	YES	4,479	37.82
	NO	7,365	62.18
PORTLAND WESTERN	YES	3,883	43.18
	NO	5,110	56.82
ST MARY EASTERN	YES	3,247	33.50
	NO	6,444	66.50
ST MARY CENTRAL	YES	5,254	47.43
	NO	5,824	52.57
ST MARY WESTERN	YES	4,811	48.13
	NO	4,464	51.87
ST ANN NORTH WESTERN	YES	4,417	62.88
	NO	2,607	37.12
ST ANN NORTH EASTERN	YES	5,341	60.45
	NO	3,494	39.55
ST ANN SOUTH EASTERN	YES	5,796	75.66
	NO	1,865	24.34
ST ANN SOUTH WESTERN	YES	2,020	31.48
	NO	4,396	68.52
TRELAWNY NORTHERN	YES	4,117	40.51
	NO	6,046	59.49
TRELAWNY SOUTHERN	YES	2,982	40.69
	NO	4,360	59.31
ST JAMES NORTH WESTERN	YES	6,360	46.92
	NO	7,194	53.08
ST JAMES SOUTH EASTERN	YES	2,929	32.11
	NO	6,194	67.89
HANOVER WESTERN	YES	3,282	32.81
	NO	6,722	67.19

PARISH AND CONSTITUENCY	ANSWER	TOTALS	PERCENTAGE
HANOVER EASTERN	YES	2,799	36.63
	NO	4,842	63.37
WESTMORELAND EASTERN	YES	3,881	47.53
	NO	4,285	52.47
WESTMORELAND CENTRAL	YES	5,496	47.60
	NO	6,049	52.40
WESTMORELAND WESTERN	YES	4,539	39.19
	NO	7,041	60.81
ST ELIZABETH SOUTH WESTERN	YES	3,017	41.23
	NO	4,300	58.77
ST ELIZABETH SOUTH EASTERN	YES	3,939	62.56
	NO	2,356	37.44
ST ELIZABETH NORTH EASTERN	YES	3,611	42.72
	NO	4,842	57.28
ST ELIZABETH NORTH WESTERN	YES	2,490	30.93
	NO	5,558	69.07
MANCHESTER NORTHERN	YES	5,201	48.06
	NO	5,621	51.94
MANCHESTER WESTERN	YES	5,974	59.15
	NO	4,125	40.85
MANCHESTER EASTERN	YES	4,657	51.36
	NO	4,410	48.64
CLARENDON NORTH WESTERN	YES	4,664	40.25
	NO	6,925	59.75
CLARENDON NORTH EASTERN	YES	3,135	26.74
	NO	8,589	73.26
CLARENDON SOUTH EASTERN	YES	2,622	23.74
	NO	8,424	76.26
CLARENDON SOUTH WESTERN	YES	3,944	34.88
	NO	7,364	65.12
ST CATHERINE WESTERN	YES	3,103	30.50
	NO	7,071	69.50
ST CATHERINE SOUTH EASTERN	YES	4,275	31.87
	NO	9,137	68.13
ST CATHERINE CENTRAL	YES	4,725	48.56
	NO	5,005	51.44
ST CATHERINE NORTH EASTERN	YES	4,815	40.81
	NO	6,981	59.19

The total number of ballots cast for the resolution was 217,319 (45.88 per cent) and the total number of ballots cast against the resolution was 256,261 (54.12 per cent). Jamaica was now poised to secede from the Federation.

It was clear that the initial reactions to the secession of Jamaica from the Federation would cause attention to shift to the attitude of Eric Williams and whether or not Trinidad and Tobago would stay in the Federation.

The acting governor general of the Federation, John Mordecai, had this to say in a secret and personal telegram to the secretary of state for the Colonies the day after the referendum:

1. I discussed with the Prime Minister early this morning and later met the Cabinet formally following their own discussion. My accompanying non-personal telegram reports conclusions reached.

2. Although Ministers appear generally to grasp the grave consequences of Jamaica's withdrawal, some of their reactions could lead one to doubt it. The Prime Minister (for one) seems ready to canvass the view that Eastern Caribbean federation with a much stronger centre than the Lancaster House scheme would be workable fairly easily. Cabinet even mentioned possibility of Britain continuing assistance to Eastern Caribbean federation to make up for Jamaica's withdrawal, but without any idea that this would be incompatible with independence. There was also some suggestion of adhering to 31st May, 1962 although it was not difficult to convince the Cabinet that this would be impracticable; at the cost of some emphasis they were however made to appreciate the likelihood (which to judge by Williams' utterances at Lancaster House and subsequently must be regarded as strong) of Trinidad following Jamaica out of the federation and the consequences of such a development.

3. I realize that you may feel different about receiving the Prime Minister without adequate preparation but in the above circumstances there seems advantage in such a visit preceding the proposed meeting with West Indian leaders. This would not only give time for Trinidad views to be ascertained but would enable you to point out some hard facts particularly as to the financial implications and thus help to prevent proposed meeting here from producing unrealistic proposals.

4. For the moment everything seems to turn on upon Trinidad's attitude. I have impressed upon the Prime Minister the importance of the reason for line in their talks which would precipitate a public statement by Williams as to Trinidad's intentions. It has not been possible to contact Hochoy today but we will discuss tonight.[4]

The British government was considering the idea of sending junior colonial office minister, Hugh Fraser, out to the West Indies on a salvage mission. Before that was decided, the views of Mordecai were sought. In replying to the secretary of state he said:

1. Key to problem of what can be salvaged is whether Trinidad will play along with the Eastern Caribbean Federation of the nine or elect to go it alone. Assuming former is the pattern to be encouraged, it is a good sign that not only Federal Prime Minister and the Government but Premiers and Chief Ministers in Barbados and the majority of the seven have already declared publicly their strong hope and determination that such an arrangement be worked. The Governor agrees with me that if there is a chance of Williams not (repeat not) following Jamaica out it rests in an <u>en bloc</u> 'appeal' being tactfully encouraged and strengthened.

2. In the above circumstances I would consider it preferable to judge the timing and advantage of Fraser's visit after (repeat after) discussions which the S. of S. may have in London with the Prime Minister and Premier (my immediately following telegram Personal refers).

3. It is also relevant that Arthur Lewis who is now in Trinidad and has seen both Prime Minister and Premier has been formally accepted by the former as dollar a year representative to work here for the next three months to examine prospect of salvage proposals. It is good sign that Williams while still non-committal personally welcomes this arrangement.[5]

These missives from Mordecai to the secretary of state for the colonies, Iain Macleod, immediately preceded a secret minute from Macleod to Prime Minister Harold Macmillan dated September 22, 1961 which read as follows:

1. The Jamaica referendum has resulted in a defeat for Manley on the Federation issue. We expected and hoped for a narrow but clear affirmative. The result is a narrow but clear negative.

2. This is a most grievous blow to the Federal ideal for which we and enlightened West Indian opinion have striven for so many years. It is certain that the federation cannot continue in its present form and must be doubtful whether it can survive at all.

3. The decision of Jamaica to quit the Federation must be taken as final. We may expect a demand that they should be allowed to go forward into Independence as a separate member of the Commonwealth. In view of the size, population (1.6 million) and economic viability of Jamaica this will be a demand which, with the precedents of Sierra Leone and Cyprus before us, we could not resist. Whether there will have to be a General Election in Jamaica or whether Manley will successfully maintain that an adverse

vote on this single issue does not constitute a vote of no confidence in his Government remains to be seen.

4. The question whether a Federation of most or all of the East Caribbean Islands can survive the defection of Jamaica depends more on the attitude of Trinidad and Tobago than any other single factor. Dr. Williams (Premier of Trinidad and Tobago) made it clear during the West Indian Conference that, if Jamaica left the Federation, Trinidad would follow suit since she would not be able or prepared to take on the financial burden of 'carrying' the Federation. (Jamaica and Trinidad contribute about 85% of Federal revenues in roughly equal shares.) If he maintains this line, we can expect a demand from Trinidad and Tobago that they too should be allowed to 'go it alone' into independent membership of the Commonwealth. This would be as difficult to resist as a similar demand from Jamaica.

5. If Trinidad takes this line, it is difficult to see a 'rump' Federation of Barbados and the smaller islands surviving. Antigua has always taken a pro-Jamaica line and is unlikely in any case to continue in a Federation that does not include Jamaica. She may well seek some form of association with Jamaica (though whether Jamaica after the referendum would be in a position to accommodate her is doubtful). Barbados is not very likely to press for independence and is more likely to want to continue as a separate self-governing Colony, possibly with some special status. This would leave us with six small Windward and Leeward islands which have no prospect of 'making independence' alone and all but one of which are budgetarily in the red and supported financially by the U.K. – a most dismal prospect.

6. It is, however, just possible that Trinidad might be prepared to lead an East Caribbean Federation – on her terms. Eric Williams has always disliked the present loose form of Federation which has been a condition of Jamaica belonging. The defection of Jamaica will give him the opportunity to press for a tighter form of Federation which he has always advocated, with strong central powers over taxation, development planning, etc. In return for that he might be prepared to make a concession over his earlier stand against the early introduction of the freedom of movement. This might overcome the prejudice of other Islands against continuing in a Federation dominated by Trinidad, since it is on this issue that they have been most bitterly critical of Trinidad. On this hypothesis we might salvage a viable Federation which could go forward to independence without Jamaica – and relieve us of the prospect of having the smaller islands indefinitely on our hands. But Eric Williams will in that case make full use of his strong bargaining position and no doubt demand a handsome financial contribution over the early years from H.M.G. on balance. However, it seems more probable that he will want to 'go it alone'.

7. We cannot, of course, express publicly our regret at the result of the referendum since that could embitter our relations with Bustamante if he returns to power in Jamaica. Our immediate line with the Press is that it was recognised that the Lancaster House Agreement was dependent on the Jamaica referendum and the endorsement by Legislatures in other Islands; that we have always regarded the form of Federation as a matter for West Indians themselves to settle; and that the referendum result is a new factor in the situation the effects of which we are studying.

8. The Americans will be extremely concerned over this development and the Foreign Office are sending an assessment to the Foreign Secretary in Washington. The Commonwealth Relations Office are also sending guidance to their High Commissioner in Ottawa.

9. I have asked for immediate assessments from the Acting Governor-General and Governors and Administrators. Hailes has broken his holiday in Scotland and I have held discussions with him. The Jamaican leaders and the Federal Prime Minister Sir Grantley Adams wish to come to London at a very early date to confer with me. I will report again in a few days on the situation as I see it.

10. I am sending copies of this minute to the Lord Chancellor, the Chancellor of the Exchequer, the Foreign Secretary, The Commonwealth Secretary, and the Minister of Defence.[6]

It was apparent that the British government was prepared to accept the strong possibility that Trinidad and Tobago was unlikely to continue in the federation based on their suspicions about whether Eric Williams was committed to the idea.

This was critical from a West Indian standpoint because it meant that independence could be handed over to Jamaica and to Trinidad and Tobago without any regard to the concept of West Indian nationhood or individual nationhood. In the case of Jamaica, Bustamante had been clear for many years before the referendum that he was opposed to any idea of Jamaica being in a federation with the smaller territories of the Eastern Caribbean.

Indeed, he had made his views about the prospect of a federation known at the Conference on the Closer Association of the British West Indian Colonies that was held in Montego Bay, Jamaica, September 11–19, 1947. In his address to the First Plenary Session of the Conference on September 11, 1947, Bustamante in response to the address by the secretary of state for the colonies, Arthur Creech Jones, stated:

> We come to federation – I can see federation one day, but now you have said in your speech today, if I understand and remember rightly, that the

first step must be federation, and then after that we may work up ourselves to self-government. I do not like that kind of promise. Work up to what? You get federation now, and this is what you are asking us to do. Jamaica is walking politically, and very rapidly so, and could walk much quicker if the British Government was just enough to give us what is ours by right – freedom so that we can prove to the world that although there are brains abroad there are brains here too.

Jamaica can walk, Trinidad is creeping, Barbados and Demerara are right behind Trinidad or almost the same, St. Kitts and St. Vincent are attempting to creep and only attempting. Antigua is creeping, and of all the other small islands some can barely creep on the palm of their hands, and others on hands and feet, and others not at all, yet you say to us, "We want you to federate". How can the walking and the creeping and the babe who has not begun to creep yet, how can they walk in the same avenue? It cannot be done.[7]

Bustamante never deviated from this position. The delegation from Trinidad and Tobago at the Montego Bay Conference consisted of three members of the executive and legislative councils in the persons of Timothy Roodal, Courtenay Hannays, and Albert Gomes with their advisers H.W. Wilson, attorney general, and R.B. Skinner, acting financial secretary.

In later years, when Eric Williams became the chief minister (1956) and then premier (1959) of Trinidad and Tobago, Bustamante, did not change his position on the federation while in opposition to Norman Manley, and it was obvious that Williams was only committed to the idea of a federation if Jamaica was going to be involved. Given Bustamante's position, Williams needed Norman Manley to succeed for Trinidad and Tobago to be involved. There was now great peril facing the future of the federation with the adverse result in the Jamaican referendum.

With the governor general of the West Indies, Lord Hailes, breaking his vacation in Scotland in order to return to the federal seat of government in Trinidad, he was able to advise the new secretary of state for the colonies, Reginald Maudling (who had assumed duties on October 9 upon succeeding Iain Macleod), of the views of the federal cabinet of Prime Minister Sir Grantley Adams on October 17, 1961 in the following terms:

1. I have the honour to inform you that the situation arising out of the Jamaica Referendum has been considered by the Federal Cabinet in the context of the recent discussions in London between your predecessor and the Federal Delegation led by the Prime Minister, and of the communiqué issued on 5th October at the conclusion of the discussions between your predecessor and the Jamaica Delegation led by the Premier of Jamaica.

2.   The Federal Government formally protests against the decision recorded in the above-mentioned communiqué that Her Majesty's Government would be prepared to introduce legislation as early as possible in the forthcoming session of Parliament to provide for Jamaica's withdrawal from the Federation, and that every effort would be made to secure the passage of this legislation before the end of March, 1962. The Federal Cabinet regards this decision as contrary to the spirit of the existing Federal Constitution, and considers that it would be highly impolitic for the act and timing of Jamaica's secession to be negotiated and decided solely between Her Majesty's Government and the Government of Jamaica, without consultation at all stages with the Federal Government and the Governments of the other Territories of the Federation. My Ministers accordingly request that any further action in regard to this matter should be taken only after consultation with the Federal Government and the nine Territorial Governments of the Eastern Caribbean.[8]

It was obvious that the federal cabinet was not facing the reality of Jamaican secession from the federation. The British government recognized what had happened and were clear about what they had to do, while the federal cabinet was seeking to restrain any such moves.

One week later, Maudling sent a confidential dispatch to Hailes in which a very clear statement of British government policy on the effect of the Jamaican referendum was expressed:

1.   I have the honour to address you on the subject of the result of the Jamaican Referendum.

2.   As you are aware Mr. Macleod discussed the implications of the result of the Referendum with delegations from the Federal Government led by the Federal Prime Minister, and from the Jamaican Government led by the Premier of Jamaica. It was agreed in these discussions that while the result of the Referendum in no way affected the juridical position of the Federation, and the Federal Government would continue to operate in accordance with its present constitution until such time as that constitution might be modified, it must nevertheless be regarded as a final verdict by the electorate of Jamaica that they no longer wish to participate in the Federation of the West Indies.

3.   In view of this, Mr. Macleod, following his discussions with the Federal delegation, informed the representatives of the Government of Jamaica that Her Majesty's Government accepted the result of the Referendum as a final indication of Jamaica's wishes and would be prepared to introduce legislation as early as possible in the forthcoming session of Parliament to provide for Jamaica's withdrawal from the Federation. Every effort would be made to secure the passage of this legislation before the end of March, 1962.

4. My predecessor also informed the Jamaican delegation that Her Majesty's Government was prepared to accede to their request that Jamaica should achieve independence in the course of 1962 and undertook, if Jamaica so desired, to seek in due course the concurrence of the Governments of the Commonwealth to Jamaica becoming an independent member of the Commonwealth. It was further agreed that the form of the future constitution of Jamaica and the date on which independence would be achieved should be settled at a conference between H.M.G. and a delegation from the Jamaican Parliament in January or February, 1962.

5. It is clear that the withdrawal of Jamaica from the Federation must have a profound effect upon the structure and constitution of the Federation and, indeed, on all aspects of Federal activity. The Federal Government proposes to consult the remaining territorial governments concerning the convening of a Conference to discuss the situation in detail, and I would be glad to be kept informed of the progress of this proposal. Following these discussions between the Federal Government and, if the governments concerned agree, I propose to call a Constitutional Conference early in 1962 to consider the problems caused by the withdrawal of Jamaica from the Federation, and its implications for the decisions contained in the Report of the West Indian Constitutional Conference (Cmnd. 1417). Without prejudice to the result of these discussions it will, I think, be generally accepted that the inevitable consequence of this situation is that it is no longer probable that the Federation will be able to proceed to independence on 31st May, 1962, and further, that it will no longer be appropriate to proceed with the conference on defence , financial, economic, international relations and other matters concerning the independence of the Federation which it had been agreed would commence on 8th January, 1962.

6. I will address you and the Governments concerned further about various matters which would be consequential upon the abandonment of the date of 31st May, 1962, e.g. the revision of the arrangements for Colonial Development and Welfare expenditure notified to you in my savingram FEDER No. 17 of 12th July, 1961, and the proposals for constitutional changes in the Leeward and Windward Islands contained in Cmnd. 1434. I shall also address you further on the question of the Report of the Joint British, Canadian and United States Economic Mission to the Leeward and Windward Islands, which is at present under consideration by the three participating governments.

7. I am sending a copy of this despatch to (FEDER Governors and Administrators).[9]

This was the roadmap for independence for Jamaica that had been laid out by the British government. There was no questioning of the referendum result as it was viewed as a clear expression of self-determination. The British government was not seeking to go backwards on the issue of independence for Jamaica and it was already prepared to smooth the way forward with the facilitation of membership of the Commonwealth as well.

There was obvious uncertainty about the future of the federation and the proposed independence date of May 31, 1962 was no longer a viable date in the eyes of the secretary of state for the colonies.

What would happen next with the future of a revised federation would depend heavily upon the attitude adopted by Trinidad and Tobago's premier, Eric Williams.

The Withdrawal of Trinidad and Tobago from the Federation

In a 1965 speech on the subject of the negotiations for a revised federation following the result of the Jamaican referendum, Eric Williams had this to say:

> The Jamaica Referendum of September 1961 spelled the doom of the Federation of the West Indies. This was immediately obvious to all of us in the P.N.M. Government. The smaller islands and the United Kingdom did not take this view of the matter, and began to put pressure on us to accept a substitute federation of nine countries, as Prime Minister Macmillan had urged on me when he visited Trinidad.

> From the West Indian point of view, Arthur Lewis prepared a memorandum at the request of Grantley Adams suggesting how the smaller federation might be organized and might operate. In summary, it involved a federal budget of 60.8 million dollars, of which Trinidad and Tobago was to contribute 45.34 million or just under 75 percent; but Arthur Lewis added that 'it is arguable that Trinidad should contribute 80 percent.'

> Where representation in the federal parliament was concerned, however, Arthur Lewis arguing on what he claimed was 'the general consensus' in the other territories that the formula arrived at in the Inter-Governmental Conferences should be maintained, committed himself to a Trinidad and Tobago representation which was not based on the fact that Trinidad and Tobago accounted for approximately 60 percent of the population of the nine territory federation. To put it bluntly, Trinidad and Tobago was to pay three quarters of the budget but to have less than half of the seats in the federal parliament. This was wholly unacceptable to the P.N.M. Cabinet.[10]

Williams's views on the subject of Jamaican withdrawal and Arthur Lewis's federal negotiation fit squarely into a narrative that had been expressed by the chief minister of Antigua, Vere Bird, mere days after the Jamaican referendum result. According to a secret and personal dispatch by the administrator in Antigua to the secretary of state for the colonies on September 25, 1961, Bird's views were summarized as follows:

> 1. Further to my Personal and Confidential telegram Personal No. 18 and my open telegram No. 149, the latter, Bird says, is "to show Antigua has not changed her mind". In effect Bird means that Antigua's sympathy always was with Jamaica: now Antigua will consider joining a Federation of the Eastern Caribbean with or without Trinidad but as equal partners only, and not in Bird's words "as little Tobagoes". Any attempt by Williams which appears to Bird to be making Antigua dependent on Trinidad, Bird says, will not be acceptable.[11]

With these competing narratives from Williams and Bird, it was inevitable that Arthur Lewis's balancing act between Trinidad and Tobago and the remaining territories in the federation in the Eastern Caribbean was going to encounter fatal headwinds that would doom the negotiations even before they started.

Bird's intense dislike of Williams and Williams's refusal to entertain any other offer besides one that would give Trinidad and Tobago the dominant position that Bird was privately rejecting meant that the federation was essentially over.

However, as the negotiator on behalf of the federal government, Lewis had to make every effort to close the gap that he knew existed. Lewis documented his meetings with Williams and his notes show the many mood swings through which Williams passed. The following are Lewis's records of his encounters with Williams in trying to renegotiate a revised Federation:

> I saw Dr. Williams four times:
>
> September 22
>
> I went to see him to persuade him to declare in favour of a strong Eastern Caribbean Federation. He was full of venom and insisted that he wanted the whole Federation to "mash up". Only then would he consider starting a new federation, on Trinidad's terms. I then switched to persuading him not to say anything at all, and he said he would propose to his party that it keep federation out of the election.
>
> Trinidad's terms would be strong federation, on the lines of the Economics of Nationhood.
>
> He welcomed the proposal that I sound out the other Governments.

He repudiated any immediate intention of declaring for the independence of Trinidad.

October 6

I reported that Mr. Bird of Antigua was willing to accept the main features of a strong federation, provided no attempt was made at a unitary state. He was pleased with my report that a reasonable settlement could be made.

He informed me that Ellis Clarke had advised that the Federation would end in March, and I tried vainly to argue him out of this.

He thought he might be ready for a meeting in January.

He undertook to read and comment on my report.

November 3

We had lunch in his house for two hours. He had previously read a first draft of my report, addressed to him.

There was a marked shift in his thinking, towards a unitary state, but his mind still seemed to be open on this subject.

The alarming shift was in his attitude to a conference. He could not have his party convention till mid-January. This would have to be followed by educating the public. Clearly he was thinking in terms of months.

By now he had also publicly committed himself to the ending of the Federation in March.

I gained the impression that destroying the Federation had become an obsession, and that his desire to bring off this coup was his main reason for elaborating a programme of public "education" which would prevent him reaching the conference table until after March.

He would circulate my report to his friends and officials, and invited me to return for further comment after my visit to B.G.

November 8

He had not yet received comments on my report. His mind was still toying with a unitary state, and seemed a little less open. But he argued in a friendly way. His attitude to a conference was much worse. He now objected even to the presence of the Federal Government at a conference, though when pressed he gave the impression that he might yield on this. It was clear that he would not come to a conference summoned by the Federal Government, which in any case would not exist for him after March.

Asked where we go from here; was he prepared to summon his own unofficial parley of Chief Ministers? He replied that the Colonial Office had got us into this mess, and had a duty to take the initiative in getting us out. There ought soon to be discussion on practical arrangements for continuing common services when the Federation came to an end. He had received a nice letter from Mr. Maudling. He would attend a conference if it was clear that the Federal Government would not keep interfering in the discussion.

He insisted that he was anxious to come to terms with the other islands, and we spent some time on steps he might take to make friends. I pointed out that he was creating an image of himself as the big bad wolf waiting to devour the little islands. He promised to mend his ways.[12]

These notes by Arthur Lewis provide a useful requiem for the federation as they show how Williams swayed from one point of view to the other. What would have been uppermost in Williams's mind during this period was whether he could win the December 4, 1961 general elections in Trinidad and Tobago.

Having won the elections and forming a new government, Williams turned his party, the People's National Movement (PNM) to the task of considering its position on the future of the federation of the West Indies. He timed a resolution that he had prepared for his party to be debated on January 14, 1962, which was the day after the secretary of state for the colonies, Reginald Maudling, arrived in Trinidad for a visit.

The resolution that was debated and adopted by the General Council of the PNM read as follows:

Be it therefore resolved that Trinidad and Tobago reject unequivocally any participation in the proposed Federation of the Eastern Caribbean and proceed forthwith to National Independence, without prejudice to the future association in a Unitary State of the people of Trinidad and Tobago with any Territory of the Eastern Caribbean whose people may so desire and on terms to be mutually agreed but in any case providing for the maximum possible degree of local government.

And be it further resolved that the P.N.M.'s Government in Trinidad and Tobago take the initiative in proposing the maximum possible measure of collaboration among the units of the disintegrated Federation in respect of such common services as the university and communications.

And be it further resolved that Trinidad and Tobago declare their willingness to associate with all the people of the Caribbean in a Caribbean

Economic Community and to take such action as may be necessary for the achievement of this objective.[13]

Trinidad and Tobago had suddenly moved from a position of negotiating its independence as part of a revised federation of the West Indies to seeking its own independence on the basis of a party resolution adopted by the general council of the PNM, whereas Jamaica had been afforded an opportunity to express its self-determination through the medium of a referendum called by its Premier Norman Manley for September 19, 1961. Trinidad and Tobago had just come out of a general election on December 4, 1961 where the issue of staying in or opting out of the federation was not on the ballot.

However, the British government had already recognized that there was very little that they could do if the government of Trinidad and Tobago did not wish to participate in a revised federation of the Eastern Caribbean.

After his visit to the region between January 13 and 28, 1962, Reginald Maudling reported to the British cabinet.

According to the declassified Cabinet Conclusions of the British cabinet for February 6, 1962, the following is recorded:

3. The Colonial Secretary said that he would be expected to make an early statement in Parliament on his recent visit to the West Indies. His primary object had been to discuss with the leaders of the Governments in the Eastern Caribbean the situation arising from Jamaica's desire to leave the West Indies Federation. The main elements in the situation were that the Government had accepted the decision of Jamaica to withdraw from the Federation; that Trinidad and Tobago had decided not to participate in any federation of the Eastern Caribbean; and that the Ministers in the Leeward and Windward Islands, while advocating a new federation between their territories, were agreed that the present federation should be dissolved. He proposed to inform Parliament that in the circumstances the Government had decided, with regret, that they had no alternative but to arrange for the Federation to be dissolved; that legislation for this purpose would shortly be introduced and that the Bill would provide for an interim organisation to be set up under a commissioner appointed by the Government to administer the common services for the time being until more permanent arrangements could be worked out in consultation with the local Governments. It would be premature to describe the suggested federation of Barbados and the Leeward and Windward Islands as more than a promising development and he would emphasise the need for further study before any final decisions could be taken on it.

In discussion there was general agreement in the Cabinet that the dissolution of the West Indies Federation could not be prevented. It was noted that officials of the Treasury and the Colonial Office were examining the economic problems involved in future constitutional developments.

The Cabinet –

Authorised the Colonial Secretary to make an early statement in Parliament, on the lines which he had indicated, on future constitutional developments in the West Indies.[14]

It was clear that the cabinet of Prime Minister Harold Macmillan had accepted the inevitability of the demise of the federation of the West Indies and that they were prepared to consider a smaller federation of the Windward and Leeward Islands together with Barbados as nothing more than 'a promising development'.

Later the same day, the secretary of state for the colonies, Reginald Maudling, made a statement in the House of Commons as follows:

With permission, Mr. Speaker, I will make a statement on the West Indies.

As the House is aware, I paid a visit to the West Indies from 13th to 28th January. My object was to discuss with the leaders of the Governments in the Eastern Caribbean the situation arising from Jamaica's desire to leave the Federation. During my visit I had talks with the Federal Government and with the Premiers of Barbados and Trinidad, as well as with Chief Ministers of all the Leeward and Windward Islands which form part of the Federation of the West Indies.

My talks revealed that we face this situation: Jamaica has declared its determination to withdraw from the Federation and this decision has been accepted by Her Majesty's Government. The Government of Trinidad and Tobago have decided not to participate in any federation of the Eastern Caribbean. Finally, the Premier of Barbados and the Chief Ministers of the Leeward and Windward Islands, while advocating a new federation between their territories, are agreed that the present one should be dissolved.

In these circumstances, Her Majesty's Government have with regret reached the conclusion that they have no alternative but to arrange for the dissolution of the present Federation. Under the Federation, however, a number of common services of great value have been operating in the area. We are anxious to ensure their continuation on a regional basis pending clarification of the constitutional position throughout the area.

Her Majesty's Government have, therefore, decided to introduce legislation into Parliament very shortly which will enable us to dissolve the present Federation, and to set up an interim organisation, under a Commissioner appointed by Her Majesty's Government, which will be responsible for running the common services for the time being, until some more permanent arrangements for their operation can be worked out in conjunction with the Governments of the West Indies.

Her Majesty's Government regard the suggested federation of Barbados and the Leeward and Windward Islands as a promising development. They consider, however, that a great deal of careful study both here and in the West Indies will be needed before any final decisions can be taken and they propose for their part to initiate this study in the very near future.[15]

When this statement was made on February 6, the Jamaican Independence Conference was simultaneously underway at Lancaster House during the period February 1–9, 1962.

Barbados Demands Independence

After his election on December 4, 1961 (the same day as the election in Trinidad and Tobago), the new premier of Barbados, Errol Barrow, wanted to pursue independence for Barbados. Indeed, the decision by the Errol Barrow administration to pursue independence for Barbados by 1966 as opposed to engaging in the pursuit of a smaller federation made up of eight of the remaining members of the former federation that was dissolved in 1962 (after the withdrawal of Jamaica and Trinidad and Tobago) is an interesting investigation.

According to page 16 of the 1961 manifesto of the Barbados Democratic Labour Party (DLP) that was prepared for the general election of December 1961: 'The road to destiny is the road to independence. Towards this goal the country must press on.'[16]

It was apparent from 1961 that Barrow and the DLP were committed to independence for Barbados. However, the British government had other ideas in the aftermath of the official withdrawal of both Jamaica (by virtue of the result of the referendum on the federation held on September 19, 1961) and the decision on January 14, 1962 of the ruling People's National Movement (PNM) led by Dr Eric Williams to approve a resolution calling for Trinidad and Tobago's withdrawal from any continued participation in a revised federation.

The position of the British government was made clear by the statement in the House of Commons by the secretary of state for the colonies on February 6, 1962. With the British government being uncertain about a revised federation of the remaining eight members of the former federation and with Errol Barrow being certain that he wished to pursue a policy of independence for Barbados as expressed in the DLP 1961 general election manifesto, the 'promising development' of a possible federation of Barbados and the Leeward and Windward Islands might not have been so promising after all if Barrow were to immediately pursue his stated policy as expressed in the DLP manifesto.

The East Caribbean Federation Conference was convened at Marlborough House in London during the period May 9–24, 1962. This conference was the culmination of a consensus agreed at a conference held in Barbados in February and March 1962. According to paragraph 6 of the Report of the East Caribbean Federation Conference held at Marlborough House:

> Between 26th February and 3rd March, 1962, representatives of the Governments of Barbados, the Leeward Islands and the Windward Islands held a Conference in Barbados to consider further the question of setting up a federation of their territories. At this Conference they confirmed their desire that such a federation should be established, and submitted detailed proposals to the Secretary of State. On 16th April, 1962, the Secretary of State informed the House of Commons that the United Kingdom Government had reached the conclusion that a federation of Barbados and the Leeward and Windward Islands appeared to offer the best solution to the problems of the area, provided that the federal constitution was such as to provide adequate powers to the central government and to offer a reasonable prospect of economic and financial stability.[17]

These discussions at Marlborough House were taking place immediately prior to the convening of the Trinidad and Tobago Independence Conference 1962 which was going to be held at Marlborough House as well during the period May 28–June 8, 1962.

What emerges here is the fact that the British government was involved in simultaneously negotiating the continuation of a federal experiment alongside the preparation of Jamaica and Trinidad and Tobago for their individual independence. Lurking beneath the East Caribbean Federation discussions was the commitment stated in the 1961 DLP manifesto in Barbados that clearly stated a desire for Barbados to proceed to its own independence.

By late1964, the federal negotiations among the remaining eight former members of the Federation of the West Indies had collapsed, and the Barrow administration in Barbados issued a white paper on independence in August 1965.[18]

Indeed, in December 1965, the British government published a white paper that included its proposals for Antigua, St Kitts/Nevis/Anguilla,

Dominica, St Lucia, St Vincent, and Grenada to move to self-government in a new relationship in association with Great Britain.[19]

The British government held the Windward Islands Constitutional Conference between April 18 and May 6, 1966 at Lancaster House to discuss the constitutional proposals for a new self-government arrangement, while the government of Antigua and the British government held a conference in March 1966 and another conference with the government of St Kitts/Nevis/Anguilla commenced on May 12, 1966.[20]

These developments cleared the way for the pursuit of a strategy of independence for Barbados in 1966. As far as Barrow was concerned, there was no need for any general election to be held before independence was granted because the DLP had campaigned in 1961 on the basis that it would pursue independence for Barbados and that mandate from the 1961 general election was already in hand.[21]

There has been uncertainty over the years about the factors that caused Errol Barrow to call a general election for November 3, 1966 (some 22 days before Independence Day on November 30, 1966) against the grain of his prior public discourse that no election was required before independence was granted. What caused all of that to change?

The Barbados Constitutional Conference 1966

In introducing a resolution on January 4, 1966 in the Barbados House of Assembly calling on the British government to convene the Barbados Independence Conference, Errol Barrow said:

> The exercise in democracy that we have gone through is that we stated our intention before an election. We faltered by the wayside to see if we could collect some of our lesser brethren – in the sense of more unfortunate brethren – together along the road to independence with us; that is where we wasted three and one half years in this exercise. Having been diverted from our main objective, we have merely returned to the mandate of the people and the expression of our intentions as demonstrated in the Manifesto of the Democratic Labour Party.[22]

Barrow's reference to wasting three and a half years was based on the fact that his government was very involved in the political negotiations for an East Caribbean Federation that were based on the Marlborough House conference in London during the period May 9–24, 1962.[23] Barrow's narrative in describing his 'lesser brethren' in the Eastern Caribbean was similar to the tone and content of Bustamante's speech at the 1947 Standing Closer Association Conference in Montego Bay.[24]

Barrow's speech was made in January 1966 and so he counted the intervening period (May 1962–December 1965) as three and a half 'wasted years'. The Barbados Constitutional Conference was subsequently held in London during the period June 20– July 4, 1966.[25]

British Government Strategy for Barbadian Independence

In the declassified file PREM 13/1326, a letter from Douglas Williams in the West Indian section at the Colonial Office to M.H.M. Reid, a private secretary to Prime Minister Harold Wilson on June 29, 1966, the following is recorded:

> Dear Reid,
>
> Barbados Constitutional Conference
>
> I enclose three copies of a paper setting out the matters concerning the Barbados Constitutional Conference which the Colonial Secretary wishes to discuss with the Prime Minister and the Commonwealth Secretary after Cabinet tomorrow.
>
> Mr. Lee was not able to see this paper in draft but it follows instructions which he gave to his officials earlier today.
>
> I am arranging for copies of this letter and the paper to go to Mr. Lee, Mr. Bottomley and their Private Secretaries tonight. Copies are also going to Heddy in the C.R.O.
>
> Yours sincerely,
>
> Douglas Williams.[26]

Attached to the letter was a confidential memorandum by the colonial secretary (Frederick Lee) on the subject of the Barbados Constitutional Conference, which was being sent to Prime Minister Harold Wilson and the secretary of state for Commonwealth relations (Arthur Bottomley).

In the declassified copy of this letter from the records held by the prime minister's office, there is a handwritten note from his private secretary dated June 29 on the letter that reads:

> 'Prime Minister,
>
> No time for you to read this:….see the last 2 pages.'[27]

The last two pages of the memorandum by the secretary of state for the colonies read as follows:

CONCLUSIONS

<u>Arguments for Granting Independence without regard to the Date of Elections</u>

9. The record of the Democratic Labour Party while in office in the past five years has been good. It had done nothing which would substantiate the Opposition's alleged fear that after independence it intends to resort to various dictatorial practices. It has produced a constitution which (with the exception of the omission of the provisions relating to the General Assembly) containing no unusual features and is a sound workmanlike democratic instrument. It can argue it has a mandate, (of sorts) in its 1961 Manifesto for taking the country to independence. Barbados is not like some of the emergent African Countries. It is a stable country and has had constitutional government for over 300 years and is accustomed to democratic practices and the rule of law. It is true that the Premier, although intelligent and frequently charming, is a bully when he is crossed and his behaviour has undoubtedly caused serious misgivings among many Barbadians. Nevertheless I have not heard him say anything in this Conference which would support the allegation that he intends to make himself a dictator after independence. In the opinion of many observers – though by no means all – he is likely to win the next elections and therefore would probably be the Prime Minister of the independent Barbados with whom we shall have to deal. For us openly to come out against him and insist upon fresh elections before he goes to independence will be a severe loss of face for him and might make him hostile to Britain afterwards for some time to come. Such a step therefore should be taken only after serious reflection.

<u>Arguments in Favour of Insisting on Elections</u>

10. We have never in the past without elections or a referendum moved a country to independence when its Parliament was so near to its natural term and when the Opposition Parties were continuing to express serious misgivings about some features of the proposed constitution. For us to attempt to do so in this instance would expose us to criticism from some of our own back-benchers. From a conversation which Mr. Maudling has had with my private office, it would appear that the Conservative Party are also expecting us to insist upon elections before Barbados goes to independence. The two Barbadian opposition parties combined did in the elections of five years ago poll the majority of the votes; and there is every reason to believe that at the very least they still control fairly widespread support in the country. Although I cannot say that if their opinion was disregarded there would be trouble in Barbados, the resultant atmosphere would scarcely be a suitable one in which the territory should move to independence.

<u>Recommendations</u>

11. I therefore incline to the view that we must insist upon fresh elections before Barbados moves to independence. I am however anxious if possible to avoid causing the Premier any loss of face. I therefore suggest that I should be authorized to handle the matter in the following way:-

The Premier and his party have an important meeting with the Canadian Government and other Caribbean Governments starting in Ottawa on the 6th July. They are due to leave London at mid-day on 4th July. With the best will in the world, it is at the present rate of progress going to be very difficult to get through the Conference business in that time. I therefore suggest that I should be authorized to tell the Premier privately and in confidence that we are unable to agree to his going to independence until fresh elections have been held. I should then bring this Conference to an end on the basis that there are a number of points which require further consideration and on which it is not possible to reach a decision within the time available. The Conference would be resumed at a later date on the understanding between the Premier (not revealed to the Opposition parties) and myself that, before this resumption, fresh elections will have been held in Barbados on the basis of single member constituencies.[28]

Although the secretary of state for the colonies was urging his prime minister in his memorandum on June 29 to agree with his proposal for general elections to be held in Barbados before independence was granted, he faced a question for oral answer in the House of Commons the next day (June 30) from Mr Nigel Fisher, MP for Surbiton, on that very subject to which Secretary of State Lee declined to share his true opinion.

Mr. Fisher asked the Secretary of State for the Colonies whether he will make a statement about the constitutional conference on Barbados.

Mr. Frederick Lee: The conference is still in progress. I hope to be able to make a statement next week.

Mr. Fisher: Will the right hon. Gentleman say whether he favours elections before independence or after independence, bearing in mind that elections are due very shortly in the Colony anyway, as he knows, and that this is a very controversial point both in Barbados at present and, I understand, at his own constitutional conference?

Mr. Lee: It is a point which has not escaped the attention of delegates at the conference. I would not at this stage like to add anything which might make the conference more difficult to pursue.[29]

Secretary of State Lee deflected the answer to Fisher's question by shifting the attention away from his personal view and using the delegates at the conference as his frame of reference. At that particular moment, he was still waiting for his prime minister's consideration of his proposal to insist on general elections before independence and so he could not give the House of Commons a straight answer.

On the following day (July 1), after Secretary of State Lee had received the concurrence of Prime Minister Wilson, he made a statement to the Barbados Constitutional Conference as follows:

> I am now in a position to inform the Conference that these consultations have taken place and that, subject to the passage of the necessary legislation by the United Kingdom Parliament, Her Majesty's Government agree that Barbados should become independent on the 30th November, 1966.

> The question of the date of the next elections in Barbados is one for the Government of Barbados to determine, bearing in mind that a Dissolution is in any case due not later than the 19th December 1966. They will doubtless be announcing their decision in due course.[30]

By this time, Secretary of State Lee had received the concurrence of his prime minister on the issue of insisting to Barrow privately, and without the knowledge of the Opposition, that a general election would have to be held before independence could be granted.

The importance of this deal between the British government and Barrow is best captured in a confidential internal note under the heading 'Barbados' for Prime Minister Harold Wilson on July 1, 1966 from A.M. Palliser, a private secretary to the prime minister, as follows:

> The Colonial Secretary sent you a message today to say that he saw the Premier of Barbados this morning. They agreed that the Colonial Secretary will announce today that H.M.G. had agreed to independence for November 30. Mr. Barrow gave the Colonial Secretary a firm assurance in strict confidence that he would hold elections before the independence Bill came to Parliament. But he said that he could not guarantee, because of the practical difficulties which he had earlier explained, that these elections would be held under the new system of single member constituencies. The Colonial Secretary accepted this position.

> The Conference is being informed of the decision regarding the date of independence at its meeting this afternoon.[31]

In returning the note to Palliser, Harold Wilson wrote in green ink at the top of the page: 'If he goes back on X, are we fine to defer independence? HW'.[32]

In green ink, Harold Wilson highlighted the specific part of the note that referred to X which was:

> '....a firm assurance in strict confidence that he would hold elections before the independence Bill came to Parliament.'[33]

The Barbados Constitutional Conference had no idea that Wilson, Lee, and Barrow had made a secret and confidential deal. Both the British government and Barrow knew that if Barrow did not dissolve Parliament that they were not obliged to bring a bill to Parliament to grant independence to Barbados.

The secretary of state was able to rely on the fact that the Barbados Parliament, if not sooner dissolved, would stand dissolved on December 19, 1966 and that a general election would have to be held shortly after that in early 1967, at the latest. No one at the conference picked up on this and it was allowed to pass virtually unnoticed, while Barrow already knew what he had to do and the Opposition did not.

This issue of a general election before independence could be granted seemed to have been placated by the Secretary of State's statement at the conference on July 1. On July 7, Nigel Fisher was again asking Secretary of State Lee in the House of Commons about the outcome of the Barbados Constitutional Conference.

> Mr. Fisher asked the Secretary of State for the Colonies whether he will make a statement on the outcome of the Barbados Conference and the date of independence for the colony.

> Mr. Frederick Lee: The Conference ended on 4th July. Subject to the agreement of Parliament, Barbados will become independent on 30th November, 1966. The report will be published as a White Paper and copies are being placed in the Library.[34]

Fisher did not follow up on his earlier request to inquire about whether or not general elections will be held before independence. That allowed Secretary of State Lee to avoid giving an answer to a question that could have compromised the secret deal that had been made between himself, Prime Minister Wilson and Premier Barrow.

The Secret Deal between Errol Barrow and Harold Wilson

In a confidential memorandum from A.M. Palliser, private secretary to the prime minister, to the Hon. A.P.H.T. Cumming-Bruce at the Colonial Office dated July 1, 1966, he stated:

> I should perhaps just confirm for the record that the Prime Minister received the Colonial Secretary and the Commonwealth Secretary in his room at the House of Commons yesterday evening at 6.00p.m. The Governor of Barbados was also present. They discussed certain problems arising out of the Barbados Constitutional Conference, about which Williams sent Reid with his letter of June 29 a memorandum by the Colonial Secretary. This was seen by the Prime Minister.

> I need not record the discussion in any detail. The conclusion reached, as summed up at the end of the meeting by the Prime Minister was that Mr. Lee could agree to independence for Barbados at the beginning of December. Before this, fresh elections would have to be held in the Colony. But in order to save Mr. Barrow's face this need not be said publicly. One way of handling the tactical problem might be to agree to adjourn the Conference until the Autumn (i.e., until after the election) and thereafter to reconvene it in order to achieve formal agreement of independence. But discretion on the tactics was left to the Colonial Secretary.

> This method of procedure was agreeable to the Commonwealth Secretary, who made the point that his main concern was to avoid a Constitution in which, if we too seriously offended Mr. Barrow, he might make a nuisance of himself within the Commonwealth as Prime Minister of an independent Barbados.

> I have since received your telephone message of this morning about the agreement reached between the Colonial Secretary and Mr. Barrow. I have reported this to the Prime Minister.

> I am sending a copy of this letter to Borster (Commonwealth Relations Office) and Reid (Cabinet Office).[35]

The British government was actually afraid of Barrow as it was felt that he might 'make a nuisance of himself within the Commonwealth as prime minister of an independent Barbados'. Additionally, the internal confidential note sent by Palliser to Wilson had received the blessing of Wilson on the condition that the Barbados independence bill would not be brought to Parliament until there was certainty that a general election was going to be held in Barbados.

It is apparent that the British government had calculated that Barrow would win the general election so they wanted to avoid embarrassing him in public by calling for a general election to be held before independence. Instead, they made a secret deal that required him to dissolve Parliament and hold a general election before the date of independence.

Barrow was able to get the British government to accept that there would be no change to single-member constituencies for this particular election. That compromise obviously assisted Barrow greatly in his election strategy.

If that deal was not kept, there would be no independence bill to be brought to the British Parliament. Another interesting aspect of this secret deal was that the governor of Barbados, Sir John Stow, who also attended the private meeting with Prime Minister Wilson and Secretaries of State Lee (Colonies) and Bottomley (Commonwealth relations) was also part of this discussion. He too kept his silence as the dissolution of Parliament would actually have to be proclaimed by him on the advice of Barrow.

At the conclusion of the Barbados Constitutional Conference on July 4, A.M. Palliser sent a note to A.P.H.T. Cumming-Bruce at the Colonial Office on July 4 as follows:

> I told the Prime Minister of the message that you sent me on July 1 about the Colonial Secretary's talk with the Premier of Barbados. He asked whether, if Mr. Barrow went back on the firm confidential assurance given to the Colonial Secretary that he would hold elections before the independence bill came to parliament, Her Majesty's Government would be free to defer independence. The Colonial Secretary may wish to take account of this question in reporting tomorrow about the Conference to OPD on the lines we agreed this morning.[36]

The conditions of the secret deal were now to be transferred to the Overseas and Defence Policy Committee of the cabinet for discussion the following day. The date for Barbados' independence had been set and the secret deal was being honoured.

The Buckingham Palace Conditional Agreement

On July 26, 1966, Sir Hylton Poynton, permanent under secretary of state at the Colonial Office, wrote to Michael Adeane, private secretary to Her Majesty Queen Elizabeth II, under the subject line 'Independence Celebrations, Barbados', as follows:

> Thank you for your letter of the 19th July about the Independence of Barbados on the 30th November.
>
> I am now writing to ask if the Queen would be prepared to nominate H.R.H. The Duke of Kent as Her Representative at the Independence Celebrations

in the island. This would give great pleasure to the people of Barbados, who would also be delighted if the Duchess were able to accompany him.

If this suggestion is approved, we should like to inform the Governor as soon as possible; but we suggest that in view of the complications explained in my letter to you of 8th July, we should not tell Barbados Ministers or authorize a public announcement until Mr. Barrow has acknowledged his undertaking to the Secretary of State about holding elections before independence. The terms of the announcement might then follow the Guyana precedent as follows:-

"The Queen has invited His Royal Highness The Duke of Kent to be Her Majesty's Special Representative at the Independence Celebrations in Barbados in November. His Royal Highness has accepted the invitation with great pleasure. He will be accompanied by the Duchess."

Could you let me know whether these proposals are approved?

I am sending copies of this letter to Garner, Buckley and Palliser.[37]

The arrangements for Her Majesty Queen Elizabeth II to be represented at the Barbados Independence Celebrations had now become a matter of some delicacy in dealing with Buckingham Palace. Sir Hylton Poynton captured the nature of that delicacy by (i) informing the Palace that there were 'complications' involved with making any public announcement about who would represent the Queen, and (ii) it would be important to have the Queen identify Her Representative pending the resolution of the 'complication' by the Secretary of State for the Colonies (iii) the Queen's representative was suggested to her for her concurrence, and, (iv) the British Guiana precedent used for announcing the Royal Visit for the independence celebrations was to be followed given that this was still fresh having regard to the fact that British Guiana attained its independence as Guyana on May 26, 1966.

Buckingham Palace, through Michael Adeane, responded the following day (July 27) as follows:

Thank you for your letter of 25th (sic) July which I have laid before the Queen.

I am to say that Her Majesty is very glad to nominate The Duke of Kent to be her Representative at the Barbados Independence Celebrations on 30th November.

Her Majesty fully understands the possible complications which may arise during the period between now and Independence. Therefore, while she approves the terms of the proposed press announcement as set out in your letter, she agrees that this announcement should not be made public until such time as the Secretary of State recommends that this should be done. No doubt you will let me know when this moment arises.

I am sending copies of this letter to Garner, Buckley. [redacted].[38]

It was apparent that Her Majesty chose to be advised by Her Secretary of State for the Colonies as to when the public announcement should be made as regards who will represent Her at the Barbados Independence Celebrations. The Duke and Duchess of Kent were chosen, but that would have to wait for a later date to be announced.

In the interim, Errol Barrow had an undertaking to keep and only when there was public compliance with it would the rest of the independence puzzle be put in place.

Independence for Barbados on November 30, 1966

The Barbados Independence Bill 1966 was not laid for First Reading in the House of Commons until October 19, 1966. By that time, Barrow had already advised the governor to dissolve Parliament on October 10 and a general election had been set for November 3.

Barrow kept his side of the deal with the British government on October 10, and they kept their side of the deal on October 19 when the Barbados Independence Bill 1966 was laid for First Reading in the House of Commons.

In piloting the bill on Second Reading in the House of Commons on October 28, the secretary of state for the colonies, Frederick Lee, said the following on the specific issue of elections:

> The people of Barbados have been given the opportunity to elect a new Legislature before independence. On the advice of the Premier, the old Legislature was dissolved on 10th October some two months before its statutory life of five years expired – and elections are to be held on 3rd November. Whatever the result of those elections, I am sure that the new Government will carry into independence the good wishes of all Members of this House.[39]

The people of Barbados never knew that Barrow had to concede to a demand that came from Prime Minister Harold Wilson himself that Barbados would not get independence unless he called a general election first. They made a significant concession to Barrow by letting him alone know that that was the demand so that he could prepare himself in advance by choosing his date.

In the case of Trinidad and Tobago (1962), a general election was held before a decision had been made about whether or not Trinidad and Tobago would remain in a revised federation without Jamaica. Independence negotiations only took place after the government of Trinidad and Tobago had decided not to participate in any further discussions for a revised federation and sought to proceed to its own independence.

This was different from the way in which Jamaica was handled. There was an independence conference in February 1962 in London after the decision by the Jamaican electorate in September 1961 to secede from the federation. That conference in February 1962 set the date for independence and then a general election was held in April 1962 which saw a change of government from the PNP led by Norman Manley to the JLP led by Alexander Bustamante.

In Trinidad and Tobago, a general election was held on December 4, 1961 and there was no mention of independence as the country was involved in negotiations with the West Indian Federal government to determine an appropriate formula for the revised federation that would not include Jamaica. However, once elected, Williams made the decision one month later to seek independence.

In the case of Barbados, the secret deal was made in such a way that the country knew it was getting independence on November 30 1966, but it had to choose whomsoever they wanted to govern them in a general election on November 3. In this way, the independence date was confirmed, but not the government.

The general election was held on November 3, 1966 with double member constituencies and the result was DLP 14 seats, Barbados Labour Party (BLP) eight seats and Barbados National Party (BNP) two seats. Errol Barrow became the first prime minister of an independent Barbados.

Independence and Nationhood

Jamaica made demands that permitted the country to exercise its self-determination whether to proceed to independence as a single nation state or as part of a federation. It was obvious that patriotism and nationalism were more powerful determinants of that self-determination than the competing emotions of West Indian regionalism and nationhood.

Trinidad and Tobago never had the opportunity to exercise that kind of self-determination as the general election of 1961 was held on the basis that the twin-island state was likely to be part of a revised federation without Jamaica on terms that were being negotiated between Eric Williams and Arthur Lewis, up to three weeks before the general election itself. Indeed, in the 1961 general election manifesto of the PNM, there was no specific mention of the party taking Trinidad and Tobago into independence in its own right.[40]

When Eric Williams greeted the secretary of state for the colonies, Reginald Maudling, on January 14, 1962 the day after his arrival in Trinidad with the news that Trinidad and Tobago was going to withdraw from the Federation of the West Indies in its revised format without Jamaica and proceed, instead, to its own independence, the final rites of the federation had been performed.

To think that Trinidad and Tobago would move from that January announcement to independence on August 31 of the same year without any self-determination on the matter left the country in a condition of having to find nationalism and patriotism out of a failed project of West Indian nationhood.

Barbados was able to enjoy its own exercise of self-determination and patriotic legitimacy out of the ashes of the failed federal project by having the issue of independence asserted as an election issue in 1961 in the manifesto of the DLP, which won the general election. The country then participated in a second failed federal project and, with the imposition of a secret deal on its leader by the British government, was able to exercise its own self-determination on November 3, 1966 before its independence on November 30, 1966.

Notes

1.   *The Report of the Jamaica Independence Conference 1962*, Cmnd. 1638/1962 (London: H.M.S.O., 1962), 5.
2.   *Report of the Chief Electoral Officer 1961*, Referendum 1961 (Kingston: Electoral Office, October 17, 1961).
3.   Ibid., 11.
4.   *UK National Archives, CO 1031/3278*, Mordecai to Secretary of State for the Colonies, Immediate, Secret and Personal, Personal No. 196, September 20, 1961.
5.   *UK National Archives, CO 1031/3278*, Mordecai to Secretary of State for the Colonies, Emergency, Secret and Personal, Personal No. 197, September 21, 1961.
6.   *UK National Archives, CO 1031/3278*, Macleod to Macmillan, Secret, P.M. [61] 73, September 22, 1961.
7.   *Conference on the Closer Association of the British West Indian Colonies 1947*, Cmnd. 7291/1948, Part Two: Proceedings (London: H.M.S.O., 1948), 23.
8.   *UK National Archives, CO 1031/3278*, Hailes to Maudling, P.M. 12/016, October 17, 1961.
9.   *UK National Archives, CO 1031/3278*, Maudling to Hailes, Confidential, No. 992, October 24, 1961.
10. Paul Sutton, *Forged from the Love of Liberty* (Trinidad: Longman Caribbean, 1981), 297–98.

11. *UK National Archives, CO 1031/3278*, Administrator, Antigua to Secretary of State for the Colonies, Immediate, Secret and Personal, Personal No. 19, September 25, 1961.

12. *UK National Archives, CO 1031/3278*, Secret and Personal, Note by Dr A. Lewis, November 9, 1961.

13. People's National Movement, *General Council Resolution*, January 14, 1962.

14. *UK National Archives, British Cabinet Conclusions*, CC (62) 11th Conclusions, February 6, 1962.

15. *UK Hansard, House of Commons Debates* February 6, 1962 Vol. 653 c. 230.

16. Mary Chamberlain, *Empire and Nation-building in the Caribbean: Barbados 1937–66* (Manchester: Manchester University Press, 2010), 180.

17. *Report of the East Caribbean Federation Conference 1962*, Cmnd. 1746/1962 (London: H.M.S.O., 1962), 6.

18. Chamberlain, *Empire and Nation-building*, 181.

19. *Constitutional Proposals for Antigua, St Kitts/Nevis/Anguilla, Dominica, St Lucia, St Vincent and Grenada*, Cmnd. 2865/1965 (London: H.M.S.O., 1966).

20. *Report of the Windward Islands Constitutional Conference 1966*, Cmnd. 3021/1966 (London: H.M.S.O., 1966), 5.

21. Chamberlain,*Empire and Nation-building*, 182.

22. Yusuff Haniff, *Speeches by Errol Barrow* (London: Hansib Publishing Ltd., 1987), 69–70.

23. See note17 above.

24. See note 7 above.

25. See *Report of the Barbados Constitutional Conference 1966*, Cmnd. 3058/1966 (London: H.M.S.O., 1966).

26. *UK National Archives, PREM 13/1326*, Letter from Douglas Williams to M.H.M. Reid, June 29, 1966.

27. *UK National Archives, PREM 13/1326*, Handwritten note by M.H.M. Reid addressed to the Prime Minister on the Letter from Douglas Williams to M.H.M. Reid, June 29, 1966.

28. *UK National Archives, PREM 13/1326*, Confidential Memorandum by the Colonial Secretary attached to the Letter from Douglas Williams to M.H.M. Reid, June 29, 1966.

29. *UK Hansard, House of Commons Debates June 30, 1966*, Vol. 730 c. 2168.

30. *Report of the Barbados Constitutional Conference 1966*, 7.

31. *UK National Archives, PREM 13/1326*, Internal Confidential Note from A.M. Palliser to Prime Minister Harold Wilson, July 1, 1966.

32. *UK National Archives, PREM 13/1326* Handwritten note by Harold Wilson addressed to A.M. Palliser on the Internal Confidential Note from A.M. Palliser to Harold Wilson, July 1, 1966.

33. *UK National Archives, PREM 13/1326*, Palliser to Wilson, July 1, 1966.

34. *UK Hansard, House of Commons Debates July 7, 1966*, Vol. 731 c. 92W.

35. *UK National Archives, PREM 13/1326*, Confidential memorandum from A.M. Palliser to A.P.H.T. Cumming-Bruce dated July 1, 1966.

36. *UK National Archives, PREM 13/1326*, A.M. Palliser to A.P.H.T. Cumming-Bruce, July 4, 1966.

37. *UK National Archives, PREM 13/1326*, A.H. Poynton to Michael Adeane, July 26, 1966.

38. *UK National Archives, PREM 13/1326*, Michael Adeane to A.H. Poynton, July 27, 1966.

39. *UK Hansard, House of Commons Debates October 28, 1966*, Vol. 734 c. 1653.

40. People's National Movement, *Election Manifesto General Elections 1961* (Port of Spain: P.N.M. Publishing Co. Ltd., 1961).

2.
The Supremacy of Parliament and the Supremacy of the Constitution

The advent of newly independent countries in the Commonwealth Caribbean that were formerly colonies of Great Britain brought with it the establishment of parliaments authorized to enact and repeal legislation in accordance with the provisions of their written independence constitutions.

The transfer of the doctrine of the supremacy of Parliament is an important matter that goes to the heart of the democracies of these countries and their simultaneous acceptance of fundamental human rights and freedoms upon becoming independent through the grant of fully responsible status to them by the British government.

The question of the supremacy of Parliament is a legal doctrine of the British system of government. According to A.V. Dicey:

> The principle, therefore, of parliamentary sovereignty means neither more nor less than this, namely that "Parliament" has "the right to make or unmake any law whatever; and further, that no person or body is recognized by the law of England as having a right to override or set aside the legislation of Parliament," and further that this right or power of Parliament extends to every part of the King's dominions.[1]

It was from the Revolution Settlement of 1688 that sovereignty was vested not in the King alone, but rather in the King in Parliament.[2] This has remained as the foundation of the British system of government for more than 300 years. To challenge this phenomenon would require a revolution as it has been recognized by the courts and by constitutional scholars alike.

This dominance was also exported to the colonies of Great Britain in such a manner that the legislatures in the colonies themselves became constrained in the exercise of their own powers by the omnipotent powers of the British Parliament. This power, though, had been erratically enforced in theory on the premise that the inhabitants of British colonies were naturally subject to British law. Indeed, in the American Colonies Act

1766[3] it was asserted that the British Parliament had '...to have full power and authority to make laws...to bind the colonies and people of America.'[4]

This dominance was later imposed on the colonies in a more forceful manner by legislating for the repugnance of colonial law in relation to the laws of the Imperial Parliament in cases where colonial law contradicted imperial law. The vehicle through which this was achieved was the Colonial Laws Validity Act 1865.[5]

The attainment of fully responsible status or independence by most of the former colonies of Great Britain brought with it the creation of parliaments that were competent to make their own laws. This was usually accompanied by a clause in the instrument granting fully responsible status that removed the applicability of the Colonial Laws Validity Act 1865 (supra).

The challenge for parliaments throughout the Commonwealth is whether they are supreme to the extent that their power to make law can disregard the instrument that established them. In the landmark Ceylonese case of *Bribery Commissioner v Ranasinghe,*[6] the Judicial Committee of the Privy Council established the principle that the power to make law is controlled by the instrument that establishes the legislative body. Such a restriction was deemed to exist notwithstanding the issue of the sovereignty of Parliament.

The Privy Council relied upon the certificate of the Speaker as being conclusive evidence of the adoption of the correct procedure in the enactment of legislation. Where the certificate of the Speaker was not available for whatever reason, there was ground to question the validity of the enactment.

The Privy Council, however, has not adopted a consistent approach on this subject of the Speaker's certificate over a period of about 20 years in different parts of the Commonwealth. In Grenada, after the restoration of civilian government, following the United States-led military intervention in the political crisis in October 1983, in the case of *Mitchell & Others v DPP and Another,*[7] the Privy Council held that knowledge of the size of the majority of the governing party provided 'common ground' to conclude that a bill had been passed by the requisite majority specified in the Constitution and that this diminished the requirement for the Speaker's Certificate.

The Doctrine of the Supremacy of Parliament in the United Kingdom

According to Dicey:

> Parliamentary sovereignty is therefore an undoubted legal fact. It is complete both on its positive and on its negative side. Parliament can legally legislate on any topic whatever which, in the judgment of Parliament, is a fit subject for legislation. There is no power which, under the English constitution, can come into rivalry with the legislative sovereignty of Parliament.[8]

Once a document is recognized as being an Act of Parliament of the United Kingdom (UK), no English court can refuse to obey it. In this way, legislative supremacy is, therefore, a legal concept owing to the fact that the courts will not refuse to recognize such laws as made by Parliament. However, the doctrine itself is grounded in a political reality that has remained unchallenged for more than 300 years. That reality is that following the Glorious Revolution of 1688, the supremacy of Parliament was established and no other authority has dared to challenge it since that time.

The legal competence of Parliament to legislate in a manner that cannot bind its future successors is also another affirmation of the doctrine of the supremacy of Parliament. For Dicey there was no statute that was more significant to proving the point about parliamentary supremacy than the Septennial Act 1715.[9]

This act extended the life of Parliament from three years to seven years. Dicey's fascination with the impact of this in relation to the doctrine was the fact that an existing Parliament was able to prolong its own legal existence. For him, this proved that Parliament was 'neither the agent of the electors nor in any sense a trustee for its constituents. It is legally the sovereign legislative power in the state, and the Septennial Act is at once the result and the standing proof of such Parliamentary sovereignty.'[10]

This discussion of the Septennial Act 1715 by Dicey must be measured against his own discussion of the impact of the Parliament Act 1911[11] on the supremacy of Parliament. The effect of the latter on the doctrine itself was that it left the powers of the House of Commons intact, but reduced the powers of the House of Lords to holding what he called 'a suspensive veto',[12] which may prevent a bill from becoming an act of Parliament for a period of two years. The Parliament Act 1911 also reduced the parliamentary term from seven years to five years thereby confirming that no Parliament may bind its future successors. The suspensive veto described by Dicey was further reduced from two years to one year under the provisions of the Parliament Act 1949.[13]

The supremacy of Parliament, therefore, is a firmly established doctrine of the British system of government whose effect has been clearly demonstrated. However, the application of the doctrine in other colonial and later Commonwealth countries provides a completely different dimension on the subject.

The Limitation of Powers of Colonial Legislatures

The conditions under which British law was received in a colony differed depending upon whether the colony was conquered or ceded, on the one hand, or was settled, on the other hand. This distinction was made in the famous case of *Campbell v Hall* [14] from the British colony of Grenada. This case arose out of a dispute between a servant of the Crown, William Hall, a tax collector, and the plaintiff, James Campbell, over the payment of a certain tax on sugar in Grenada (a former French colony captured by British forces in 1762 and ceded to Great Britain by France by the Treaty of Paris in 1763).

In delivering the judgment of the Privy Council, Lord Mansfield, stated, inter alia,

> A country conquered by the British arms becomes a dominion of the King in the right of his Crown; and, therefore, necessarily subject to the Legislature, the Parliament of Great Britain.
>
> The 2d is, that the conquered inhabitants once received under the King's protection, become subjects, and are to be universally considered in that light, not as enemies or aliens.
>
> The 3d, that the articles of capitulation upon which the country is surrendered, and the articles of peace by which it is ceded, are sacred and inviolable according to their true intent and meaning.
>
> The 4th, that the law and legislative government of every dominion, equally affects all persons and all property within the limits thereof; and is the rule of decision for all questions which arise there. Whoever purchases, lives, or sues there, puts himself under the law of the place. An Englishman in Ireland, Minorca, the Isle of Man, or the plantations, has no privilege distinct from the natives.
>
> The 5th, that the laws of a conquered country continue in force, until they are altered by the conqueror: the absurd exception as to pagans, mentioned in Calvin's Case, shews the universality and antiquity of the maxim. For that distinction could not exist before the Christian era; and in all probability

arose from the mad enthusiasm of the Croisades. In the present case, the capitulation expressly provides and agrees, that they shall continue to be governed by their own laws, until His Majesty's further pleasure be known.

The 6th, and last proposition is, that if the King (and when I say King, I always mean the King without the concurrence of Parliament) has a power to alter the old and to introduce new laws in a conquered country, this legislation being subordinate, that is, subordinate to his own authority in Parliament, he cannot make any new change contrary to fundamental principles: he cannot exempt an inhabitant from that particular dominion, as for instance, from the laws of trade, or from the power of Parliament, or give him privileges exclusive of his other subjects; and so in many other instances which might be put.[15]

This argument clearly established that in conquered or ceded colonies the existing law remained until altered by the Crown under its prerogative or by the legislature.

According to Sir William Dale:

1. In a settled colony the basic law was the law of England, because Englishmen carried it there with them, as their personal law. The common law, equity and the statutes were included.

2. But the settlers took with them only so much of the English law as was applicable to their own situation and the condition of an infant colony.[16]

This view was confirmed by Roberts-Wray when he said:

At common law, British subjects who settle in a country without an organised government carry English law with them; and though the Crown has a constituent power, it cannot make ordinary laws for them. They appear to have some sort of inherent right to expect the Crown to grant them the means to legislate for themselves, but being unenforceable, it cannot be a legal right; and it is submitted below that, if the Crown remains inactive, they have a common law right to provide those means for themselves until the prerogative power is brought into action.

These general principles can, it is submitted, apply only to settlers properly so called; they cannot extend to a remote area, for example in the Antarctic, where there are no permanent residents and human beings reside only for short tours of service.[17]

The reality expressed here is that English law was exportable by settlers to colonies and would have the force of law there. Therefore, Roberts-Wray concluded as follows:

> In a settled Colony, established or recognized by the Crown, the legislature owes its existence and its authority to the exercise of the Prerogative. The Sovereign's will might be expressed in a charter (Letters Patent) or by instructions to the Governor given by his Commission or otherwise.[18]

Having established that colonial legislatures were created under certain limitations, the question of the competence of these legislatures to function in competition with the Imperial Parliament in London was subsequently addressed in the nineteenth century.

The Colonial Laws Validity Act 1865[19] came into being out of a response to a number of judgments given by Mr Justice Boothby of the Supreme Court of South Australia. While the issues that his judgments raised became the subject of three opinions of the Law Officers of the UK (March 25 and April 12, 1862 and September 28, 1864), the act itself cleared up many doubts about the powers of colonial legislatures.

The long title of the act is 'An Act to remove Doubts as to the Validity of Colonial Laws' and the preamble to the Act read as follows:

> Whereas Doubts have been entertained respecting the Validity of divers Laws enacted or purporting to have been enacted by the Legislatures of certain of Her Majesty's Colonies, and respecting the Powers of such Legislatures, and it is expedient that such Doubts should be removed....[20]

This act introduced the concept of repugnancy as a basis to void any law enacted by a colonial legislature if that law was deemed to be repugnant to British law. That doctrine would remain in place until the Statute of Westminster 1931[21] when it was removed for the Dominion of Canada, the Commonwealth of Australia, the Dominion of New Zealand, the Union of South Africa, the Irish Free State and Newfoundland.

This alteration emerged out of resolutions adopted at two Imperial Conferences that were held in 1926 and 1930. Section 2 of the Statute of Westminster read as follows:

> 2. – (1) The Colonial Laws Validity Act, 1865, shall not apply to any law made after the commencement of this Act by the Parliament of a Dominion.

> (2) No law and no provision of any law made after the commencement of this Act by the Parliament of a Dominion shall be void or inoperative on the ground that it is repugnant to the law of England, or to the provisions of any existing or future Act of Parliament of the United Kingdom, or to any order, rule or regulation made under any such Act, and the powers of the Parliament of a Dominion shall include the power to repeal or amend any such Act, order, rule or regulation in so far as the same is part of the law of the Dominion.[22]

This particular collection of words would come to represent the template that would be used in many independence acts for various former colonies of Great Britain when they became independent. Indeed, section 2 of the Statute of Westminster can be found almost verbatim in sections 1 and 2 of the First Schedule of the Trinidad and Tobago Independence Act 1962.[23]

A part of the independence arrangements for former colonies of Great Britain was the removal of the doctrine of repugnancy to British law in respect of the powers of the parliaments that were created in these former colonies.

The Creation of Parliaments in Independent Commonwealth Countries

The new constitutions of these former colonies of Great Britain created parliaments for them that were bestowed with the following main characteristics:

i.   the doctrine of repugnancy to British law was abolished;

ii.   the new Parliament was empowered and authorized to enact legislation that would have extra-territorial effect; and

iii. the powers of the British Parliament were curtailed in relation to the independent country by provisions that prohibited the application of British law to the independent country from an appointed day and thereafter.

The effect of a written constitution on these powers of Parliament was such that the Parliament of newly independent countries could not exist unless there was such a document that prescribed the existence of Parliament and bestowed powers upon it. Unlike Great Britain, the parliaments of independent countries of the Commonwealth can all trace their existence and their powers to an instrument that was made under the authority of an act of the British Parliament. This would also apply in cases where there was constitutional amendment to provide for an autocthonous arrangement.

In all cases, the Constitution would provide for its own amendment by Parliament which begs the question that without a constitution, can Parliament exist? It is this question that provides the basis for a debate about whether the Westminster doctrine of the supremacy of Parliament can be exported to the parliaments of the former colonies.

The only way that a parliament could exist without an instrument making provision for it is if there were to be a revolution similar to the Glorious Revolution of 1688 in Great Britain. Without such an event, the parliaments of the Commonwealth cannot claim legitimacy to be supreme to the extent that no power may come into rivalry with it.

The constitutions may themselves remove judicial review of legislation enacted by Parliament or alter the procedure for making laws or abolish the phenomenon of entrenchment of constitutional articles. However, the reality is that Parliament has to depend upon the existence of an instrument that makes provision for its powers and procedure that gives effect to its laws.

To this end, the doctrine of the supremacy of the Constitution has emerged as a superior force that has curtailed the supremacy of Parliament. Indeed, many constitutions have a clause that proclaims that 'this constitution is the supreme law and any other law that is inconsistent with this constitution is void to the extent of the inconsistency.'

The Limitation on the Doctrine of the Supremacy of Parliament by a Written Constitution

The doctrine of the supremacy of the constitution has been discussed by constitutional scholars and judges alike. In taking this discussion outside of the British Parliament, the terms 'sovereignty' and 'supremacy' have been used interchangeably. The distinction between the two in respect of the British Parliament and the legislatures established in former British colonies is best captured by B.O. Nwabueze:

> The U.K. Parliament is therefore not only sovereign but supreme, by which is meant that there is no law to which it is subject as regards either the content of its power or the procedure for exercising it, and it is this supremacy that really excludes the supremacy of the constitution. A legislature operating under a written constitution may be sovereign, even to the extent of having power to amend the constitution in the same way as it makes ordinary law, but it can hardly be supreme, since it is inconceivable that the constitution should fail at least to prescribe a quorum and the method of arriving at decisions by a simple majority. Such a provision binds the legislature, and disregard of it will invalidate any purported exercise of power. The supremacy of the constitution can co-exist with the sovereignty of parliament, but it necessarily excludes the supremacy of parliament.[24]

Nwabueze elegantly articulates the effect of a written constitution upon a legislature, and we are able to better appreciate the reasons why the doctrine of the supremacy of Parliament can truly exist in the British Parliament and not in the former colonies of Great Britain.

Perhaps, it is in the area of procedural requirements that the differentiation can be best understood. The British Parliament does not have its enacted legislation subject to scrutiny by the courts to determine whether the legislation has been validly passed in accordance with any specified procedure. The act of Parliament on the face of it is good enough to establish its validity.

It is at this point that the supremacy and the sovereignty of Parliament part company in the legislatures of former British colonies. According to Nwabueze:

> The courts are bound to accept and act upon the official copy of the act, and cannot go outside it to ascertain whether it was passed in the manner and form prescribed by the constitution. On this view of sovereignty, a sovereign legislature operating under a written constitution is clearly above the constitution just like one operating under an unwritten constitution. However, the Judicial Committee of the Privy Council has in a recent appeal from Ceylon emphatically rejected this view, holding that under a written constitution which prescribes a procedure for law-making, the courts are not only entitled to go outside the official copy of the act in order to enquire into the question of procedure, but have a duty to declare the act invalid if in fact it was passed without due form. For where a legislature is given power subject to certain manner and form, whether it be a simple or special majority, that power does not exist unless and until the manner and form is complied with.[25]

The case to which Nwabueze refers is *Bribery Commissioner v Ranasinghe* (supra), in which the landmark judgment established the doctrine of the supremacy of the Constitution in law and curtailed the doctrine of the supremacy of Parliament outside of Westminster.

The Parliamentary Power to Amend the Constitution

The power of Parliament to make laws and to amend the constitution is derived from the constitution itself. According to the Privy Council in *Ranasinghe*:

> The legislative power of Parliament is derived from section 18 and section 29 of the Constitution. While section 29(3) expressly makes void any Act passed in respect of the unalterable provisions entrenched in section 29(2), which shall not be the subject of legislation, any Bill which amends or repeals any other provision in the Constitution in terms of section 29(4) but does not have endorsed on it a certificate under the hand of the Speaker is also, even though it receives the Royal Assent, invalid and ultra vires.[26]

The Privy Counci made the certificate of the Speaker the centrepiece of its ruling in respect of determining whether a parliament has complied with the provisions of the Constitution in respect of the legislative procedure on a bill for an act that seeks to amend the Constitution.

It is, indeed, at this point that a parliament operating under a written constitution will have its supremacy diminished when compared to the British Parliament. The issue of amending a constitution does not arise for the British Parliament owing to the fact that there is no written constitution.

However, the Privy Council has created some doubt as to the extent to which it will uphold its own rules of interpretation on this point based on its judgment in the case of *Mitchell and Others v Director of Public Prosecutions and Another* (supra) from Grenada more than 20 years after *Ranasinghe.*

The offending portion of their judgment reads:

> The Act received the assent of the Governor General on 21 February 1985. Although there is not among the papers lodged with the petition a certificate by the Speaker or Deputy Speaker under section 39(8) of the Constitution to the effect that Act No. 1 of 1985 was supported by two-thirds of all members of the House of Representatives, no point was taken as to this either before their Lordships or in the courts of Grenada; for it is common ground that the Bill which became Act No. 1 of 1985 received the support of at least two-thirds of all members of the House of Representatives, where the Bill passed unopposed as it did also in the Senate.[27]

This approach is in stark contrast to *Ranasinghe* where the issue of the Speaker's certificate in constitutional amendments was handled as follows:

> Where an Act of Parliament involves an amendment of any alterable provision in the Constitution, the Speaker's certificate under section 29(4) of the Constitution, stating that the number of votes cast in favour of the Bill in the House of Representatives amounted to not less than two-thirds of the whole number of Members of the House (including those not present), is an essential part of the legislative process necessary for amendment. The Courts of law therefore have a duty to look for the certificate in order to ascertain whether the Constitution has been validly amended. Statutory provisions enabling the subsequent reprint of an Act cannot validate an invalid Act.[28]

The unmistakable contrast between the approach of Viscount Radcliffe, Lord Evershed, Lord Morris of Borth-y-Gest, Lord Hodson and Lord Pearce (the *Ranasinghe* case) and Lord Fraser of Tullybelton, Lord Scarman, Lord Diplock, Lord Keith of Kinkel and Sir Owen Woodhouse (the *Mitchell* case), on the issue of the Speaker's certificate in constitutional amendments in Commonwealth legislatures, is confusing and controversial.

The precise nature of the Grenada matter will be highlighted below. However, the specific issue of the importance of the Speaker's certificate in validating an act that amends the Constitution must be highlighted.

The Privy Council moved from a position of the courts having 'a duty to look for the certificate in order to ascertain whether the Constitution has been validly amended' to the relaxation of this principle in the absence of the certificate where it relied on 'common ground that the Bill which became Act No. 1 of 1985 received the support of at least two-thirds of all members of the House of Representatives, where the Bill passed unopposed as it did also in the Senate.'

Has the Privy Council diminished the principle and did it give to the Parliament of Grenada a level of sovereignty and supremacy in 1985, in the aftermath of its return to civilian rule, that it refused to give to the Parliament of Ceylon in 1964? Indeed, did it permit the Parliament of Grenada the same level of supremacy as enjoyed by the UK Parliament of the United Kingdom in the particular matter before it?

In order to appreciate this better, it will be useful to highlight the key issues involved in the Grenada situation.

The Uncertainties of Grenada

In Grenada in 1979, the New Jewel Movement led by Maurice Bishop overthrew the administration of Prime Minister Sir Eric Gairy in a coup d'état after which Maurice Bishop declared himself prime minister and led an administration called the People's Revolutionary Government (PRG). The PRG governed on the basis of enacting People's Laws which became valid after publication in the Gazette or announcement on Radio Free Grenada by the prime minister.

The Crown was not overthrown as the governor general, Sir Paul Scoon, continued to remain in office even though his office was not used to give effect to any executive or legislative acts.

In 1983, there appeared a schism in the Central Committee of the PRG, and Maurice Bishop was put under house arrest by Bernard Coard, a minister in the PRG. Bishop was later freed by his supporters and paraded through the streets of St George's, the capital. He was captured and subsequently executed by firing squad together with some of his ministers.

General Hudson Austin, commander of the People's Revolutionary Army (PRA) declared himself head of a Revolutionary Military Council (RMC) during this period and declared a state of emergency and a 96-hour curfew during which time the PRA disposed of the bodies of Bishop and his ministers.

Governor general Paul Scoon is reported to have issued an invitation to the US government to intervene in the affairs of the island during this period of crisis. This led to the arrival of US Army Rangers on the island between October 25 and 31, 1983. The revolution was put down and the governor general assumed control of the island in the name of Her Majesty Queen Elizabeth II, Queen of Grenada. This he accomplished initially by the issuance of proclamations.

He then established an interim government to advise him on the exercise of his powers and, eventually, a general election was held in November 1984. A Parliament assembled in December 1984 in which the party led by Herbert Blaize had won 14 of the 15 seats in the House of Representatives at the general election. Mr Blaize was appointed prime minister by the governor general and he formed a government.

The Blaize administration moved swiftly to rectify the legal nightmare facing Grenada in the aftermath of the resumption of constitutional government following the general election. This it accomplished by enacting the People's Laws, Interim Government Proclamations and Ordinances Confirmation of Validity Act (Act No. 1 of 1985). The long title of this Act is: 'An Act to confirm the validity of laws made during the period between March 1979 and November 1984 when the Constitution of Grenada was suspended.'[29] The governor general assented to this act on February 21, 1985.

The issue that is related to how this act got entangled in the *Mitchell* case relates to the charges of murder, etc., that were brought against Andy Mitchell and 18 others who were captured during the American intervention. They had argued that they could not be tried under the court system, which they had established when they were in power as the PRG, because that system had been overthrown by the actions of the governor general in seeking to restore constitutional government under the Constitution of Grenada.[30] Their basic argument was that they ought to be tried under the provisions of the Constitution of Grenada before they suspended it and, therefore, they were seeking the special leave of Her Majesty to be heard by the Privy Council.

The facts of the case were as follows:

Petition for special leave to appeal from the judgment of the Court of Appeal of Grenada (Haynes P., Peterkin and Liverpool JJ.A.) given on 10 May 1985 dismissing an appeal by Andy Mitchell and 18 other petitioners from a judgment of Nedd C.J. in the High Court of Grenada on 19 November 1984 dismissing the petitioners' motion for redress under section 101 of the Constitution of Grenada 1973. By that motion the petitioners sought a declaration, inter alia, that the High Court of Grenada as then established was unconstitutional, not competent to try them in respect of the charges preferred against them and not legally constituted; that they were entitled to be tried by a properly constituted court under the provisions of the Constitution; that they had a right of appeal to the Court of Appeal established by the Constitution; and that the Privy Council (Abolition of Appeals) Law 1979 was a nullity.

At the close of the hearing before the Judicial Committee Lord Fraser of Tullybelton announced that their Lordships would advise that they did not have jurisdiction to hear the petition for reasons to be delivered later.[31]

In writing for the Board, Lord Diplock took note of the absence of the Speaker's certificate among the documents lodged in the case[32]. However, rather than declaring Act No. 1 of 1985 null and void and of no effect by using the strict application of the doctrine of the supremacy of the Constitution that was applied by the Board in *Ranasinghe* in Ceylon in 1964, Lord Diplock substituted the 'common ground' principle to validate the act, owing to the fact that there was no opposition to the bill and because the government commanded the support of 14 of the 15 members of the House of Representatives and, therefore, had more than the two-thirds majority vote that was required to pass the bill in the House. The absence of the Speaker's certificate was a major deficiency that the Board ought to have addressed more forcefully because it is still not known how many MPs voted for the bill that was, in effect, amending the Constitution.

The fact that the matter that concerned the application for special leave emerged out of a judgment given on November 19, 1984 in the High Court and a judgment given on appeal by the Court of Appeal on May 10, 1985 and the special leave hearing before the Privy Council on July 10, 1985 was immaterial as events had overtaken the proceedings. By the time the application for special leave had come before the Board, the act had already come into force on February 21, 1985. This permitted the Board to hold that it had been deprived of jurisdiction to hear the application and, in the process, confirmed that the Constitution had, in fact, been amended to abolish appeals to the Privy Council.

It is this latter point that has undermined the determination of how supreme Commonwealth parliaments really are when this is compared to the judgment in *Ranasinghe*.

Indeed, there was some doubt about whether Act No. 1 of 1985 had been properly passed based on the dictum of Lord Diplock. In order to address this possible anomaly, the Parliament of Grenada confirmed Act No. 1 of 1985 a second time by the enactment of Act No. 16 of 1987.

This action of the Parliament of Grenada was clearly designed to ensure that the amendment to the Constitution was confirmed for the removal of all doubt. However, it was also embracing the judgment in *Ranasinghe* by doubting its own competence to amend the Constitution without recourse to the Speaker's certificate. If the Privy Council had no problem with it, why should the Parliament of Grenada doubt its own competence? Was the Grenada situation one of political convenience for the Board to find a way out of having to rule in favour of those who terrorized the state or was it a case where the Parliament of Grenada was elevated to the same level as the British Parliament in its competence to amend the Constitution without reliance on the procedural requirements enforced elsewhere?

Conclusion

The supremacy of the Constitution and its effect on the doctrine of parliamentary supremacy in post-independence Commonwealth legislatures has been clearly decided before the courts. However, the arguments advanced by the Privy Council in 1964 in Ceylon are inconsistent with the arguments advanced by that same body in 1985 in Grenada.

The immediate suggestion that emerges out of the Grenada case is that a government that controls more than a special majority in the elected House of Parliament in a Commonwealth Caribbean legislature may be able to rely upon the 'common ground' theory enunciated by Lord Diplock to effect an amendment to the constitution by avoiding the scrutiny of procedural requirements outlined in Ceylon some two decades earlier.

The Privy Council was questioned in 2006 in the case of *Coard and Others v The Attorney General*[33] over whether the *Mitchell* case had been wrongly decided. According to the judgment of the Board (Lord Bingham of Cornhill, Lord Hoffman, Lord Phillips of Worth Matravers, Lord Carswell and Lord Brown of Eaton-under-Heywood) delivered by Lord Hoffman:

> 20. Mr. Fitzgerald submitted that *Mitchell v Director of Public Prosecutions* [1986] AC 73 was wrongly decided. The arguments which he advanced against the decision were in substance the same as those which the

Board then rejected. In essence, he argued that section 3 of the West Indies Associated States (Appeals to the Privy Council) (Grenada) Order 1967 (S.I. 1967 / No. 224), which has been quoted above, did not merely provide machinery for such right of appeal as the Constitution might from time to time create but directly conferred a right of appeal which could be abolished only by the special voting procedure prescribed by section 39(5) of the Constitution for an amendment of section 3. It is common ground that the 1987 Act complied with section 39(2) but not with section 39(5).

21. Their Lordships reject this argument for the reasons given by Lord Diplock in *Mitchell*. The 1967 Order was made under powers conferred by the Judicial Committee Act 1844 and the language of section 3 shows clearly that it is concerned not with the constitutional question of whether a right of appeal should exist but with the procedural question of how such an appeal should be exercised. Once the Constitution was amended to abolish the right of appeal, there was nothing upon which the 1967 Order could operate.[34]

The reference to *Mitchell v Director of Public Prosecutions* [1986] AC 73 in the above judgment is the same case as cited in this chapter as *Mitchell & Others v DPP and Another* [1985] 3 WLR 724 (P.C.). These paragraphs demonstrate some diplomatic language that reveals the deftness of the Privy Council on the decision in the *Mitchell* case. Instead of making reference to Act No. 1 of 1985 (which was before the Board in 1985), Lord Hoffman made reference to the fact that 'the 1987 Act complied with section 39(2) but not with section 39(5).' At the time when Lord Diplock introduced his 'common ground' argument there was no 1987 act, yet Lord Hoffman rejected Mr Fitzgerald's argument by reference to the 1987 act.

The *Mitchell* case may well have been wrongly decided when held up against the standard of the *Ranasinghe* case at the time of its decision in July 1985. However, when the judgment was delivered in the *Coard* case on February 7, 2007, the Privy Council refused to concede that the *Mitchell* case was wrongly decided. To that extent, the *Coard* case confirms the undermining of the *Ranasinghe* case by the *Mitchell* case.

The cases of *Mitchell* and *Coard* may very well open the door to further arguments about the doctrine of the supremacy of Parliament where procedural requirements are involved in relation to confused opinions from the Privy Council which may have been based on political convenience in post-revolutionary Grenada as opposed to strict legal interpretation. But they cannot undermine the basic premise that without a written constitution the right of a parliament to exist and to have the power to make laws would have to emerge from a revolution or popular consent in order to give it such undocumented legitimacy. This is what applies to Commonwealth Caribbean countries in the absence of revolutionary situations.

Notes

1. A.V. Dicey, *Introduction to the Study of the Law of the Constitution*, 8th ed. (London: Macmillan and Co. Ltd., 1927), xviii–xix.
2. 'Legalization of the Convention Parliament, 1 Will and Mary, Cap. I. 1689,' in *Select Statutes Cases and Documents*, ed. Sir Charles Grant Robertson (London: Methuen & Co. Ltd., 1935), 105–106.
3. *Laws of the United Kingdom* 6 Geo. 3, c. 12.
4. Sir Kenneth Roberts-Wray, *Commonwealth and Colonial Law* (London: Stevens and Sons, 1966), 140.
5. *Laws of the United Kingdom* 28 & 29 Vict. c. 63.
6. *Bribery Commissioner v Ranasinghe* [1965] AC 172.
7. *Mitchell & Others v DPP and Another* [1985] 3 WLR 724 (P.C.).
8. Dicey, 66–68.
9. *Laws of the United Kingdom* 1 Geo. 1, St. 2, c. 38.
10. Dicey, 45–46.
11. *Laws of the United Kingdom* 1 & 2 Geo. 5, c. 13.
12. Dicey, xxiii.
13. *Laws of the United Kingdom* 12, 13 & 14 Geo. 6, c. 103.
14. *Campbell v Hall* (1774) 1 Cowp. 204, 98 ER 1045.
15. Ibid., 208–209.
16. Sir William Dale, *The Modern Commonwealth* (London: Butterworths, 1983), 7.
17. Roberts-Wray, op. cit., 151.
18. Ibid., 151–52.
19. See note 5 above.
20. *Laws of the United Kingdom* 28 & 29 Vict. c. 63, Preamble.
21. *Laws of the United Kingdom* 22 Geo. 5, c. 4
22. Ibid., s. 2.
23. *Laws of the United Kingdom* 10 & 11 Eliz. 2, c. 54.
24. B.O. Nwabueze, *Constitutionalism in the Emergent States* (London: C. Hurst & Co., 1973), 8.
25. Ibid., 7.
26. *Bribery Commissioner v Ranasinghe, Privy Council Appeal No. 20 of 1963*, 74.
27. *Mitchell v Director of Public Prosecutions* [1985] 3 WLR 724 (P.C.) at 728C.
28. *Bribery Commissioner v Ranasinghe*, 73.
29. *Laws of Grenada*, Act No. 1 of 1985.
30. *Grenada Constitution Order 1973*, S.I. 1973 / No. 2155 (London: H.M.S.O., 1973).
31. *Mitchell v Director of Public Prosecutions*, 725 E to G.
32. See note 27 above.
33. *Coard v Attorney General* [2007] UKPC 7.
34. Ibid., paras. 20–21.

3.
Magna Carta and Human Rights

Introduction

> The whole history of the African population of the West Indies inevitably
> drives them towards representative institutions fashioned after the British
> model. Transplanted by the slave trade or other circumstances to foreign
> soil, losing in the process their social system, language and traditions, and
> with the exception of some relics of obeah, whatever religion they may
> have had, they owe everything that they have now, and all that they are, to
> the British race that first enslaved them, and subsequently to its honour
> restored to them their freedom. Small wonder if they look for political
> growth to the only source and pattern that they know, and aspire to share
> in what has been the peculiarly British gift of representative institutions.[1]

This excerpt from Major Wood's 1922 report best encapsulates the story
of how the principles of Magna Carta came to be included in the later
constitutions of the former colonies of the British West Indies and had
been excluded before. Major Wood (later Lord Halifax) was expressing a
view that confirmed the superiority factor that underscored much of the
political thought that drove the slave trade and slavery in the British West
Indies.

Such political thought was devoid of any reference to Magna Carta as the
basis for the organization of slave society and its sustenance. Indeed, most
of the constitutional law texts on the Commonwealth Caribbean make
absolutely no mention of Magna Carta whatsoever with the exception
of Sir Fred Phillips's *Commonwealth Caribbean Constitutional Law* in
which he argues that the foundations of the protection of the right to life,
the right to personal liberty, the right to the protection of property, and
the right to due process of law were established for Caribbean societies
through Magna Carta.[2]

The significance of this fact is that many constitutional law scholars in
the region have not made the connection between Magna Carta and many
of the human rights features of Commonwealth Caribbean constitutions.

Of the 12 independent states in the region, 11 of them have included a Bill of Rights in their constitutions that is based on the European Convention on Human Rights 1950,[3] and one of them (Trinidad and Tobago) has modelled its Bill of Rights in accordance with the Canadian Bill of Rights 1960.[4]

The influence of Magna Carta on these two source documents has been well-established. In the case of the Canadian Bill of Rights 1960, the following is useful:

> Magna Carta informed the development of Canada's Bill of Rights, a federal statute from 1960 that was the earliest written expression of human rights law at the federal level in Canada. The Bill of Rights replaced the unwritten rights implied by the 1867 Constitution Act that the new nation would be created "with a Constitution similar in Principle to that of the United Kingdom," a statement that indicates Magna Carta, the Petition of Right, and the Bill of Rights are all part of the Canadian constitutional tradition.[5]

This link between Magna Carta and the Canadian Bill of Rights 1960 is an important dimension in understanding the link of Magna Carta to the constitution of Trinidad and Tobago.

The European Convention on Human Rights 1950 also has a direct link to Magna Carta. This is best captured in an essay by Mark Rathbone. Rathbone states:

> The European Convention on Human Rights was an international agreement which aimed to establish common standards of human rights in the aftermath of the Second World War and the Holocaust. Yet the fact that British lawyers, notably David Maxwell Fyfe, Conservative MP, later Home Secretary and Lord Chancellor, took a leading role in the drafting of the Convention meant that it was heavily influenced by British legal traditions, including the Magna Carta. There were other historic sources of inspiration, notably the French revolutionary Declaration of the Rights of Man, dating from 1789, the US Bill of Rights, ratified in 1791, and the Universal Declaration of Human Rights, adopted by the United Nations in 1948. The fact, however, that in March 1951 Britain was the first country to ratify the ECHR suggests that it sits comfortably within British legal traditions. The ECHR came into force in 1953 and was eventually incorporated into British domestic law as the Human Rights Act in 1998.[6]

Rathbone's assertions are very useful for making the link with 11 independent countries in the Commonwealth Caribbean whose Bills of Rights have been modelled after the European Convention on Human Rights 1950. Those Commonwealth Caribbean countries are: (i) Antigua and Barbuda, (ii) The Bahamas, (iii) Barbados, (iv) Belize, (v) Dominica, (vi) Grenada, (vii) Guyana, (viii) Jamaica, (ix) St Kitts-Nevis, (x) St Lucia, and (xi) St Vincent and the Grenadines.

The enactment of human rights provisions in the constitutions of all 12 independent Commonwealth Caribbean countries represents the final culmination of the journey of Magna Carta and its principles into these constitutions.

In 2011, Jamaica enacted The Charter of Fundamental Rights and Freedoms (Constitutional Amendment) Act, 2011,[7] which repealed and replaced chapter three of the Constitution of Jamaica (the human rights chapter) that had been drafted at independence in 1962. The provisions of this amendment to the human rights chapter of the Jamaican Constitution represented a blend of the Universal Declaration of Human Rights,[8] the European Convention on Human Rights (supra), the Canadian Bill of Rights 1960 (supra), and the Canadian Charter of Rights and Freedoms 1982.[9] All four of these source documents trace their core provisions back to Magna Carta.

There is clear evidence to show that the colonial state that existed in these Commonwealth Caribbean countries in the centuries before their independence operated on the basis of exploitation, inequality, and injustice at different stages of their development, especially prior to the abolition of slavery in 1834.

The existence of Magna Carta was ignored by British settlers and officials in the British West Indies as well to the extent that the philosophy of regarding enslaved Africans as property and not as people was a core legal philosophy of the pre-emancipation era. This philosophy was reinforced by case law in *Gregson v Gilbert*[10] otherwise known as the Zong massacre. In arriving at a decision in this case, Lord Mansfield confirmed his view of the slaves as property which is best captured as follows:

> The captain of the Zong, en route from West Africa to Jamaica with a cargo of several hundred slaves, lost his way in the Caribbean and was delayed at sea for several days. With water running out, 60 slaves died of thirst, 40 desperately threw themselves into the sea and drowned, and another 150 were thrown overboard. The ship owner brought a lawsuit against the insurer of the ship and its cargo for recovery of the value of the slaves who had been thrown overboard.

A jury gave a verdict against the insurer, on the ground that the loss of the slaves was a result of the normal perils of the sea. On appeal, Mansfield ruled that there had to be a new trial, because the ship owner had not shown that it was necessary to throw the slaves overboard. Apparently it had rained before the ship arrived in Jamaica; it was therefore possible that some water was available for the slaves. It was implicit in Mansfield's decision that if the ship owner could prove that sufficient water was lacking it would have been legal – and within the terms of the insurance policy as one of the normal perils of the sea – to throw the slaves overboard. Nowhere in his short opinion was there any suggestion that the captain and crew of the Zong were murderers.[11]

This judgment by Lord Mansfield on May 22, 1783 confirmed that slaves were regarded as property and not as human beings in the context of the British West Indies. However, this judgment rests upon the thinking applied by Lord Mansfield in an earlier opinion that he had expressed in the case of *Somerset v Stewart* [12] given on June 22, 1772 which established that slavery could not be practised in England, but left open the issue of whether it could be practised in other parts of the British Empire by virtue of the ambiguity of his judgment in this regard.

One of the final paragraphs of the judgment in the *Somerset* case read as follows:

> We are so well agreed, that we think there is no occasion of having it argued (as I intimated an intention at first) before all the judges, as is usual, for obvious reasons, on a return to a habeas corpus; the only question before us is, whether the cause on the return is sufficient ? If it is, the Negro must be remanded; if it is not, he must be discharged. Accordingly, the return states, that the slave departed and refused to serve; whereupon he was kept, to be sold abroad. So high an act of dominion must be recognized by the law of the country where it is used. The power of a master over his slave has been extremely different, in different countries. The state of slavery is of such a nature, that it is incapable of being introduced on any reasons, moral or political; but only positive law, which preserves its force long after the reasons, occasion, and time itself from whence it was created, is erased from memory: it's so odious, that nothing can be suffered to support it, but positive law. Whatever inconveniences, therefore, may follow from a decision, I cannot say this case is allowed or approved by the law of England; and therefore the black must be discharged.[13]

This ambiguity suggested that in England slave compulsion and domination could not be accepted, but left open the question of acceptance 'in different countries'. That would seem to suggest that the principles of Magna Carta might not have been universally recognized throughout the British Empire in the context of any general application.

Imperial Design and British Presence in the West Indies

The issue of how Great Britain came to acquire colonies in the West Indies is an important part of any discussion about Magna Carta in the region. Essentially, the Treaty of Tordesillas 1494, concluded between Spain and Portugal, revised a papal bull of 1493 by fixing a line 370 leagues west of the Cape Verde Islands that ceded to Portugal all territory to the east of that line and ceded to Spain all territory to the west of that line.[14]

This partition of the world between Spain and Portugal was soon challenged by other imperial powers. According to Eric Williams:

> On March 5, 1496, Henry VII issued a patent to another sailor, John Cabot, to undertake a voyage of discovery. The date has been called the birthday of the British Empire. Whilst no concrete results were obtained, the patent is of significance. It omitted the words "Southern Seas", thus giving tacit recognition to Spanish and Portuguese discoveries and, to that extent, to the papal document. But its very issuance rejected any interpretation of a partition of the entire world between Spain and Portugal, and was a warning that the English Government regarded ownership as based at least on discovery.[15]

This approach by Great Britain ushered in an era of overseas exploration that would facilitate the export of English settlers and their values and beliefs to a so-called New World where colonies would be established in the name of the Crown. According to Williams:

> Sir William Cecil (later Lord Burleigh), the Elizabethan statesman, told the Spanish Ambassador to England in 1562 that 'the Pope had no right to partition the world and to give and take kingdoms to whomsoever he pleased.' The British Government countered Spanish claims with the doctrine of effective occupation.[16]

The first method of challenging the Spanish hegemony secured by the Treaty of Tordesillas 1494 by other imperial powers was the use of piracy. This led to a period of plunder and warfare in the Caribbean that is best described by Williams as follows:

> The undeclared war in the Caribbean, in the sixteenth century phrase, 'no peace beyond the line', was enshrined in the Treaty of Cateau-Cambrésis of 1559 between France and Spain: "west of the prime meridian and south of the Tropic of Cancer…violence by either party to the other side shall not be regarded as in contravention of the treaties." The incarnation of this phase of Caribbean history is Sir Francis Drake.[17]

As the sixteenth century gave way to the seventeenth and the exploits of Francis Drake on the high seas put Great Britain in a better position to challenge Spanish hegemony, it was the commencement of colonization in the West Indies by Britain that would lead to the export of Magna Carta to the region. According to Williams:

> It was to permanent settlements in the Caribbean that England and the other European nations turned. In an effort to reinforce one of the expeditions to Guiana, the English made their first attempt to settle in the West Indies, in St. Lucia, in 1605. But the settlement was a failure as a result of the hostility of the Carib Indians. A similar attempt to settle in Grenada four years later failed for the same reason. The Dutch landed on the barren rock of St. Eustatius in 1600, and the Dutch West India Company was established in 1621. In 1623 the English landed in St. Kitts, and in 1625 in Barbados.[18]

The arrival of English settlers in the West Indies would open the door to a prolonged period of colonization that would later come to include the movement of thousands of persons of African descent to the region from West Africa.

They would come as slaves to work on the sugar plantations as part of what was to become a slave trade that would support the institution of slavery. A triangular trade developed and is adequately described by Williams as follows:

> The combination of the Negro slave trade, Negro slavery and Caribbean sugar production is known as the triangular trade. A ship left the metropolitan country with a cargo of metropolitan goods, which it exchanged on the coast of West Africa for slaves. This constituted the first side of the triangle. The second consisted of the Middle Passage, the voyage from West Africa to the West Indies with the slaves. The triangle was completed by the voyage from the West Indies to the metropolitan country with sugar and other Caribbean products received in exchange for the slaves.[19]

Magna Carta in the British West Indies

The issue of the influence of Magna Carta on a worldwide scale has been expressed by the Magna Carta 800th Anniversary Committee. This has been challenged by James Melton and Robert Hazell in their co-edited book *Magna Carta and its Modern Legacy* as follows:

> The world is poised to celebrate the 800th anniversary of Magna Carta in 2015. One reason for such a celebration is the Great Charter's "influence". In the words of Sir Robert Worcester – writing on behalf of the Magna Carta

2015 Committee – Magna Carta "has influenced constitutional thinking worldwide including in France, Germany, Japan, the United States and India as well as many Commonwealth countries, and throughout Latin America and Africa." According to the celebration committee, then, Magna Carta has shaped theories of constitutionalism, and perhaps even the contents of constitutions in virtually every corner of the world. Despite the claims of the celebration committee, Magna Carta's influence is unclear because the term influence itself is unclear.[20]

This line of argument suggests that Magna Carta has been more influential in the United Kingdom (UK) than it has been overseas. In the case of the West Indies, that argument may be substantiated in the colonial past, but there is good reason to believe that the adoption of Bills of Rights at independence, based on either the European Convention on Human Rights 1950 or the Canadian Bill of Rights 1960, would confirm the direct influence of Magna Carta.

Derek O'Brien confirms the absence of the influence of Magna Carta on the legal codes of the slave colonies of the British West Indies. According to O'Brien:

The idea that English liberty was inextricably linked to English ancestry is particularly helpful in understanding why these settlers did not think twice about denying the freedoms guaranteed by English liberty to the slaves in their midst, who were being imported in increasingly large numbers from West Africa to work on the sugar plantations that sprang up across the region from the mid-seventeenth century onwards. Instead, the slave population was governed by a set of laws known as Slave Code Acts. These laws were enacted by colonial assemblies, which were composed mainly of slave owners. Unsurprisingly, the laws that they enacted were designed to promote the collective interests of the slave owners and offered absolutely no protection or redress to the enslaved population. As we shall see in the next section, these laws were as far removed from Magna Carta and the tradition of English liberty as it is possible to conceive.[21]

The picture painted by O'Brien captures the complete absence of Magna Carta in the evolution of slave society in the British West Indies. However, O'Brien does not address the source of the political and social thought that led British settlers in the West Indies to adopt the approach of superiority over the enslaved Africans that allowed the continuation of slave society until emancipation in 1834, nor does he address the issue of imperial design that led to a British presence in the West Indies.

The sociological insight expressed in the dictum of Major E.F.L. Wood, parliamentary under-secretary of state for the colonies, in his report to the then secretary of state for the colonies, Winston Churchill, in 1922[22] is reflective of the philosophy of racial superiority.

O'Brien does not address the phenomenon of racial superiority as the mindset that drove the perpetuation of the legal and political thought that regarded the slaves as property and not as persons. Nor does he address the issue of the economic value of enslaved Africans as the basis for the operation of the slave trade and slavery. While the brutality of the slave codes regarded the slaves as deviant persons who had to be controlled, it was their classification as property that set them apart from the settlers who enslaved them. This was best captured in the *Zong* massacre and the judgment by Lord Mansfield in the *Gregson v Gilbert* case.[23]

This case provided an adequate example of the legal philosophy that informed maritime insurance law at the time, but also confirmed the absence of any Magna Carta influence in those laws. O'Brien mentions the case *en passant*; however, its significance is far more profound in understanding the dichotomy between the foundation of the legal system in England and the application of insurance law in the British colonies and on the high seas.

According to James Walvin:

> What stunned people about the Zong in March 1783 was not simply the murderous brutality of events on that ship, but the incredible legal saga played out in London – and the implications of that legal debate. An English jury, sitting under the watchful gaze of the Lord Chief Justice, Lord Mansfield, "rendered a verdict wholly favourable to the owners of the Zong for the loss of 130-plus slaves at £30 each".[24]

For many scholars, the *Zong* massacre marked a turning point in the debate over the continuance of the slave trade and ultimately slavery itself. Walvin explains as follows:

> But the Zong case offered a totally new approach to the entire business of maritime insurance. Did an insurance policy cover the deliberate killings of Africans? The Zong legal hearings in 1783 revealed the links between the staid world of insurance and the violent world of the slave ships – and, in the process, the matter was transformed. The insistence of William Gregson and his colleagues that they receive compensation for murdered Africans shifted the entire debate from a technical decision about the law of insurance into a public discussion about the very nature of slavery itself. Before 1783, arcane matters of maritime insurance had been the preserve of specialist legal debate. Now they were thrown into full public and political view.[25]

Articles 39 and 40 of Magna Carta 1215 confirm their inconsistency with slavery in the British West Indies and the slave trade that lay at the heart of the triangular trade between England, West Africa, and the West Indies. According to Article 39 of Magna Carta:

> No free man shall be seized or imprisoned, or stripped of his rights or possessions, or outlawed or exiled, or deprived of his standing in any other way, nor will we proceed with force against him, or send others to do so, except by the lawful judgement of his equals or by the law of the land.[26]

Article 40 of Magna Carta 1215 read as follows: 'To no one will we sell, to no one deny or delay right or justice.'[27]

Objectively speaking, the operative words in article 39 would be 'free man' which could be used as a justification to separate the legal status of the English settlers in the British West Indian colonies as opposed to the enslaved Africans who were brought to those colonies who would not have been classified as 'free men'.

This could account for the differential treatment meted out to slaves under the Slave Codes as highlighted by O'Brien.[28] However, article 40 is very specific insofar as it does not use any classification between those who are regarded as 'free men' and those who are not by virtue of the fact that there is a blanket statement that: 'To no one will we sell, to no one deny or delay right or justice'.[29]

In respect of conquered or ceded colonies, where the laws of those colonies would remain in force until such time as English law was introduced by the King or Queen in Parliament, there also appeared to be a clear distinction between the European inhabitants and the enslaved Africans in respect of how the law would view them and the way in which the colonial authorities who took control of colonies after conquest or cession in the name of the Crown would regard them.

There was no distinction about whether or not the recognition of slavery (before 1834) and the slave trade (before 1808) would be deemed unlawful. The 1772 case of *Somerset v Stewart*[30] established that slavery was not legal in England, but in the colonies there was no statement in this case that outlawed it.

British Law in the Colonies

The 1763 Treaty of Paris that ended the Seven Years' War between Britain, France, and Spain made the following declarations at Articles VIII and IX that pertained to the West Indies:

VIII. The King of Great Britain shall restore to France the islands of Guadeloupe, of Mariegalante, of Desirade, of Martinico, and of Belleisle; and the fortresses of these islands shall be restored in the same condition they were in when they were conquered by the British arms, provided that his Britannick Majesty's subjects, who shall have settled in the said islands, or those who shall have any commercial affairs to settle there or in other places restored to France by the present treaty, shall have liberty to sell their lands and their estates, to settle their affairs, to recover their debts, and to bring away their effects as well as their persons, on board vessels, which they shall be permitted to send to the said islands and other places restored as above, and which shall serve for this use only, without being restrained on account of their religion, or under any other pretence whatsoever, except that of debts or of criminal prosecutions: and for this purpose, the term of eighteen months is allowed to his Britannick Majesty's subjects, to be computed from the day of the exchange of the ratifications of the present treaty; but, as the liberty granted to his Britannick Majesty's subjects, to bring away their persons and their effects, in vessels of their nation, may be liable to abuses if precautions were not taken to prevent them; it has been expressly agreed between his Britannick Majesty and his Most Christian Majesty, that the number of English vessels which have leave to go to the said islands and places restored to France, shall be limited, as well as the number of tons of each one; that they shall go in ballast; shall set sail at a fixed time; and shall make one voyage only; all the effects belonging to the English being to be embarked at the same time. It has been farther agreed, that his Most Christian Majesty shall cause the necessary passports to be given to the said vessels; that, for the greater security, it shall be allowed to place two French clerks or guards in each of the said vessels, which shall be visited in the landing places and ports of the said islands and places restored to France, and that the merchandize which shall be found therein shall be confiscated.

IX. The Most Christian King cedes and guaranties to his Britannick Majesty, in full right, the islands of Grenada, and the Grenadines, with the same stipulations in favour of the inhabitants of this colony, inserted in the IVth article for those of Canada: And the partition of the islands called neutral, is agreed and fixed, so that those of St. Vincent, Dominico, and Tobago, shall remain in full right to Great Britain, and that of St. Lucia shall be delivered to France, to enjoy the same likewise in full right, and the high contracting parties guaranty the partition so stipulated.[31]

The protection of commercial property and the grant of religious freedom were significant aspects of this treaty. The treatment of the transfer of Grenada and the Grenadine islands on the same basis as the transfer of Canada from France to Britain was significant as it was the basis of guaranteeing religious freedom as between Catholics and Protestants.

This particular aspect of the Treaty of Paris is important, because it would become the centerpiece of a groundbreaking legal judgment in 1774 in the famous case of *Campbell v Hall*[32] from Grenada which defined the manner in which English law was to be received in settled, conquered and ceded colonies.

In respect of the doctrine of repugnancy to British law that emerged in the second half of the nineteenth century, British colonial legislatures had previously enacted laws or measures that violated Magna Carta and its principles in British West Indian colonies prior to 1834.

Adoption of Magna Carta Principles

The adoption of Magna Carta principles into the constitutions of the independent Commonwealth Caribbean countries did not happen by direct acknowledgement. Instead, these principles came to the region through the adoption of the principles contained in either the European Convention on Human Rights 1950 or the Canadian Bill of Rights 1960, suitably modified for insertion in the constitutions of the respective countries adopting them.

Commonwealth Caribbean law books are devoid of references to the Magna Carta in their indices with the exception of Sir Fred Phillips's *Commonwealth Caribbean Constitutional Law*.[33] One of the more recently published books on constitutional law in the Commonwealth Caribbean, namely the second edition of the book *Changing Caribbean Constitutions* by Dr Francis Alexis in 2015[34] makes no mention of Magna Carta in its 671 pages.

There is a debate that O'Brien engages on the issue of the influence of Magna Carta in the Commonwealth Caribbean. He engages it on the following grounds:

> In the post-independence era, the legacy of English liberty bequeathed by the original settlers has continued to define and shape the rights and freedoms of Commonwealth Caribbean citizens by restricting them to their pre-independence incarnation. Not only has this undermined the normative force of the Independence Constitutions, but in so doing, it has evoked a source of law that is inextricably associated with the colonial era and slavery.[35]

O'Brien relies too heavily on the link between British settlers and the era of slavery to undermine the reliance on Magna Carta that was largely ignored in the pre-emancipation period to make his point. He does not make the connection between the influence of Magna Carta on either the European Convention on Human Rights 1950 or the Canadian Bill of Rights 1960 and their adoption in the independence constitutions of the 12 independent countries of the region, far less the Jamaican reforms of 2011.

Reliance on the slave trade and slavery narrative causes O'Brien to miss the incorporation of Magna Carta principles in the Bills of Rights of these countries that go beyond the issue of English common law and its reception in the legal systems of these countries.

The fact that all of the independent countries of the Commonwealth Caribbean, with the exception of Trinidad and Tobago, adopted the model of the European Convention on Human Rights 1950 at their independence raises the question of why Trinidad and Tobago deviated in its adoption of the Canadian Bill of Rights 1960 model for its independence constitution.

This came about as a consequence of proposals advanced by the Bar Association of Trinidad and Tobago at the Meeting of Commentators on the Draft Constitution at Queen's Hall, in Port of Spain, over the period April 25–27, 1962. The president of the Bar Association at that time, Mr (later Sir) Hugh Wooding, made a plea at the Queen's Hall Conference for the adoption of the Canadian Bill of Rights 1960, suitably amended, to replace the model of the European Convention on Human Rights that was included in the Draft Constitution for Trinidad and Tobago's Independence.

Mr Wooding said, inter alia:

> Surely if we find that the principle or the form or the contents of the Canadian Bill of Rights is such as can be acceptable generally, we can adapt it to circumstances. We can surely adapt the thing as at the present time this Draft Constitution has taken a number of its provisions from precedents which have gone before. We have adapted things, amended them, added certain things, deleted certain things, and in the same way we can take the Canadian Bill of Rights and adapt them to suit us, and I do not see why we should be limited to choosing the Canadian Bill of Rights as it is or refusing to consider it altogether. I put forward, on behalf of the Bar Association, that it should be taken as a model, and it should be used as a means whereby we can help to shape our thinking in the matter, modifying it to the extent that may be necessary, and remembering also that this Canadian Bill of Rights is something which came into existence in 1960 and forms no part of the Constitution of Canada.[36]

The proposals advanced by Wooding and the Bar Association of Trinidad and Tobago were considered by the cabinet, together with other proposals made at the meeting. The chairman of the Queen's Hall Conference made the following statement at the commencement of the proceedings on Friday, April 27, 1962:

> I am happy to be in a position to inform you, on the authority of the Cabinet, that your written comments and your suggestions made in this Hall have received preliminary consideration. Further detailed consideration will of course be given to them but already certain decisions have been taken. These decisions are that at the Joint Select Committee to begin on Monday the Government representatives will propose:...(c) the substitution for Chapter II of a Bill of Rights along the lines of the Canadian Bill of Rights with appropriate modifications including the introduction of safeguards (Applause).[37]

This extract from the verbatim record of the Queen's Hall Conference is crucial to an understanding of how Trinidad and Tobago deviated from the European Convention on Human Rights 1950 and adopted the model of the Canadian Bill of Rights 1960 for its Bill of Rights in its independence constitution. The above quotation marks the exact moment of transfer from one model to the other and that change was retained throughout the Joint Select Committee that considered the revised draft constitution (April 30–May 16, 1962) as well as the Marlborough House Conference that considered the Independence constitution (May 28–June 8, 1962).

It is through these Bills of Rights that the principles of Magna Carta worked their way into Commonwealth Caribbean constitutions as opposed to any reliance on English Common Law.

Magna Carta was absent from the colonial past of Commonwealth Caribbean countries and only arose with the adoption of Bills of Rights in the constitutions of those countries when they attained their independence. In dealing with this matter in the drafting of independence constitutions, it was necessary to establish a clear line of separation between the pre-independence past that had no recognition, declaration and protection of fundamental human rights and freedoms.

As a consequence, the concept of existing laws was introduced into the independence constitutions to protect and preserve all laws enacted prior to the proverbial appointed day when independence constitutions came into effect as a marker in law where pre- and post-independence applications of human rights considerations could be separated.

Writing in *Transitions in Caribbean Law*, Tracy Robinson argues as follows:

> We should be slow to promote implied constitutional norms that have no textual grounding and the provisions of the constitutions should remain important to constitutional interpretation even when we accept that they

rest on or are evidence of implied norms. Judges will have the exacting task of deciding whether the provisions reflect an implied principle but do not exhaust it.[38]

This uncertainty arises from the fact that the Commonwealth Caribbean cannot definitively trace its human rights past to a place where 'constitutional norms' would have arisen.

Robinson continues as follows:

> There is a risk that the 'common law' might derail the progressive development of implied constitutional norms. Caribbean common law constitutionalism relied heavily on existing laws and the common law as the source of constitutional fundamentals. Post independence common law constitutionalism gained a bad reputation for elevating ordinary or existing or colonial laws to high order norms, giving them normative force as the repository of constitutional and human rights principles. There have been repeated calls for models of interpretation less burdened by coloniality. Implied norms cannot ethically be made to rest on fantasies of empire or the "inferred framers intentions".[39]

The only legacy that exists will be Magna Carta, but it was absent in its application during the colonial past in the former British West Indies from which 12 independent countries of the Commonwealth Caribbean have been drawn and became present at independence when those Commonwealth Caribbean independence constitutions were drafted that included models based either on the European Convention on Human Rights 1950 or the Canadian Bill of Rights 1960 for their bills of rights.

Notes

1. *Report by the Hon. E.F.L. Wood, MP (Parliamentary Under Secretary of State for the Colonies) on his Visit to the West Indies and British Guiana, December 1921–February 1922*, Cmnd. 1679/1922 (London : H.M.S.O., 1922), 6.
2. Fred Phillips, *Commonwealth Caribbean Constitutional Law* (London and Sydney: Cavendish Publishing Ltd., 2002), 1–2.
3. Council of Europe, *The European Convention on Human Rights* (Strasbourg: Directorate of Information, 1952).
4. *Canadian Bill of Rights* S.C. 1960, c. 44.
5. Carolyn Harris, *Magna Carta and Its Gifts to Canada* (Toronto: Dundurn Publishers, 2015), 108.
6. Mark Rathbone, 'The Human Rights Act: A Magna Carta for the Twenty-first Century?' *Political Studies Association Essay* (May 2014): 1–2.
7. *Laws of Jamaica: The Charter of Fundamental Rights and Freedoms (Constitutional Amendment) Act, 2011* (Act No. 12 of 2011).
8. UN General Assembly, *Universal Declaration of Human Rights*, December 10, 1948, 217 A (III).

9. *Canadian Charter of Rights and Freedoms, Part I of the Constitution Act, 1982,* being Schedule B to the Canada Act 1982 (UK), 1982, c 11.
10. *Gregson v Gilbert* (1783) *3 Doug. KB 232.*
11. Norman Poser, *Lord Mansfield: Justice in the Age of Reason* (Montreal and Kingston: Mc Gill-Queen's University Press, 2013), 297–98.
12. *Somerset v Stewart* (1772) 98 ER 499.
13. Ibid., 510.
14. Eric Williams, *From Columbus to Castro: The History of the Caribbean 1492–1969,* (London: Andre Deutsch Ltd., 1970. First Vintage Books Edition, February 1984), 70–71.
15. Ibid., 71.
16. Ibid., 72.
17. Ibid., 73.
18. Ibid., 79.
19. Ibid., 140–41.
20. James Melton and Robert Hazell, 'Magna Carta…Holy Grail?' in *Magna Carta and its Modern Legacy,* ed. Robert Hazell and James Melton, 8 (Cambridge and New York: Cambridge University Press, 2015).
21. Derek O'Brien, 'Magna Carta, the "Sugar Colonies" and "Fantasies of Empire,"' in *Magna Carta and Its Modern Legacy,* ed. Robert Hazell and James Melton, 101–102 (Cambridge and New York: Cambridge University Press, 2015).
22. See note 1 above.
23. See note 10 above.
24. James Walvin, *The Zong: A Massacre, the Law and the End of Slavery* (New Haven and London: Yale University Press, 2011), 106.
25. Ibid., 115–16.
26. Hazell and Melton, eds., Magna Carta, Appendix, 238.
27. Ibid., 238.
28. See note 21 above.
29. See note 25 above.
30. See note 12 above.
31. *The Definitive Treaty of Peace and Friendship between his Britannick Majesty, the Most Christian King, and the King of Spain. Concluded at Paris the 10th day of February, 1763 to which the King of Portugal acceded on the same day (Articles VIII and IX).* Located in the Lillian Goldman Law Library at Yale University in the Avalon Project and accessed on November 14, 2015 at http://avalon.law.yale.edu/18th_century/paris763.asp
32. See note 2 above.
33. *Campbell v Hall* (1774) 1 Cowp. 204.
34. Francis Alexis, *Changing Caribbean Constitutions* (Barbados: Carib Research & Publications, Inc., Second Edition, 2015).
35. Derek O'Brien, Magna Carta, 122.
36. *Meeting of Commentators on the Draft Constitution at the Queen's Hall,* Wednesday April 25, 1962, XXV and XXV-2, 2.40-2.50 p.m.
37. Ibid., 186.
38. Tracy Robinson, 'Our Inherent Constitution,' in *Transitions in Caribbean Law,* ed. David S. Berry and Tracy Robinson, 273 (Kingston: The Caribbean Law Publishing Company, 2013).
39. Ibid.

4.

Parliamentary Structures and Composition

Parliamentary Structures

There are eight bicameral parliaments in the Commonwealth Caribbean and four unicameral ones. The first bicameral Parliament in the region in the era of representative and responsible government was introduced into Jamaica in 1944 by way of a new Constitution for the colony.[1]

According to Lloyd Barnett:

> The Legislature was bi-cameral, consisting of a Legislative Council and a House of Representatives. The former comprised three official members and ten unofficial members nominated by the Governor and holding office "during pleasure". The House of Representatives consisted of thirty-two members elected on the basis of single-member constituencies.[2]

In 1959, when reforms were being considered for this system, Barnett indicates that there was some debate about retaining the bicameral structure, however it was retained. There was some innovation in respect of composition with a non-political element being brought into its membership. According to Barnett:

> When the self-governing Constitution of 1959 was being prepared doubts were expressed as to the advisability of retaining a Second Chamber but it was decided that such a body might serve some useful purpose if it were so composed that it could operate on a somewhat different plane from the House of Representatives and would not be capable of obstructing the implementation of the decisions made by the elected Chamber. In an effort to satisfy these two requirements the Governor was allowed to appoint a small number of members representing non-political interests and the leaders of the political Parties, the remaining members in proportion to their strength in the House of Representatives.[3]

The actual provisions to which Barnett is referring here were spelt out in the 1959 Jamaican Constitution as follows:

> Eighteen Persons appointed by the Governor, in his discretion, after consultation with such persons that he considers can speak for the differing points of view groups represented in the House of Representatives.

> Two or three persons, as the Governor acting on the advice of the Premier shall decide, shall be appointed as members of the Legislative Council acting as aforesaid.[4]

Barnett indicates that when the time came to draft a constitution for Jamaica's independence, a decision was taken to remove those two or three senators appointed by the governor to represent 'non-political interests'. For the independence constitution, the decision of the framers was to only allow the prime minister and the leader of the opposition to recommend the appointment of senators.

Barnett states:

> The arguments in favour of making appointments in a prescribed manner which would ensure the representation of certain sections of the community concerned with agriculture, industry, commerce, religion and other important interests were rejected as being nationally divisive and undemocratic in effect. It was thought that the leaders of the Parties should be relied on to select suitable candidates who would be able to speak with knowledge of, and sympathy for, all the important interests in the community and at the same time "raise" the level of the deliberations in the Chamber above that of party politics.[5]

The introduction of a category of senators who were 'non-political' in the Jamaican Constitution in 1959 confirmed the existence of a trend elsewhere in the British West Indies primarily because Trinidad and Tobago embraced the idea as well for (i) the introduction of a Senate in 1961, and (ii) the creation of a category of senators who came to be described as 'independent senators' owing to the fact that they were not in receipt of a party whip for their participation and voting.

The fundamental difference between Jamaica and Trinidad and Tobago emerged in 1962 when both countries attained their independence from Great Britain. Jamaica removed the 'non-political' category of senators and Trinidad and Tobago retained the 'independent senators'.

In many respects, the model of having 'non-political' or 'independent' senators was copied by other Commonwealth Caribbean countries when they attained their independence from Great Britain after 1962. However, the evolution of this model of having the 'non-political' or 'independent' senators can be appreciated in the context of some British imperial history and the export of an idea that was considered for the House of Lords in 1918 and never implemented in Great Britain, but was certainly exported to the British colonies overseas.

Structural Evolution of Political and Non-Political Membership of Senates

All of the second chambers in the Commonwealth Caribbean are called senates and they are all nominated. There is no security of tenure for their members (who are called senators), who are all required to vacate their seats at the next dissolution of Parliament. The fact that all of the senates in the Commonwealth Caribbean are nominated is perhaps a direct result of the Crown Colony system of government that was introduced into the British West Indian colonies in the nineteenth century. That system of government had as its hallmark the substitution of the principle of election by the principle of nomination in the colonial legislatures of the region. At the same time, the shape, methods of composition and features of the senates in the Commonwealth Caribbean appear to have been influenced by policy developments in Britain and other parts of the British Empire concerning proposals for the reform of the House of Lords and the export of those reform proposals to colonial legislatures (even though the reforms were not implemented in Britain itself). The genesis of the eventual shape, methods of selection, and features of Commonwealth Caribbean senates (with the exception of Jamaica on the issue of non-political senators) may be traced to 1918 and the Conference on the Reform of the Second Chamber [6] in the United Kingdom (UK) under the chairmanship of Lord Bryce.

The Bryce Conference recommended the reform of the House of Lords in the following way:

I.   One section shall consist of 246 persons elected by panels of Members of the House of Commons distributed in the geographical groups hereinafter mentioned.

II.   The other section shall consist of persons chosen by the Joint Standing Committee of both Houses hereinafter mentioned. Their number shall be about one-fourth of the whole Second Chamber (excluding ex officio members).[7]

The essence of the Bryce Conference proposals accepted and recommended a second chamber that would be chosen by the House of Commons on the basis of indirect election with proportional representation of the single transferable vote type being used to secure a due representation of all the political parties. The members so elected would number 246 in all, while another 81 were to be elected by a Joint Standing Committee of both Houses of Parliament.[8]

The 1921 Senate of Malta

A consideration that was rejected by the Bryce Conference was, in fact, implemented in Malta in 1921. According to the Bryce Report:

> The Conference rejected the idea of having a Chamber elected on the basis of a property qualification, possessed by a privileged class of voters, and also that of requiring a property qualification for the persons to be elected, restrictions which have been adopted in some countries, but which were deemed unsuitable to modern conditions. Neither was it thought that the plan (sometimes suggested) that the persons chosen to sit should be taken from certain prescribed categories (e.g., from those who had filled some public office) would work well, for it would be very difficult to draw up any satisfactory list of categories which might not be either too large to be useful or too restricted to permit many men of eminence and worth to be admitted as nominees.[9]

While this approach was rejected for the reform of the second chamber in the UK, it was apparently suitably modified and implemented in Malta in 1921. The 1921 Maltese Senate comprised of 17 members, of whom ten were 'Special Members' and seven 'General Members' who were chosen as follows:

- Two members to represent the Clergy nominated by the Archbishop of Malta.

- Two members to represent the Nobility elected by a special class of electors for that category.

- Two members to represent the Graduates elected by a special class of electors for that category.

- Two members to represent the Chamber of Commerce elected by a special class of electors for that category.

- Two members to represent the Trade Union Council elected by a special class of electors for that category.

- The seven 'General Members' were elected with Malta and Gozo divided into two constituencies, one of which (Valletta and its environs) returned four Senators, and the other (the remoter portions of Malta and Gozo), three Senators.[10]

The franchise in Malta for election to the Senate established in 1921 was that the voters for the special classes had to be male British subjects over 21 years of age and had to have special qualifications which were laid down in the Constitution Letters Patent. The voters for the General members had to be male British subjects over 21, able to read and write, and either paying £20 a year from real property in Malta or other capital. Any person who was entitled to vote as a special elector was also entitled to stand for election by his special class. A person who was qualified to vote for the general senators would have been eligible to be elected to the Senate upon fulfilling certain conditions of which the most important were that he be an ecclesiastic of the higher orders, or hold a degree of the University, or be worth £100 a year, or pay rent to that amount.[11]

The similarities between the franchise for, and the composition of, the Senate in Malta in 1921 and the remarks of Lord Bryce[12] in 1918 evidences a correlation between the two. In rejecting the above recruitment methodology for a second chamber, the Bryce Conference accepted and recommended a second chamber that would be chosen by the House of Commons on the basis of indirect election with proportional election of the single transferable vote type being used to capture as many of the political interests represented in the House of Commons which would number 246, while another 81 were to be elected by a Joint Standing Committee of both Houses.

The Maltese Senate of 1921 was abolished in 1936,[13] while the enactment of the Government of India Act 1935[14] established that the export of the agreed Bryce second chamber reforms, suitably modified, were introduced into the Indian subcontinent. That act provided for the separation of India and Burma and introduced a bicameral system into Burma and the following Indian provinces – Madras, Bombay, Bengal, the United Provinces, Bihar, and Assam.

There would be a direct line of development from the 1933–34 discussions on Indian constitutional reform to the establishment of bicameral legislatures in the Commonwealth Caribbean. It is at this point in the evolution of British imperial history that the bicameral model based on a mixture of political and non-political representation emerged, firstly, in the legislatures of the Indian subcontinent and later in the legislatures of the British West Indies, starting with Jamaica. However, Jamaica would end this model of senatorial membership at its independence in 1962 and Trinidad and Tobago would inherit it and continue the tradition when it attained its independence in 1962.

Burma and the Indian Provinces

In Burma, there were to be 36 members of the Senate with 18 being chosen by members of the House of Representatives using the system of proportional representation of the single transferable vote type. The other 18 members were to be chosen by the governor of Burma at his discretion. To some extent, a similar formula was applied in the Indian provincial legislatures named above. The lower House was known as the Legislative Assembly and the upper House was known as the Legislative Council.

The members of these legislative councils were elected by a combination of special electorates – the General electorate, the Moslem electorate, the European electorate, and the Indian-Christian electorate – for some of the seats. Other members were elected on the basis of indirect election by members of the legislative assemblies in those provinces on the basis of proportional representation of the single transferable vote type. The remainder were appointed by the governor in his discretion.

This rather unique type of second chamber had apparently been exported by Britain to the Indian subcontinent by 1935. However, the model did not resemble the House of Lords, but in fact resembled the Bryce proposals for the reform of the House of Lords. The continued export of this model did not end with the Burmese and Indian provincial bicameral systems.

Ceylon

In 1945, a constitutional commission under the chairmanship of Lord Soulbury visited Ceylon and subsequently recommended a bicameral system for Ceylon that was based on the Burmese Senate of 1935. This Ceylonese Senate was to consist of 30 members, 15 of whom were to be elected by members of the lower House on the basis of proportional representation of the single transferable vote type. The remaining 15 were to be chosen by the governor general in his discretion from among persons who had distinguished themselves in the public service, education, medicine, law, science, engineering, banking, commerce, industry, or agriculture. These appointments would be made after the governor-general had consulted the representatives of the appropriate occupation or profession.[15]

Indeed, in respect of Ceylon, the Soulbury Commission conceded the link with Burma in the following way:

> We prefer the proposal that the Second Chamber should be selected partly
> by the First Chamber by means of the single transferable vote, and partly by

nomination by the Governor-General; and we think that this method would ensure adequate representation of minorities in the Second Chamber. We understand that it has been adopted in Burma with satisfactory results.[16]

These recommendations were accepted and embodied in the Ceylon (Constitution) Order-in-Council 1946.[17]

British Guiana

In 1950, a constitutional commission visited British Guiana under the chairmanship of Sir John Waddington and had as its other members Professor Vincent Harlow and Dr Rita Hinden. The commission, in its report, was divided two to one in favour of a bicameral system for British Guiana. Both Harlow and Hinden were in favour of a bicameral system, while the chairman recommended a unicameral system.

The upper House recommended by Harlow and Hinden was to be called the State Council and was to consist of nine members. The suggested formula was that six were to be nominated by the governor from among outstanding persons in the counties of Berbice, Demerara, and Essequibo (two persons from each county). Of the remaining three members, two were to be appointed by the governor on the recommendation of the majority group in the House of Assembly (the lower House) and one was to be appointed by the governor on the recommendation of the Opposition in the House of Assembly.[18]

The specific reasons given by Harlow and Hinden in their majority report for this formula were as follows:

> Of the members nominated by the Governor, two should be chosen to represent the county of Berbice, two the county of Demerara, and two the county of Essequibo. The three counties have a long history as separate colonies and we were much impressed by the vigourous local patriotism which still exists. By this device, the State Council would be given a valuable territorial basis. We do not suggest a rigid residential qualification, since this might unduly restrict the field of choice, but the Governor should satisfy himself that the persons whom he selects have an adequate first-hand knowledge of conditions in the respective counties, as for example, by virtue of practicing a profession or having business interests therein.[19]

The qualifications suggested by Harlow and Hinden for members of the State Council resemble those that were implemented in Ceylon in 1946. Insofar as a trend can be identified, the case for the non-political or independent senator was gathering momentum at this time. However, a new feature emerged in this codicil to the main report by Harlow and Hinden, which saw the creation of a new type of composition in second chambers for the Commonwealth Caribbean that were to come a decade later and beyond.

The specific recommendation by Harlow and Hinden was as follows:

> Turning now to the three other members of the State Council whom we recommend should be appointed by the Governor on the recommendation of the House of Assembly, two should be selected by the majority-group holding office, and the third by the opposition...The presence of these spokesmen for both sides of the House of Assembly would be of great assistance to the State Council in reviewing legislative measures, and would more closely associate the two Chambers.[20]

The idea of government and opposition members in a second chamber was being advocated openly on the basis of recommendation from the lower House. This procedure would undoubtedly be far simpler than an election being held among members of the lower House using the format of the single transferable vote of proportional representation. In a strict two-party split in the lower House, the result would inevitably be the same where small numbers are involved; however, the method of recommendation guarantees the Opposition a certain degree of representation as long as it can obtain a minimum of one seat in the lower or elected House.

It is quite clear that the single transferable vote could not be employed in this instance because the numbers involved were too small. As a result, there was the introduction of nomination by political recommendation with the majority party being given the larger share of nominated seats. Naturally, indirect election would have produced a similar result for any party with a majority in the lower House.

Trinidad and Tobago

The British Guiana experience might have been less significant were it not for the fact that Professor Harlow had supervised the doctoral thesis of Eric Williams at Oxford. Indeed, Williams did not hide the fact that he was in some way influenced by what Harlow had recommended for British Guiana. At a public meeting in Port of Spain on July 19, 1955, he said:

> In 1951 the two university members of the three-member British Guiana Constitutional Commission, one of whom supervised my doctor's thesis at Oxford, recommended the establishment of a bicameral legislature for

British Guiana. What they had to say is of direct concern to the people of Trinidad and Tobago.[21]

At the same meeting, Williams proposed his own Senate for Trinidad and Tobago which would have consisted of 16 members comprised in the following way:

1. Six members representing special economic interests, chosen by those interests themselves, namely oil, sugar, commerce, cocoa, shipping and local industries.

2. Five members representing the religious denominations, namely the Archbishop of Port-of-Spain, the Bishop of Trinidad, the Head Pundit of the Hindu Faith, the Moulvi of the Moslem Faith, and one representative selected by agreement from among all the other religious denominations.

3. Three ex-officio members, namely the Chief Justice, the Colonial Secretary and the Attorney General.

4. Two men or women of distinction in public life appointed by the Governor on the recommendation of the Chief Minister.

Analysis of Williams's Proposals for Bicameralism

In examining the 1955 proposals advanced by Williams on the question of a bicameral legislature for Trinidad and Tobago, he was clearly suggesting a modified version of the House of Lords. His desire to name religious and economic interests as well as to include men and women of distinction in public life resembled the concept of the Lords Spiritual and Temporal. The idea of placing the chief justice as the presiding officer in this proposed second chamber mirrored the role played by the lord chancellor in the UK at that time as head of the judiciary and presiding officer of the House of Lords. This was part of his belief, at the time, that the British Constitution, suitably modified, was appropriate for Trinidad and Tobago.

However, the proposals would have been largely unworkable as the method of selection of the economic interests was left to those interests themselves. That might have been far more difficult to achieve than was anticipated, because, there were significant areas of overlap between representatives of the various interests, e.g., commerce and shipping. Likewise, his proposal for the other religious denominations to agree to a single representative among themselves must be viewed in the same way.

Nevertheless, it was a mechanism that was designed to gain the support of special interests in the society by allowing them the privilege of choosing their own spokesmen for the Senate. At the same time, it went against the report by the Constitution Reform Committee,[22] which recommended a unicameral system. In this way, unicameralism was portrayed as being disadvantageous to those special interests and Williams was carving a niche for himself as the champion of bicameralism that he suggested had benefits for the special interests themselves.

When Williams and the People's National Movement (PNM) came to power in 1956, constitutional reform was on their agenda. However, Williams altered his ideas to dispense greater patronage. In 1958, he suggested the following formula through the Report of a Select Committee of the Trinidad and Tobago Legislative Council:[23]

1. The Senate would consist of 18 members nominated by the Governor on the advice of the Premier.

2. Of the 18, seven members would be appointed from the main religious and economic interests.

3. The remaining eleven members would be chosen from among other persons in the Territory.

The PNM Victory and Changes to Williams's Proposals

Although the PNM won 13 of the 24 elected seats in the legislative council at the 1956 general elections, this did not guarantee the party control of the council as there were also five nominated members to be appointed by the governor. There were negotiations with the governor and the Colonial Office over the appointment of some nominated members on the advice of the chief minister.

As far as getting the permission of the Colonial Office on the nomination of at least two nominated members by way of the governor acting on the advice of the chief minister was concerned, the Colonial Office made a policy shift in respect of Trinidad and Tobago as well as its other colonies. Evidence of this can be gleaned from a confidential intel from the Foreign Office to certain of Her Majesty's Representatives. It was labelled for Foreign Office and Whitehall distribution. The appropriate excerpt from the intel read as follows:

5. Immediately after the election the Governor, Sir Edward Beetham, sent for Dr. Williams and offered him his co-operation in forming a Government. Dr. Williams then asked that his nominees should be appointed to fill the nominated seats, and this request at first threatened to give rise to some constitutional difficulty. The reason for this request was that the People's National Movement, holding thirteen out of thirty-one seats in the new Legislative Council, would, even with the votes of the two official members

have to command the vote of at least one other member to give them an overall majority in the Council. Dr. Williams was not prepared to have to rely on the votes of independent nominated members to implement the Movement's programme which he claimed he had a clear mandate from the electorate to pursue.

6.   The revised constitution was designed (by a Constitutional Reform Committee in Trinidad which included all the members of the previous Legislative Council) to suit the continuation of a situation where the electorate had not returned a majority of one party. The basis on which Nominated Members are appointed remains as it was set out in 1949 in a despatch from the Secretary of State to the Governor, namely that such members should "strengthen the experience and knowledge of the Council in dealing with the complex issues of Government" and should be appointed not to represent any particular interest, but "to serve the broad and best interests of the Colony as a whole".

In one or two other colonial territories with advanced constitutions, it has, however, been recognized recently that nominated members could not be appointed to a Legislature to oppose the policy of the majority of the elected members, and in those territories the Governors have consulted with the Leaders of the majority parties as to how the nominated seats should be filled.

In Trinidad, therefore, the emergence of a majority party was recognized as calling for some modification of the principles of the 1949 despatch. The Secretary of State therefore authorized the Governor to "take such steps by way of nominating suitable persons to the Legislative Council, after consultation with the leader of the majority party, as will provide a reasonable working majority for that party".

Discussions between the Governor and Dr. Williams have now taken place and two Nominated Members who may be expected to support the P.N.M. have been appointed. The new Legislative Council met on October 26 and elected a P.N.M. Government with Dr. Williams as Chief Minister.[24]

The two nominated members chosen by the PNM were W.J. Alexander and C.A. Merry. The governor Sir Edward Beetham was quite cooperative on this issue and had excellent relations with Williams and the executive council. To quote Williams:

The first stage in the process of Constitution reform was, as my honourable Friend the Leader of the House indicated, in October 1956 when a sufficient number of nominated members (2) was obtained by the Party that received a majority of the elected seats in the election, to ensure to that majority, political stability...based on precedents already established in Malaya and

> Singapore, the Secretary of State for the Colonies said so. We requested it
> on the basis of the precedents set in those countries. It did not have to be
> granted, Sir.[25]

On November 21, 1958, a Select Committee of the Legislative Council
was appointed to make recommendations for a new constitution for
Trinidad and Tobago. That committee recommended the introduction
of a bicameral legislature with a lower (or elected) House to be called a
House of Representatives and an upper (or nominated) House to be called
a Senate.[26]

Williams made significant changes to his original 1955 proposals. He
was now recommending a Senate of 18 members to be nominated by the
governor on the advice of the premier. Seven of these members were to be
chosen from the main religious and economic interests and the other 11
were to be chosen from persons in the territory.

Furthermore, it seemed as though Williams had been influenced by the
proposals for a Senate as contained in the Constitution of the Federation
of the West Indies.[27] In addition, four members of this Select Committee
all served on the previous Constitution Reform Committee of 1955.
At that time, there were no provisions that would have allowed for a
government and an opposition; however, the 1956 amendments[28] to the
1950 Constitution[29] created the framework for this to become possible.

Those four members who had formed part of a wider majority in the
legislative council prior to 1956 and had advocated the retention of a
unicameral system for Trinidad and Tobago were now in an opposition
minority. It was Williams and his PNM colleagues who were going to be
dominant in this select committee and their views would prevail. A useful
example of this can be seen in the following excerpt from the committee's
report as follows:

> By a majority vote it was agreed, and we recommend, that there shall be
> a bicameral legislature in the place of the unicameral Legislative Council
> which exists at present.

Mr. T.U.B. Butler and Mr. S. Capildeo voted against. Butler was of
the opinion that the legislature should continue to be of a unicameral
character and that it should consist entirely of elected members. Capildeo
believed that the legislature should continue to be unicameral consisting
of Elected Members, Nominated Members and ex officio Members.[30]

Williams was also seeking a method for creating political stability by
ensuring majority rule and political patronage at the same time. The

Senate he had proposed in 1955 would not have guaranteed him majority rule and political stability which he came to realise as being necessary in 1956 when the PNM won 13 seats out of 24, but was still in a minority overall in the legislative council. That situation was altered in favour of the PNM through the appointment of two of the five nominated members of the legislative Ccouncil which allowed the party majority rule.

In order for him to hold on to political power and to entrench the PNM, Williams had to have an adequate amount of political patronage at his disposal which would have assured him of an entrenched base of political support. The party was now in power and, therefore, it was necessary for changes to be made to ensure the dominance of the party, especially when the results of the general election were so close and there had to be a policy shift on the part of the British government to ensure a majority in the legislative council.

Williams was clearly not comfortable with such a dependence on the British government, and he needed to propose reforms that would serve the best interests of the party if he was ever going to have an impact on the political, economic, and social development of Trinidad and Tobago. There was also another phenomenon which clearly influenced Williams to alter his proposals for a Senate in Trinidad and Tobago and that was the West Indian Federation.

The Influence of the Federal Constitution on Williams

The British Caribbean Federation had been established by an act of the UK Parliament, namely the British Caribbean Federation Act 1956.[31] Its Constitution came into effect on July 31, 1957 in the form of the West Indies (Federation) Order in Council 1957.[32] However, there were significant areas of overlap between the recommendations of the 1958 select committee of the legislative council on Constitution reform and the 1957 Federal Constitution. These areas of overlap included the following:

(a) The term of office of Senators would be five years;

(b) the Senate would be presided over by a President elected by and from its membership;

(c) the Senate would have no power to delay money bills but would have the right to delay any other bill for not more than one year or two consecutive sessions;

(f) the Senate would remain in session so long as the House of Representatives so remains.[33]

It was apparent that Williams had not dealt in detail with the tenure of office and functioning of his proposed Senate in 1955, but having become chief minister he was modifying his proposals in a more realistic way, and he seemed to have been influenced by the mechanics of the federal Senate and the realities of maintaining stable majority rule. Indeed, it was on the basis of these proposals that a delegation was sent to London in October 1959 to negotiate with the Colonial Office on the wider issue of constitutional reform.

Reasons for Williams's Alteration of his 1955 Proposals in 1958

Williams's emphasis in his new proposals in 1958 was on political stability through a government majority in an Upper House. This was to be achieved through greater flexibility in the system and method of appointment of the senators to his proposed Senate than had previously been advocated in 1955 as well as greater political control. His alteration of ideas on the Senate can be attributed to three significant factors which were:

1. The courtesy extended to him by the Secretary of State for the Colonies to choose two of the five nominated members in the Legislative Council to ensure a government majority. This was done on the basis of precedents already set in Malaya and Singapore at that time. This experience in itself would have made Williams realise the importance of the need for control of the nominated element in any legislature following an electoral victory that carried with it control of the elected seats in a legislature.

2. The experience gained by Williams in office as Chief Minister leading a government that controlled the Legislative Council went a long way towards increasing his political understanding by 1958. Whereas his 1955 proposals were somewhat idealistic, his 1958 proposals reflected the ideas of a man who knew the importance of ensuring a government majority at all times in a nominated House and this could be combined with a judicious use of political patronage which would ensure the development of the entrenchment of the P.N.M. as a major political force in Trinidad and Tobago.

3. The establishment of the Legislature of the British West Indian Federation in Trinidad and Tobago brought with it a first-hand view of the operation of a bicameral system in 1958. Williams had previously (1955) only described the composition of his proposed Senate and had not dealt with the actual working of such a body. The Federal Senate, therefore, provided the necessary mechanical input into his revised (1958) proposals that made them politically negotiable insofar as the Colonial Office was concerned.

> In other words, the Federation had a significant impact upon Williams's ideas for a Senate in Trinidad and Tobago.

By 1961, what was implemented was a Senate with the following composition:

1. Twelve Senators appointed by the Governor on the advice of the Premier.

2. Two Senators appointed by the Governor on the advice of the leader of the opposition.

3. Seven Senators appointed by the Governor in his discretion after consultation with such persons as he might wish to consult to represent special interests.[34]

Essentially, this formula for the Trinidad and Tobago Senate was the result of the cumulative British imperial experience with bicameral institutions in its Asian and Caribbean colonies. Eric Williams had also been influenced in his views on bicameralism by Professor Harlow as well as the model of the West Indian Federation and it is reasonable to assume that Harlow would have been aware of the models that were being exported to Ceylon, Burma, and the Indian provinces as well as the recommendations of the Bryce Committee. In other words, what was exported to these colonies of Britain were the Bryce proposals for the reform of the House of Lords suitably modified with the passage of time. This was not the Westminster model.

Since 1961 eight of the English-speaking countries that attained their independence from Britain have adopted a bicameral formula reasonably similar (with the exception of Jamaica and the Bahamas) to the Trinidadian provisions of 1961, whereas Jamaica opted to remove the non-political or independent senators that formed part of its own bicameral arrangements from 1944 to 1962 when it became independent in 1962.

When consideration was being given to the composition of the senates for Burma in 1935 and Ceylon in 1945, Jamaica formed part of that British imperial thinking about second chambers in 1944. The fact that Jamaica opted to remove the non-political component of their Senate for independence was an act of autochthony on the part of the framers of their constitution who opted to delete that method of composition from their constitutional evolution rather than to perpetuate it.

What was retained in Jamaica was the idea of bicameralism based on the principle of nomination for seats in the legislature which was the original basis of the system of Crown Colony government that was implemented widely by the British government in its Caribbean colonies. Under this system, it was the governor of the colony who nominated persons to the legislative council to serve as legislators. The concept of representative government emerged in the twentieth century alongside the principle of nomination as the franchise was gradually extended and the number of elected seats in the legislative councils of the region was also increased.

Bicameralism provided a way for the elected members of the legislative councils to be separated from the nominated members who could be placed in another chamber so as to ensure the continued representation of various special interests in the legislative process. However, the concept of ensuring that a variety of interests would be represented in the legislative process through the concurrence of the political directorate was addressed in the 1918 Bryce Conference Report.

By Jamaica deviating from this component of the formula of non-political or independent senators in 1962, the bicameral model that included it was to be found in Trinidad and Tobago in its independence Constitution and that model has been widely implemented in the Commonwealth Caribbean.

There has been no attempt to alter these legislative systems in the post-independence era. In Trinidad and Tobago, there was constitutional reform in 1976 whereby the country became a republic and the Senate was retained and enlarged so that the new formula of appointment according to section 40(2) of the Constitution is as follows:

Of the 31 Senators –

(a) sixteen shall be appointed by the President acting in accordance with the advice of the Prime Minister;

(b) six shall be appointed by the President acting in accordance with the advice of the Leader of the Opposition; and

(c) nine shall be appointed by the President in his discretion from outstanding persons from economic or social or community organisations and other major fields of endeavour.[35]

That this format of an elected lower House and a nominated upper House has not been altered is a reflection of the political determination of Eric Williams in his efforts to reform the Constitution in such a way as not to part with the principle of bicameralism as he first established it with the concurrence of the Colonial Office in 1961 in Trinidad and Tobago. Furthermore, the independence Constitution of 1962 contained essentially the same provisions for bicameralism as the 1961 Constitution with some modifications.

Basically, there have always been three categories of senators since the 1961 model was introduced in Trinidad and Tobago: government, opposition and independent senators. The last category owes no allegiance to any party or anyone and can vote without supporting a party line. Apart from Jamaica and the Bahamas, all of the other independent countries of the Commonwealth Caribbean have included these three categories of senators with minor variations in some cases. This model of non-political senators was strengthened in Belize in 2001[36] when the size of its Senate was increased from eight to 12 senators. Jamaica only has a divide between government and opposition senators. Belize subsequently increased its Senate to 13 senators.

The majority that any government earns after a general election may vary in the elected House depending on the outcome of every general election. However, there is always a fixed arithmetic in the Senate, and this means that the bicameral system does offer a check and balance against extreme executive action by virtue of constitutional provisions that impose requirements for special parliamentary majorities in substantial cases of constitutional amendment.

The composition of the other Senates in the region, besides Trinidad and Tobago, is set out below:

Antigua and Barbuda

1.   Ten Senators appointed by the Governor-General on the advice of the Prime Minister.

2.   Four Senators appointed by the Governor-General on the advice of the Leader of the Opposition. (Where there is a vacancy in the office of Leader of the Opposition or the Governor-General considers that it is impracticable to obtain the advice of the Leader of the Opposition, the Governor-General may exercise in his own discretion those functions he is required to exercise on the advice of the Leader of the Opposition.)

3.   One Senator appointed by the Governor-General in his discretion from outstanding persons or persons representing such interests as the Governor General considers ought to be represented in the Senate.

4.   One Senator appointed by the Governor-General on the advice of the Barbuda Council.

5.   One Senator, being an inhabitant of Barbuda, appointed by the Governor- General on the advice of the Prime Minister.[37]

Barbados

1.   Twelve Senators appointed by the Governor-General on the advice of the Prime Minister.

2. Two Senators appointed by the Governor-General on the advice of the Leader of the Opposition. (Where there is a vacancy in the office of Leader of the Opposition, the Governor-General shall act in his discretion in respect of the exercise of any function that he is required to exercise on the advice of the Leader of the Opposition.)

3. Seven Senators appointed by the Governor-General in his discretion to represent religious, economic or social interests or such other interests as the Governor-General considers ought to be represented.[38]

Belize (at independence)

1. Five Senators appointed by the Governor-General on the advice of the Prime Minister.

2. Two Senators appointed by the Governor General on the advice of the Leader of the Opposition. (Where the office of Leader of the Opposition is vacant, the Governor-General shall select a person in his own deliberate judgment who shall tender such advice to him. Or he may select two persons in his own deliberate judgment each of whom shall tender advice to him in respect of the appointment of one Senator each.)

3. One Senator appointed by the Governor-General after consultation with the Belize Advisory Council.[39]

Belize (after 2001)
Of the twelve Senators –

(a) six shall be appointed by the Governor-General acting in accordance with the advice of the Prime Minister; and

(b) three shall be appointed by the Governor-General acting in accordance with the advice of the Leader of the Opposition; and

(c) one shall be appointed by the Governor-General acting in accordance with the advice of the Belize Council of Churches and Evangelical Association of Churches; and

(d) one shall be appointed by the Governor-General acting in accordance with the advice of the Belize Chamber of Commerce and Industry and the Belize Business Bureau; and

(e) one shall be appointed by the Governor-General acting in accordance with the advice of the National Trade Union Congress and the Civil Society Steering Committee.[40]

Belize (after 2016 when the Prime Minister fixed the date of commencement of the thirteen senators)

(f) one shall be appointed by the Governor-General, acting in accordance with the advice of non-governmental organisations.[41]

The Bahamas

1. Nine Senators appointed by the Governor-General on the advice of the Prime Minister.

2. Four Senators appointed by the Governor-General on the advice of the Leader of the Opposition. (Where there is a vacancy in the office of Leader of the Opposition, the Governor-General shall act in his own deliberate judgment in the exercise of any functions that he is required under the Constitution to exercise on the advice of the Leader of the Opposition.)

3. Three Senators appointed by the Governor-General on the advice of the Prime Minister after consultation with the Leader of the Opposition. (The Prime Minister is required to exercise this function to secure that the political balance of the Senate reflects that of the House of Assembly at the time.)[42]

Grenada

1. Seven Senators appointed by the Governor-General on the advice of the Prime Minister.

2. Three Senators appointed on the advice of the Leader of the Opposition. (Where there is a vacancy in the office of Leader of the Opposition, the Governor-General may act in his own deliberate judgment in the exercise of any power where he is required under the Constitution to exercise such power on the advice of the Leader of the Opposition.)

3. Three Senators appointed by the Governor-General on the advice of the Prime Minister after the Prime Minister has consulted the organizations or interests which the Prime Minister considers the Senators should be selected to represent.[43]

Jamaica

1. Thirteen Senators appointed by the Governor-General on the advice of the Prime Minister.

2. Eight Senators appointed by the Governor-General on the advice of the Leader of the Opposition. (Where there is a vacancy in the office of Leader of the Opposition, the Prime Minister shall advise the Governor-General on the exercise of any power in respect of

which the Constitution provided for its exercise by the Governor-General on the advice of the Leader of the Opposition).[44]

St Lucia

1. Six Senators appointed by the Governor-General on the advice of the Prime Minister.

2. Three Senators appointed by the Governor-General on the advice of the Leader of the Opposition. (Where there is a vacancy in the office of Leader of the Opposition or the Governor-General, in his own deliberate judgment, considers that it is not practicable for him to obtain the advice of the Leader of the Opposition within the time required to act, he may act in his own deliberate judgment where the Constitution provides that he is required to act on the advice of the Leader of the Opposition.)

3. Two Senators appointed by the Governor-General in his own deliberate judgment after consultation with those religious, economic or social bodies from which the Governor-General considers that such Senators should be selected.[45]

The Leader of the Opposition

The Office of Leader of the Opposition was created in the first two independence constitutions of the Commonwealth Caribbean (Jamaica and Trinidad and Tobago) based on the corresponding provision in the Ministers of the Crown Act 1937,[46] with the exception that the governor general or president, as the case may be, makes the appointment instead of the Speaker of the House of Commons as obtains at Westminster.

This was confirmed by the response of the Minister of State for Colonial Affairs (The Marquess of Lansdowne) to a parliamentary question for written answer in the House of Lords asked by Viscount Alexander of Hillborough on July 19, 1962.

Viscount Alexander of Hillborough asked:

> What considerations led to the adoption of the proposal in paragraph 36 of the report of the Trinidad and Tobago Independence Conference, 1962 (Cmnd.1757) relating to the appointment of the Leader of the Opposition, and for information as to the occasions on which the Governor-General will not be required to consult and act on the advice of the Cabinet.[47]

The reply by the Minister of State read, in part, as follows:

> The proposal in paragraph 36, which was put forward by the Trinidad and Tobago delegation and accepted by the Conference, follows closely

the corresponding provision in the proposed Jamaica Independence Constitution. It is modelled on the appropriate provision in the Ministers of the Crown Act 1937, except that it is the Governor-General who will be required on all occasions to determine who shall be Leader of the Opposition. In this country the Speaker is required to determine who shall be Leader of the Opposition only in the event of any uncertainty as to which party in opposition has the greatest numerical strength in the House of Commons or as to who is the leader in that House of such a party.[48]

The model outlined by the Minister of State for Colonial Affairs is the model that has largely been copied in the Commonwealth Caribbean. The logical extension of this model is for the governor general to usurp the functions of the leader of the opposition in cases where that office is vacant. Constitutional draftsmen have been able to make provisions to this effect in respect of Commonwealth Caribbean constitutions.

Trinidad and Tobago does not have any constitutional provisions that will allow for the appointment of opposition senators in cases where there is no leader of the opposition. Indeed, it was only after the reform of the Constitution in 1976 that provision was made for the president to act without consulting the leader of the opposition in cases where mandatory consultation is required with the leader of the opposition, and there is no holder of that office at the time when the consultation is required.[49]

The first country in the region in the independence era to encounter such a phenomenon was Trinidad and Tobago itself as a consequence of the general elections on May 24, 1971 where the ruling party (the People's National Movement led by Dr Eric Williams) won all of the parliamentary seats and there was no appointment of anyone to the office of leader of the opposition at the opening of the Parliament that assembled on June 18, 1971 after that general election because of constitutional inadequacy.

Comparatively speaking, the most extreme case of substituting the advice of the leader of the opposition by the deliberate judgment of the governor general obtains in St Lucia where a time factor for tendering advice is also included. So that even if there is a leader of the opposition there must be a timely response from that person otherwise the governor general may proceed to usurp the functions of leader of the opposition and exercise those functions in his own deliberate judgment.[50]

In the Commonwealth Caribbean, up to the time of writing, there have been five occasions on which there has been no opposition membership in the Parliament after a general election. These situations occurred in Trinidad and Tobago (1971), Jamaica (1983), St Vincent and the Grenadines (1989), Grenada (1999), and Grenada (2013).

Unicameralism in the Commonwealth Caribbean

There are four unicameral legislatures in the Commonwealth Caribbean. These are to be found in Dominica, Guyana, St Kitts-Nevis, and St Vincent and the Grenadines. The general characteristics of these legislatures are essentially the same except in Guyana, where the composition of the National Assembly is fundamentally different from the other three legislatures. The principle of nomination is used alongside the principle of election in Dominica, St Kitts-Nevis, and St Vincent and the Grenadines. This is one of the legacies of the modifications to the Crown Colony system in the British West Indies that had as its hallmark the composition of legislatures with only nominated members.

The parliamentary structure of these four unicameral legislatures is as follows:

Dominica

The House of Assembly consists of such number of elected representatives as corresponds to the number of constituencies into which Dominica is divided and includes as well nine senators. Of these senators, five are appointed by the president on the advice of the prime minister and four are appointed by the president on the advice of the leader of the opposition.[51]

St Kitts-Nevis

The National Assembly consists of such number of elected Representatives as corresponds to the number of constituencies into which St Kitts-Nevis is divided as well as three senators or such greater number not exceeding two-thirds of the number of representatives as may be prescribed by Parliament. At any time when the holder of the office of attorney general is a senator, the number of senators shall be increased by one. One-third of the senators (excluding any senator who holds the office of attorney general) shall be appointed by the governor general on the advice of the leader of the opposition. The remaining senators shall be appointed by the governor general on the advice of the prime minister.[52]

St Vincent and the Grenadines

The House of Assembly consists of such number of elected representatives as corresponds to the number of constituencies into which St Vincent and the Grenadines may be divided as well as six senators. Of these, four are appointed by the governor general on the advice of the prime minister and two are appointed by the governor general on the advice of the leader of the opposition.[53]

Guyana

The National Assembly consists of 65 members. After the introduction of a new constitution in 1980, the Parliament was to be comprised of 53 members who were to be elected in accordance with the party list system of proportional representation. There are ten representatives from the regional democratic councils (one for each of the ten regions into which Guyana is divided). These representatives were elected by the regional democratic councils from among their members to serve in the National Assembly. There were two representatives elected from among the members of the National Congress of Local Democratic Organs. The members of this body consisted of persons elected to it from among members of regional democratic councils.[54]

This was altered in 2000 by an amendment to the Constitution that made the following new provisions to section 60 and section 160 of the Constitution:

> 60. (1) Election of members of the National Assembly shall be by secret ballot.
>
> (2) Subject to the provisions of article 160(2), such number of members of the National Assembly as determined by the Assembly, shall be elected in accordance with the system of proportional representation prescribed by article 160(1).
>
> 160.(1)Subject to the provisions of the next following paragraph the system of proportional representation referred to in article 60(2) for the election of such number of members of the National Assembly as shall be determined by the Assembly, shall be as follows –
>
> (a) votes shall be cast throughout Guyana in favour of lists of candidates;
>
> (b) each elector shall have one vote and may cast it in favour of any of the lists; and
>
> (c) the seats of the said elected members in the Assembly, as determined under this paragraph, shall be allocated between the lists in such a manner that the proportion that the number of such seats allocated to each list bears to the number of votes cast in favour of that list is as nearly as may be the same for each list, thus minimizing the level of disproportionality between the percentages of votes earned by lists and the percentages of seats allocated to lists in the cases of individual geographical constituencies, if they exist, and of the Assembly taken as a whole.[55]

In Guyana, the composition of the National Assembly is designed to reflect as far as possible the will of the electorate on a mathematical basis through the use of the party list system of proportional representation.

Conclusion

Overall, bicameralism has emerged as the dominant parliamentary structure in the Commonwealth Caribbean. The evolving British imperial model that can trace its source to the Bryce Conference proposals of 1918 arrived in the British West Indies in Jamaica in 1944 with an elected House of Representatives and a nominated Legislative Council with the reforms in India and Burma in 1935 and Ceylon in 1946 on either side of it.

Eric Williams embraced the evolution of this model using a combination of the British Guiana proposals of 1951 which involved his former doctoral supervisor at Oxford, Professor Harlow, as well as the model for the West Indian federal Senate and his own political windfall as conveyed by the British government upon his election in 1956 using the experiences of Malaya and Singapore.

The principle of nomination that evolved from the Crown Colony era of the nineteenth-century lies at the heart of the model and only Jamaica's deviation in 1962 from the non-political or independent membership of the second chamber left the Trinidad and Tobago bicameral model as the composition of choice for a majority of the latter day bicameral systems that would adorn the parliamentary landscape of the region in the post-independence era. The Whitehall version of the Senate was born with the three main categories of government, opposition and non-political or independent senators. In 1962, Trinidad and Tobago became an independent, sovereign nation and this Whitehall version of the bicameral system was retained with some modifications. The model has survived up to the time of writing.

Notes

1. *The Jamaica (Constitution) Order-in-Council 1944* (S.I. 1944 / No. 1215).
2. Lloyd Barnett, *The Constitutional Law of Jamaica* (Oxford: Oxford University Press, 1977), 15–16.
3. Ibid., 209.
4. *The Jamaica (Constitution) Order in Council 1959* (S.I. 1959 / No. 862), s. 15.
5. Barnett, 209.
6. *The Conference on the Reform of the Second Chamber* Cmnd. 9038 /1918.
7. Ibid., 19.
8. Ibid., 9–11.
9. Ibid., 5–6.
10. *The Colonial Office List for 1922* (London: Waterlow and Sons Ltd.), 268.
11. Ibid.
12. See note 9 above
13. *Malta Letters Patent* S.R. & O. 1936, 3681
14. *Laws of the United Kingdom* 25 & 26 Geo. 5, c. 42.
15. *Ceylon: Report of the Commission on Constitutional Reform* Cmnd. 6677 /1945.

16. Ibid., para. 303.
17. *Ceylon (Constitution) Order-in-Council 1946* S.R. & O. 1946, 2248.
18. *British Guiana : Report of the Constitutional Commission 1950–51 and Dispatch from the Secretary of State for the Colonies to the Governor of British Guiana dated October 6, 1951* Colonial No. 280, 1951.
19. Ibid., para. 20.
20. Ibid., para. 21.
21. Eric Williams, *Constitution Reform in Trinidad and Tobago.* Public Affairs Pamphlet No. 2 (Trinidad: Teachers' Educational and Cultural Association, 1955), 23.
22. *Trinidad and Tobago Legislative Council, Report of the Constitution Reform Committee 1955*, Council Paper No. 16 /1956.
23. *Trinidad and Tobago Legislative Council, Report from the Select Committee on a New Constitution for Trinidad and Tobago* Council Paper No. 11 / 1959.
24. *UK National Archives CO 1031 / 1301, No. 198 Intel, Confidential*, November 8, 1956.
25. *Official Report, Debates of the Legislative Council*, Vol. 9, 1958–59, 131.
26. *Trinidad and Tobago Legislative Council*, Council Paper No. 11/1959.
27. *The West Indies (Federation) Order in Council 1957* (S.I. 1957 / No. 1364).
28. *Trinidad and Tobago (Constitution) (Amendment) Order in Council 1956*, S.I. 1956 / No. 835.
29. *Trinidad and Tobago (Constitution) Order in Council 1950*, S.I. 1950 / No. 510.
30. *Trinidad and Tobago Legislative Council*, Council Paper No. 11/1959, para. 26.
31. *Laws of the United Kingdom* 4 & 5 Eliz. 2, c. 63.
32. See note 26 above
33. *The West Indies (Federation) Order in Council 1957*, Ch. II and also *Trinidad and Tobago Legislative Council*, Council Paper No.11/1959, para. 29.
34. *The Trinidad and Tobago (Constitution) Order in Council 1961*, S.I. 1961, No. 1192.
35. *Laws of Trinidad and Tobago, Chapter 1:01, Schedule*, s. 40(2).
36. See note 27 above and 37 below
37. *Antigua and Barbuda Constitution Order 1981*, S.I. 1981/No. 1106, ss. 28 and 80.
38. *Barbados Independence Order 1966*, S.I. 1966/No. 1455, ss. 36 and 75.
39. *Belize Independence Order 1981*, S.I. 1981/No. 1107, ss. 47 and 61.
40. *Belize Constitution (Fourth Amendment) Act, 2001,* Act No. 39 of 2001. This Act amended section 61 of the *Belize Independence Order 1981*, S.I. 1981/No. 1107 (see notes 26 and 36 above).
41. Belize Constitution (Sixth Amendment Act) 2010, Act No. 13 of 2008, s.7. This Act further amended section 61 of the Belize Independence Order 1981, S.I. 1981/No. 1107.
42. *The Bahamas Independence Order 1973*, S.I. 1973/No. 1080, ss. 39, 40 and 83.
43. *Grenada Constitution Order 1973*, S.I. 1973/No. 2155, ss. 24 and 62.
44. *Jamaica (Constitution) Order in Council 1962*, S.I.1962/No. 1550, ss. 35 and 81.
45. *St Lucia Constitution Order 1978*, S.I. 1978/No. 1901, ss. 24 and 64.
46. *Laws of the United Kingdom* 1 Edw. 8 & 1 Geo. 6, c. 38.
47. *Parliamentary Debates, Lords, 1961–62,* Vol. 242, 859.
48. Ibid.
49. *Laws of Trinidad and Tobago, Chapter 1:01, Schedule*, s. 83(6).
50. *St Lucia Constitution Order 1978*, S.I. 1978/No. 1901, s. 64(2).
51. *Dominica Constitution Order 1978*, S.I. 1978/No. 1027, ss. 30, 33 and 34.
52. *St Kitts-Nevis Constitution Order 1983*, S.I. 1983/No. 881, ss. 26 and 30.
53. *St Vincent Constitution Order 1979*, S.I. 1979/No. 916, ss. 24 and 28.
54. *Constitution of Guyana 1980, Act No. 2/1980, Schedule*, ss. 52, 72, 80.
55. *Laws of Guyana* The Constitution Amendment (No. 3) Act No. 14 of 2000.

5.
Commonwealth Caribbean Presidencies

In the post-independence era in the Commonwealth Caribbean, three presidencies have been created in Guyana, Trinidad and Tobago, and Dominica. In Guyana and Trinidad and Tobago, an independent republic was created after the initial period of independence as an independent monarchy which saw the transfer of the personal authority of Queen Elizabeth II as in the Head of State to a president as Head of State.

In Dominica, the transfer was a direct one from associated statehood to an independent republic in 1978 with Queen Elizabeth II ceasing to exercise her personal authority over Dominica as its Queen to a Head of State in the person of the president of Dominica.

Guyana was an independent monarchy between 1966 and 1970 and became a republic with a ceremonial president in 1970. However, in 1980, its presidency was altered from ceremonial to executive. Trinidad and Tobago was an independent monarchy from 1962 to 1976 when it became an independent republic in 1976 with a quasi-ceremonial president. The presidency of Dominica may be described as quasi-ceremonial.

The Transfer of the Source of State Power

The creation of independent monarchies changed the relationship between Queen Elizabeth II as Queen of the colonies of Trinidad and Tobago and of British Guiana where she acted on the advice of British ministers, to the status where she was Queen of these independent monarchies acting on the advice of her Guyanese and Trinidad and Tobago ministers.

Owing to the fact that it is impossible for Queen Elizabeth II to reside in all of the countries of which she is Queen, it is, therefore, necessary for her to have a personal representative in each independent country of which she is Queen. That personal representative is the governor general. The authority of the governor general is grounded in the Royal Prerogative of the British Monarchy and in the local statute conferring powers upon the office, and it is those powers that are exercised by the governor general on behalf of Her Majesty on the advice of local ministers.

The executive authority of the state is grounded in the Royal Prerogative of the British Monarchy. Ministers pledge an oath of allegiance to Queen Elizabeth II, her heirs, and her successors upon taking office.

The transfer from monarchical to republican status in Trinidad and Tobago saw the transfer of the Royal Prerogative to the new republic as the basis of their state power and the inclusion of transitional provisions in the Act of Parliament[1] and the new republican Constitution.[2] In Guyana, provision was already made in the Independence Constitution of 1966[3] for Guyana to become a republic upon the approval of a resolution to that effect in the National Assembly by simple majority vote.[4] There were no transitional provisions in the Constitution, but rather replacement provisions. In 1980, Guyana enacted a new Constitution[5] to become the Co-operative Republic of Guyana.

Dominica had become an associated state in 1967 under the provisions of the West Indies Act 1967.[6] Under the provisions of this Act, the United Kingdom (UK) created associated status for Antigua and Barbuda, Dominica, Grenada, St Kitts-Nevis, St Lucia, and St Vincent and the Grenadines. The Associated States were granted full internal self-government, while citizenship, defence and external affairs remained the responsibility of the UK. Either party (the UK or an Associated State) could withdraw from the arrangement unilaterally under the provisions of the Act.[7] This meant that the associated states were granted the right to self-determination.

The Independence Constitution of Dominica of 1978[8] came into force on November 3,1978 together with an Order[9] made after a resolution was passed in the Dominica House of Assembly on July 12, 1978 that terminated Dominica's associated statehood following discussions with the British government. Transitional provisions relating to the transfer from associated statehood to a sovereign democratic republic were included in the Constitution.

Methods of Election

The removal of monarchy and its replacement by republicanism in Trinidad and Tobago and in Guyana; and the creation of a republic at independence in Dominica removed the power of the prime minister to advise Queen Elizabeth II, in her personal capacity as Queen, in two of these three countries on the appointment of a governor general who would serve as Her Majesty's personal representative in each of these countries. With Dominica advancing directly to being an independent republic upon attaining its independence, such a transition was not required from having a governor general to a presidency and so a new formula was required.

This transition, in all three cases, created the need to design a method of election to choose an indigenous head of state, namely the president of the Republic.

During the period of the monarchy, the appointment of the governor general was based on Letters Patent from Her Majesty given on the advice of the prime minister of the independent monarchy. The governor general in both Trinidad and Tobago and in Guyana held office 'during Her Majesty's pleasure.'[10] This expression has traditionally been an eloquent form of expressing the complete dominance of the prime minister over the appointment and tenure of office of the governor general.

Owing to the fact that Queen Elizabeth II was Queen of Trinidad and Tobago and also Queen of Guyana, it was evident that there was no need to devise any formula for succession. The heir to the British Throne would become the new head of state of independent monarchies in the Commonwealth upon succession.

There have been changes to the manner of succession to the British Crown. The Succession to the Crown Act 2013[11] removed male primogeniture and replaced it with general primogeniture and also removed barriers for Roman Catholics to marry a British monarch. Retention of the succession plan for Commonwealth Caribbean monarchies was agreed by Antigua and Barbuda, The Bahamas, Barbados, Belize, Grenada, Jamaica, St Kitts-Nevis, St Lucia, and St Vincent and the Grenadines together with the UK, Canada, Australia, New Zealand, Papua New Guinea, the Solomon Islands, and Tuvalu in the Perth Agreement 2011.[12]

In 2011, all of these countries shared a common monarch in the person of Queen Elizabeth II and the reforms proposed by the British government required concurrence across all Commonwealth countries who would be affected by the reforms. Dominica, Guyana, and Trinidad and Tobago, as members of the Commonwealth, were not affected as these countries had introduced a new form of election for their Heads of State upon their accession to republican status seeing that the direct link to the British Crown had been severed by virtue of that accession.

In Guyana, the president is elected by direct election; in Trinidad and Tobago, the president is elected by an electoral college which consists of a joint sitting of both Houses of Parliament, while in Dominica the president is elected by the House of Assembly only if the prime minister and the leader of the opposition are unable to agree on a single nominee for the office.

These methods vary from the direct choice of the electorate to the indirect choice of the Legislature to the concurrence of the prime minister and the leader of the opposition. In all instances the president serves for a period of five years.

Guyana

In Guyana, the president is elected directly by the people at a national election. His election is linked with the elections of members to the National Assembly insofar as the party list system of proportional representation is used for the National Assembly. The presidential candidate heads the list of his party; however, the president is elected on a first past-the-post basis in relation to the other presidential candidates. The Constitution of Guyana provides for this as follows:

> 177.(1) Any list of candidates for an election held pursuant to the provisions of article 60(2) shall designate not more than one of those candidates as a Presidential candidate. An elector voting at such an election in favour of a list shall be deemed to be also voting in favour of the Presidential candidate named in the list.
>
> (2) Where –
>
> (a) there is only one Presidential candidate at the election; or
>
> (b) there are two or more Presidential candidates, if more votes are cast in favour of the list in which a person is designated as Presidential candidate than in favour of any other list, that Presidential candidate shall be deemed to be elected as President and shall be so declared by the Chairman of the Elections Commission acting only in accordance with the advice of the Chief Election Officer, after such advice has been tendered to the Elections Commission at a duly summoned meeting.[13]

The provisions in subsection (2) above were introduced by an amendment to the Constitution of Guyana by virtue of the provisions of Act No. 2 of 2000 which received presidential assent on April 11, 2000.[14] The previous section 177(2) read as follows before it was amended:

> (2) A Presidential candidate shall be deemed to have been elected as President and shall be so declared by the Chairman of the Elections Commission -
>
> (a) if he is the only Presidential candidate at the election; or
>
> (b) where there are two or more Presidential candidates, if more votes are cast in favour of the list in which he is designated as Presidential candidate than in favour of any other list.[15]

The members of the National Assembly are chosen by proportional representation, while the presidency is determined by the first-past-the-post system within the confines of a system of proportional representation. With each elector only having a single vote for one list there can be no splitting of votes between presidential and assembly candidates. The terms of office of both the president and the National Assembly are co-terminous and last for five years, unless the president sooner dissolves the National Assembly in which case the president will also be subjecting himself/herself to a general election for his/her office. The president is only eligible to be re-elected once.[16]

This amendment was introduced after the experiences of the 1997 general election when the presidency was declared without all of the results being verified. According to the Report on the 1997 Elections by the Guyana Elections Commission:

9.5 Receiving Results at the Command Center

Results were received at the Command Center from approximately 9:30 p.m .on the night of December 15, 1997. This continued until the afternoon of December 16, 1997 by means of telephones. Telephone and radio operators upon receipt of information prepared a report on a standard format. Such reports were channeled through several stages of verification involving members of the Elections Commission and assigned Senior Staff. The reports were then passed to the computer section for encoding. Once the reports were entered, the information was made available to the Chairman of the Elections Commission who made the announcement to those present in the media center. While reports were being processed from several outlying areas, concern was expressed about feedback from District # 4 Demerara/Mahaica. Reports from this district were a mere trickle and as far as Georgetown sub-district was concerned not a single report was received by midnight of December 15, 1997. The Commission did not hesitate to express its concern over such state of affairs and instructed the Chief Elections Officer to intervene immediately to ensure that Presiding Officers comply with established procedures.

This intervention resulted in a submission of some Statements of the Poll by the Returning Officer of District 4 at approximately 2:30 am on December 16, 1997. By Thursday December 18, 1997 all Statements of Poll were submitted by Returning Officers to the Command Center.

9.6 Declaration of Results

As the results came in, the method of announcing of results by the Chairman at the media center continued with the exception of District No.4. A verification process was implemented to deal with the late Statements of

Poll submitted by District 4. While this process was in progress, the Chief Elections Officer after an assessment of the results already verified made a preliminary declaration to the Chairman on Friday December 19, 1997. This declaration cited the PPP/C as having won the General Elections and six of the ten (10) regions. This was followed by the PNC securing the second largest number of votes at the General Elections and majority in the four remaining districts. The Chairman of the Elections Commission without hesitation made a declaration on the Presidency immediately. This resulted in a halt to the verification process underway for District 4 and a closure of the computer operations.[17]

The controversies that followed the 1997 elections led to civil disturbances in Guyana which caused negotiations to be held between the two main parties, the People's Progressive Party/Civic led by Janet Jagan and the People's National Congress/Reform led by Desmond Hoyte. After these negotiations, there was the signing of an accord between these leaders on January 17, 1998 that became known as the Herdmanston Accord that was brokered by the Caribbean Community (CARICOM) Mission to Guyana.[18]

This led to a reduction in the marches and demonstrations that were taking place in Guyana in the aftermath of the official declaration of the presidential election without all of the results having been verified.

There was, however, another controversy involving the 1997 general elections in Guyana that involved court proceedings that were filed on February 25, 1998 in the matter of *Esther Perreira vs the Chief Election Officer and Others*. Judgment in this matter was delivered by Madam Justice Claudette Singh in the High Court of Guyana on January 15, 2001. The specific complaints made by Perreira in her petition to the court were recited by Singh J in her judgment as follows:

The petition consists of thirty seven (37) paragraphs with particulars and a prayer. Among the complaints of the petitioner against the validity of the elections were:

  i.   That the elections were not held in conformity with the law as to elections, particularly the Constitution and the Representation of the People Act;

  ii. That the requirement of the voters' ID card as a qualification to be an elector at the elections as provided for under the Elections Laws (Amendment) Act 1997 is ultra vires Article 159 of the Constitution of Guyana;

  iii. That the unlawful acts and omissions set out herein affected the results of the said elections which would otherwise have lawfully resulted in different placing of the respective list of candidates.[19]

This election petition sought to overturn the result of the 1997 general election which would have created the need for fresh elections to be held if the petition succeded.

Singh J concluded in her written judgment:

> Accordingly I hold that the 1997 elections were not conducted in accordance with the law. I therefore grant the following declarations:
>
> i.   that Act 22/97 is ultra vires, null and void Articles 59 and 159 of the Constitution.
>
> ii.   That the 1997 elections were not conducted in accordance with the provisions of the Representation of the People Act Chapter 1:03 and articles 59 and 159 of the Constitution of Guyana.[20]

This judgment was delivered some three years and one month after the 1997 general election was held. On January 26, 2001, Singh J made an order that constrained both the presidency and the legislature from taking further action in the execution of their duties and also directed that 'fresh national and Regional Elections shall be held in the republic of Guyana on or before March 31, 2001.'[21]

Fresh national and regional elections were held on March 19, 2001 resulting in Bharrat Jagdeo being elected president of Guyana. The 2001 elections were also mired in controversy.

There was an attempt to prevent the swearing-in ceremony for Bharrat Jagdeo being held after the general election. The PNC/Reform brought a court action in the name of one of its executive members, Joseph Hamilton, by making an application for prerogative orders that sought to prevent the swearing-in ceremony for President-elect Jagdeo.[22] The application failed on the ground that it was not an election petition, but rather an attempt to require the chief election officer to comply with his statutory duties under the Representation of the People Act, Cap. 1:03.

Chief Justice Desirée Bernard said:

> I agree that if the results of the election were tainted by disenfranchisement of voters or multiple voting these issues can only be ventilated at the hearing of an election petition. I have no power in these proceedings to deal with such unlawful acts or omissions...However, the applicant's complaint is not about the validity of the results of the elections; he seeks compliance by the Chief Elections Officer with his statutory duties.[23]

The process for electing the president of Guyana has had its fair share of controversy between 1997 and 2001, which was a pivotal period for elections to the presidency. The need for CARICOM intervention in 1998 following the 1997 general elections that produced the Herdmanston Accord and the historic ruling by Singh J that forced an early general election in 2001 when such an election was not due until 2002 were crucial landmarks along the way to settling the mechanisms by which future presidents of Guyana would be elected.

Trinidad and Tobago

In Trinidad and Tobago, the president is chosen by indirect election through the legislature. An electoral college[24] has been established for this purpose, which is a joint sitting of both the House of Representatives (an elected House) and the Senate (a nominated House). The House of Representatives determines the nomination of candidates for the presidency as the nomination papers of candidates must be signed by at least 12 members of that House.[25] At the time of writing, there were 41 members of the House of Representatives.

The Speaker of the House of Representatives presides at sittings of the electoral college and voting is by secret ballot among the elected MPs and the 31 senators. Once elected, the president serves for a term of five years that is not co-terminous with the life of the Parliament.[26] There may be changes in the composition of the Parliament as a result of a dissolution and general elections, but these will not affect the tenure of the office of the president.

However, in 2001, there was a tied election result after the general election of December 10 which produced an 18-18 deadlock. President A.N.R. Robinson eventually appointed Patrick Manning as prime minister without a majority leading to a sequence of events that caused no Speaker to be elected.

After President Robinson made his announcement to the nation, Patrick Manning was sworn into office as prime minister on December 24, 2001 and on December 26, 2001, the majority of the Cabinet was sworn into office. The next sitting of Parliament had to be held no later than six months after the last sitting[27] (the House of Representatives had last met before the dissolution on October 5, 2001 and the Senate last met on October 9, 2001). This meant that a sitting of Parliament had to take place by April 8, 2002.

The government advised the president to summon Parliament to meet on Friday, April 5, 2002 and while there were no problems in the Senate, there were serious problems in the House of Representatives. This started with the election of a Speaker of the House of Representatives.

The House of Representatives was unable to elect a Speaker after two days of nominations and, in some instances, lengthy speeches.

The clerk of the House of Representatives presided over the first stages of the first sitting of the House after a general election as is the customary practice in Trinidad and Tobago, owing to the fact that the incumbent Speaker ceases to hold that office once the Proclamation by the president summoning a new Parliament is read out by the clerk of the House.

In the circumstances, the clerk was required to interpret the standing orders in relation to the controversies that arose over the votes that were cast for the election of a Speaker where the nominees from one side of the House earned an 18-18 vote, while the nominees from the other side of the House earned a 36-0 result.

The following excerpt from the Hansard of the House of Representatives for April 5, 2002 reveals the substantive issues raised:

Election of Speaker Friday, April 5, 2002

[DR THE HON. K. ROWLEY]

...I second the nomination of Prof. Max Richards to sit in the Chair as Speaker of the Parliament of Trinidad and Tobago. [Desk thumping]

Mr Ganga Singh (Caroni East): Madam Clerk, I beg to propose Mr. Robin Montano of No. 3 Henderson Road, Maraval, to take the Chair of this honourable House as Speaker. In so doing I, unlike the hon. Member for San Fernando East, do not intend to breach Standing Order 3(4) which reads: 'No debate shall be allowed upon proposals for filling the office of Speaker, but any member may call for a division after the decision on the proposal has been announced.'

Miss Gillian Lucky (Pointe-a-Pierre): Madam Clerk, if it pleases you, I beg to second the nomination of Robin Montano. [Desk thumping]

Madam Clerk: Are there any further nominations? There being no further nominations, hon. Members, the question is that Prof. Max Richards do take the Chair of this House as Speaker. All in favour say "Aye".

Government Members: Aye.

Madam Clerk: Any against?

UNC Members: No.

Madam Clerk: Hon. Members, the voices appear equally divided. I must take a division.

Ayes 18 Noes 18

Madam Clerk: There being an equality of votes, the proposal is declared lost.

The Minister of Science, Technology and Tertiary Education (Hon. Hedwige Bereaux): Madam Clerk, I would like to point out that in accordance with the provisions of Standing Order 3(3) the condition precedent for putting the question in respect of any other person who has been proposed has not been fulfilled. In respect of the nomination of Prof. Max Richards, the proposal has not been negatived and accordingly you cannot now, in accordance with the Standing Orders, put the question.

Madam Clerk, Standing Order 3 refers to the election of a Speaker. It says: 'If another such Member or person, willing to serve if elected, be proposed and seconded, the Clerk shall propose the question that the Member who was first proposed should be the Speaker. If that proposal be agreed to, the Member or other person so chosen shall be Speaker, but if the proposal be negatived, the Clerk shall propose a like question in respect of any other such Member...'

Madam Clerk, as you have just indicated, there have been 18 votes for and 18 votes against; that is an equality and as such it has not been negatived and in accordance, therefore, the question cannot be put and in fact, Prof. Max Richards has been duly elected Speaker. [Desk thumping]

Madam Clerk: Hon. Members, with a division of 18/18 the proposal is declared lost. [Desk thumping] Therefore hon. Members the question is that Mr. Robin Montano do take the Chair of this House as Speaker. All in favour say "Aye". Any against?

Hon. Members: No!

Madam Clerk: The noes appear to have it.

[Calls for a division]

Madam Clerk: The result of the division, hon. Members, is no Member voted for, 36 Members voted against.

The Minister of Science, Technology and Tertiary Education (Hon. Hedwige Bereaux): Madam Clerk, I rise again to draw your attention to Standing Order 3(2) which says:

'A Member, having first ascertained that the Member or other person to be proposed, is willing to serve if elected, may, rising in his place and addressing the Clerk, propose any other Member (not being a Minister or Parliamentary Secretary), or any other person who is not a Member of either Chamber of the Legislature, to the House as Speaker of the House; and if that proposal be seconded, the Clerk, if no other such Member or person be proposed for the office, shall declare the Member or the person so proposed and seconded to be Speaker of the House.' That is, if there is a proposal and nobody else, that person becomes the Member of the House. In this instance, Madam Clerk, what we have is a situation where we had one person proposed and that person had 18 votes for and 18 votes against which, as I indicated previously, and you ruled upon I was prepared at that time to consider it. However, what we have now is a situation where, in fact, not even the persons who have nominated and seconded the second nominee proposal, have voted for their own nominee.

In fact, therefore, logic says that we have only had one nomination and, accordingly, Prof. Max Richards is the Speaker of this House. [Desk thumping]

The Minister of Planning and Development (Hon. Dr Keith Rowley):

Madam Clerk, I rise to get a clarification. I am labouring under the impression, and I would like clarification given to your account. I was talking to my colleague and I might have missed the count.

Am I correct in understanding that 18 votes were cast for Prof. Max Richards and zero for Robin Montano? [Crosstalk]

Madam Clerk: Hon. Members, you all know very well that I am not empowered to make rulings.

Dr K. Rowley: Just a clarification. I just want to get the numbers clear. Am I correct with the numbers? Madam Clerk, I want to be very clear. I am not inviting you to take part in the House proceedings. I understand your position, but I want to be clear for the record. What were the numbers? I might have missed the vote.

How many votes were cast for Prof. Richards and how many for Robin Montano?

Madam Clerk: On the question that Prof. Richards take the Chair as Speaker of this House, 18 Members voted for and 18 Members voted against. On the question that Mr. Robin Montano take the Chair of this House as Speaker, no Members voted for and 36 Members voted against. Accordingly, hon. Members, I once again call upon this House to elect a Speaker. [Desk thumping]

The Minister of Health (Hon. Colm Imbert): Madam Clerk, we are proceeding under protest; we do not agree. [Desk thumping]

The Minister of Energy and Energy Industries (Hon. Eric Williams):

Madam Clerk, it is under duress and under protest in this House that I rise to make another nomination for the post of Speaker of this honourable Chamber. [28]

The fundamental issue was whether or not an 18-18 tie in a vote for the election of a Speaker meant that the resolution had been 'negatived'. There was no doubt that the 36-0 vote was clearly negatived, but what about a tie?

It appeared that the clerk of the House took the view that she needed to maintain the status quo where there was a tie. That status quo was that there was no Speaker at the time of the vote and, therefore, it would have been improper for her to impose a Speaker on the House in a situation where the House had neither a positive nor negative view about who should preside over it.

The premise upon which the standing orders of the House of Representatives operated was that a Speaker will always be elected so that the clerk is expected to be no more than a functionary in carrying out the election of a Speaker. Instead what occurred on April 5, 2002 was an unprecedented situation where the clerk was required to give a ruling on a procedural point regarding the interpretation of the word 'negatived' in relation to the election of a Speaker.

The argument from the government benches was that Professor Max Richards had earned more votes in a tie (18-18) than Robin Montano who got no votes (36-0). However, the system of voting is designed to ensure that the nominee from the government side will always be elected first because that nomination is usually made by the Leader of the House and is to be considered first and once they have a majority there will be no need for any further nominations to be entertained. Any other nomination would be negatived.

The 18-18 vote was the first sign that the government did not control the House and this allowed a nominee from the opposition benches to be considered in the voting for a Speaker. In order to frustrate the process and ensure that it would be prolonged and as a mark of protest against the decision of the President Republic, Arthur N.R. Robinson, in which the incumbent government had become the Opposition after an election result that produced an 18-18 tie, the Opposition decided to nominate persons to become the Speaker and then promptly voted against their own nominees.

This was a political gamble by the Opposition as it seemed as though they also had to ensure that they nominated persons whom they were sure the government would vote against. After all, what would have been the situation if the government benches had voted for one of the opposition nominees and someone on the opposition benches abstained instead of voting against their own nominee?

Ordinarily, the election of a Speaker ought not to be a matter of political patronage to be dispensed by the government, but rather a matter for the House of Representatives to elect the person whom it deems to be most capable of performing the task of presiding over the House.

The House of Representatives could not be adjourned and the government found themselves trapped in a sitting that they could not end. The only way out for the government was for the prime minister to advise the president to prorogue Parliament on April 6, 2002.

The first session of the new Parliament ended one day after it started. There was no Speaker of the House of Representatives and the second session of Parliament was convened on August 28, 2002 when another attempt was made to elect a Speaker. This also failed and the prime minister announced to the House of Representatives that he was going to advise the president to dissolve Parliament later that day and that general elections would be held on Monday, October 7, 2002.

The significance of the failure of the House of Representatives to elect a Speaker impacted upon the ability of the electoral college to meet to elect a new president in 2002 seeing that President Robinson had assumed the office of president in March 1997 for a five-year term.

The time for an election to be held was no later than 30 days before the expiration of his term of office which meant that the election ought to have been held before February 17, 2002 given that he assumed office on March 17, 1997.

In those circumstances, it was necessary for section 33(3) of the Constitution to be invoked. The section provides:

> Where for any reason at the date on which the term of office of the President is due to expire under subsection (1) or (2) there is no person entitled by election under section 26(4) to fill the office of President upon its expiration, the current term of that office shall continue until thirty days after a person is elected to the office of President whereupon the current term of that office shall expire.[29]

President Robinson remained in office beyond the end of his five-year term until he was replaced by Professor George Maxwell Richards on March 18, 2003. The inability to elect a Speaker in 2002 had hampered the ability of the Electoral College to meet when it ought to have met to elect a president by virtue of the delay in convening the First Session of the Seventh Parliament of the Republic after the date on which such an election ought to have been held up to and including February 18, 2002.

The fact that the entire period of the Seventh Parliament (April 5–August 28, 2002) passed without a Speaker being elected pushed the date for the sitting of the electoral college into 2003 after the general election was held on October 7, 2002 and the Eighth Parliament assembled on October 17, 2002.

Dominica

In Dominica, the president may be chosen primarily through the concurrence of the prime minister and the leader of the opposition after their consultation and their proposal of a joint nomination to the Speaker of the House of Assembly of a candidate for the presidency. The Speaker, in these circumstances, will only be required to inform the House of Assembly of the nomination and declare the candidate elected without putting the question to a vote.[30]

If, however, there is no concurrence between the prime minister and the leader of the opposition on a joint nomination, the Speaker shall inform the House of Assembly and within 14 days of so being informed the Speaker may receive nominations for the presidency. The prime minister or the leader of the opposition or any three members of the House of Assembly may submit nominations to the Speaker. The Speaker shall put the nominations to the vote by secret ballot and then declare the winning candidate elected. The president serves for a period of five years and his term in not co-terminous with Parliament.[31] Unlike Trinidad and Tobago, there is a term limit of two five-year terms imposed on the office of president in Dominica.[32]

Comparative Analysis of Methods of Election

The election of presidents in Trinidad and Tobago and in Dominica highlight the challenges of devising methods of election that allow the holder of the office of president an important measure of legitimacy without competing with the prime minister and the Cabinet for dominance in the system.

The method of indirect election dominated by the elected representatives of the people in Trinidad and Tobago caters to that need. In Dominica, what is addressed primarily is the political acceptance of the president to both the government and the Opposition insofar as the prime minister and the leader of the opposition are required first of all to seek a joint nomination.

Guyana differs substantially from these two republics owing to the method of direct election used for the presidency. This places the office in a position to exercise its own powers directly, rather than on the advice of the Cabinet, and makes it an executive presidency. Trinidad and Tobago and Dominica may be described as having quasi-ceremonial presidencies based on the mixture of advisory and discretionary powers exercised by both presidents.

The Exercise of Presidential Powers

The powers of the Presidencies of Dominica, Guyana, and Trinidad and Tobago are exercised in differing ways:

Dominica

In general, the president exercises his powers on the advice of the cabinet or a minister acting under the general authority of the cabinet. However, the Constitution or any other law may specify, in certain circumstances, that the president is authorized to act on the advice of, or after consultation with, any person or authority other than the cabinet or that he may act in his own deliberate judgment.[33]

Guyana

In general, the president exercises his powers in his own deliberate judgment. However, the Constitution or any other law may specify, in certain circumstances, that he be required to act in accordance with the advice or recommendation of any person or authority. In such cases, the president may, in his own deliberate judgment, refer any such advice or recommendation back for reconsideration to the person or authority concerned. After reconsideration by the person or authority concerned, the president shall act in accordance with either the original or substituted advice or recommendation as the case may be.[34]

Trinidad and Tobago

In general, the president exercises his powers on the advice of the cabinet or a minister acting under the general authority of the cabinet. However, the Constitution or any other law may specify, in certain circumstances, that the president is authorized to act on the advice of, or after consultation with, any person or authority other than the cabinet or in his discretion or that he may act in his own deliberate judgment.[35]

Consultation

The introduction of Commonwealth Caribbean presidencies brought about a new method of exercising presidential power. A formal recognition has been given to 'consultation' as a method to be employed in the exercise of presidential powers. No specific definition has been included in these constitutions to govern the exercise of consultation so that controversies have arisen about its exercise in various cases.

Executive powers had previously only been exercised by governors general on the advice of ministers or at their discretion or in their own deliberate judgment. The provisions allowing heads of state to exercise some of their powers 'after consultation' can draw the presidency into controversy, especially in situations such as the transition from one presidency to another. While this technique has been viewed as a means of reducing the powers of the prime minister in quasi-ceremonial presidencies, it has caused controversies between outgoing presidents and newly appointed prime ministers in respect of appointments to high offices of state in such presidencies.

For example, in Trinidad and Tobago there was a change of government on December 16, 1986 and soon after the new government announced the replacement of the incumbent, President Ellis Clarke. The outgoing president made appointments to the Public Service Commission and the Police Service Commission on December 31, 1986 and to the Judicial and Legal Service Commission on March 14, 1987. His term of office expired on March 19, 1987. The new prime minister, A.N.R. Robinson, complained that he had not been consulted (as required by the Constitution) in respect of the December 31 appointments. The outgoing president claimed that he had already consulted a prime minister (the previous one) and had made up his mind on the appointments, but had omitted to make them before the general elections. With regard to the appointment made on March 14, the outgoing president claimed that the new prime minister was uncooperative in the consultation process despite all of his attempts. The prime minister claimed that the appointment could be left for the new president to make after his inauguration. The outgoing president did not wish to leave any vacancies at the end of his tenure on March 19 and went ahead with an appointment on March 14.

Essentially, provision has been made in the constitutions of Dominica and of Trinidad and Tobago for appointments to a number of high offices of the state to be made, for the most part, by the president after consultation with the prime minister and the leader of the opposition. This power, as has been shown above, is to be exercised independently of the cabinet and represents only a requirement to be observed by the president before deciding in his own mind what appointment he will make.

In Guyana, provision is also made for the president to make appointments, for the most part, after consultation with the leader of the opposition. This power, as has been shown above, is to be exercised in his own deliberate judgment and represents only a requirement to be observed by the president before deciding in his own mind what appointment he will make.

Perhaps, the most interesting aspect of the exercise of powers 'after consultation' is that there is no definition of what it means constitutionally, legally or otherwise. In Guyana, it is clear that the nature of the consultation falls within the confines of the exercise of presidential powers 'in his own deliberate judgment.' In Trinidad and Tobago and in Dominica, it appears as though consultation falls in a no man's land between cabinet advice and deliberate judgment. In these cases, the implication is that the consultation be held at the behest of the president. This would seem to cloak it more firmly within the confines of 'discretion' or 'deliberate judgment'.

In Guyana, constitutional reforms in 2001, Act No. 5 and Act No. 6, created new requirements for the exercise of presidential power. Act. No 5 of 2001 created a category now described as 'meaningful consultation', while Act No. 6 of 2001 imposes the agreement of the leader of the opposition in making appointments to the offices of chancellor and chief justice.

Deliberate Judgment

In Guyana, the general method of exercising state power is by way of the deliberate judgment of the president. In Dominica and Trinidad and Tobago, deliberate judgment is, like consultation, an exception to the general principle of the president acting on the advice of the cabinet or a minister acting under the general authority of the cabinet.

Presidential Responsibility

The key factor that needs to be examined here is the absence of any kind of real political responsibility for the presidents of Dominica and, to a greater extent, Trinidad and Tobago for the exercise of their powers after consultation or in their own deliberate judgment or discretion. The constitutions of these two countries only provide for their removal from office on a variety of grounds that do not relate to political responsibility for proper decisions taken while in office.

In the 1978 Constitution of Dominica, the grounds of removal of the president are laid out in section 24 to include (i) wilful violation of the Constitution; (ii) misbehaviour that may cause hatred, ridicule or contempt for the presidency; (iii) endangering the security of Dominica; (iv) physical or mental incapacity affecting the performance of duty; (v) any circumstances that arise that would disqualify him to be elected to office; (vi) if he engages in any other occupation or is appointed to any other office.

In the 1976 Constitution of Trinidad and Tobago, the grounds of removal of the president are the same as Dominica with the exception of (v) and (vi) which do not apply in Trinidad and Tobago.

The fact that these presidents in Dominica and Trinidad and Tobago are able to shape the nature and character of the consultation exercise in such a way that excludes the influence of the political directorate is constitutionally questionable. This must be coupled with their wide exercise of powers in their own deliberate judgment (or discretion where stated). They are not accountable to any other authority, whereas the political directorate, in the form of the cabinet, is collectively responsible to Parliament.[36] This is a new trend in the exercise of state power because the governor general did not enjoy these powers of consultation in Trinidad and Tobago between 1962 and 1976 and likewise Guyana between 1966 and 1970.

This desire to introduce consultation was measured against a desire to reduce the powers of patronage being enjoyed by the prime minister, particularly in Trinidad and Tobago. This point of view was expressed in the Report of the Constitution Review Commission under the chairmanship of Sir Hugh Wooding that served during the period June 1971–January 1974 in Trinidad and Tobago.

According to the Commission:

> We propose a substantial reduction of the area of patronage at the disposal of the Prime Minister. The Chief Justice, the other members of the Judicial and Legal Service Commission, the Chairman and other members of the other Service Commissions, and the Chairman of the Boundaries Commission should all be appointed by the President after consultation with the Prime Minister and the Leader of the Opposition instead of being appointed, as now, in accordance with the advice of the Prime Minister. The Prime Minister will quite properly have influence but he will not have the final say. This modification of the powers of the Prime Minister is in line with the overwhelming majority of views expressed to us. The diffusion of power seems to us desirable as a matter of principle. We recommend accordingly.[37]

This outlook was endorsed by the government of the day when the Report of the Constitution Commission was debated in the Trinidad and Tobago House of Representatives on December 17, 1974. The then prime minister, Dr Eric Williams, had this to say on the subject:

They recommend – and the People's National Movement entirely supports the view – that the President is to be the person responsible, after consultation with the Prime Minister, Leader of the Opposition, and such other persons as he thinks fit in his discretion, for appointments to a number of offices.[38]

In agreeing to this proposal by the Constitution Review Commission, Dr Williams and the People's National Movement (PNM) did not address the question of any political responsibility for the president. When the prime minister held these powers, he was politically responsible for them. To whom was the president going to be responsible now?

This is part of the dilemma facing countries that emerge out of a colonial past and desire to create an indigenous head of state. In the UK, the monarch exercises the Royal Prerogative on the advice of ministers and there are very few aspects of the Royal Prerogative that are exercised in the discretion of the Monarch.

Unlike the UK, Trinidad and Tobago and Dominica do not have any tradition of royalty that has emerged as part of their political culture. The election of an indigenous head of state gains its legitimacy from the concurrence of the prime minister and the leader of the opposition (in Dominica) or the indirect election of the legislature (in Trinidad and Tobago or in Dominica if there is no concurrence between the prime minister and the leader of the opposition). Without that, the office of president would have no constitutionally sound basis for the exercise of its powers. The office of governor general was able to claim a direct linkage to the British Monarch and thereby earn its legitimacy through the exercise of the Royal Prerogative on the advice of local ministers. There were very few areas of personal authority to be exercised by the governor general and this state of affairs mirrored the constitutional position of the British Monarch in many respects.

In addressing the issue of presidential responsibility, there must be some appreciation of the political reality of the exercise of powers after consultation. The urgency for such an appreciation is heightened by the fact that the jurisdiction of the court is excluded from the process. According to section 80(2) of the Trinidad and Tobago Constitution:

Where by this Constitution the President is required to act in accordance with the advice of, or after consultation with, any person or authority, the question whether he has in any case so acted shall not be enquired into in any court.[39]

A somewhat similar provision is also found in the Dominica Constitution at section 118(3) as follows:

> Where by this Constitution the President is required to perform any function in accordance with the advice of, or after consultation with, any person or authority, the question whether the President has so exercised that function shall not be enquired into in any court of law.[40]

The exclusion of judicial review of the functions of the president when combined with an absence of any meaningful political responsibility for the exercise of those functions after consultation creates a constitutional loophole.

This was the prevailing view until a Privy Council decision in the case of *Attorney General v. Dumas*[41] was delivered on May 8, 2017. The case was a challenge to the decision of the president to make two nominations to the Police Service Commission of Trinidad and Tobago for the ratification or rejection by the House of Representatives. In ruling for Dumas on the issue of whether or not the court could inquire into the actions of the president, Lord Hodge writing for the Board said, inter alia:

> It has long been recognised that a statutory ouster clause, which provides that a determination shall not be called into question in any court of law, will not protect a purported determination from a legal challenge that it is ultra vires and therefore a nullity: Anisminic Ltd v Foreign Compensation Commission [1969] 2 AC 147. Thus in Attorney-General of Trinidad and Tobago v Phillip [1995] 1 AC 396 the Board considered the validity of a pardon which the President had purported to grant during the armed insurrection in July 1990. Lord Woolf, who delivered the Board's judgment, stated (412E-G):
>
> > 'Where the head of state has made a formal decision which in normal circumstances would constitute a pardon, it is important that the state should not be able to resile from the terms of that pardon except in the most limited of circumstances...The Constitution of Trinidad and Tobago supports this approach by providing in section 38(1) that the President shall not be answerable to any court for the performance of the functions of his office or for any act done by him in the performance of those functions. However section 38(1) does not go so far as to prevent the courts from examining, as did the courts below, the validity of the pardon (emphasis added).[42]

This is one instance where presidential power must now bear some judicial responsibility. The citizens are no longer bound to accept the appointees of the president made after consultation, discretion or deliberate judgment and there can be real judicial scrutiny of those appointees so as to enhance the accountability process.

In Trinidad and Tobago, there was an attempt to use the judicial process to query the December 31, 1986 appointments made by the outgoing president, Ellis Clarke and the High Court ruled that it could not inquire into the matter as its jurisdiction was ousted by the provisions of section 80(2) of the Constitution.[43] In the circumstances, the procedure employed by the outgoing president could not be questioned in a court of law, in the opinion of Blackman J at the time, and the appointment of James Alva Bain to the Public Service Commission as well as his appointment to the Police Service Commission remained valid. The absence of any other process of scrutiny at that time made the point about the exercise of power without any responsibility. However, since the Dumas judgment in May 2017 that position has changed.

There is a need to ensure that presidential appointments to national offices carry with them the stamp of political neutrality which only the office of the president can offer. While this may be so, there is now an overwhelming reason why the president should have his appointments scrutinized by the courts in order to ensure accountability and responsibility.

The president of Guyana is politically responsible for the performance of all of his functions in that he is elected directly at a general election and he and his party are accountable to the population at the next general election, not to mention that the Guyanese cabinet is responsible to Parliament and is subject to a motion of no confidence, which if lost, will result in a general election.[44] The presidents of Dominica and of Trinidad and Tobago will now no longer be treated differently as far as responsibility goes with the advent of the Dumas decision.

It appears as though the concept of 'The Monarch can do no wrong' has been transferred from the office of governor general to the presidency in Trinidad and Tobago. This concept and its immunities are best expressed as follows:

> English law has always clung to the theory that the king is subject to law and, accordingly, can break the law...The courts were the king's courts, and like other feudal lords the king could not be sued in his own court. He could be plaintiff - and as plaintiff he had important prerogatives in the law of procedure - but he could not be defendant. No form of writ or execution would issue against him, for there was no way of compelling his submission to it. Even today, when most of the obstacles to justice have been removed, it has been found necessary to make important modifications of the law of procedure and execution in the Crown's favour.

> The maxim that 'the king can do no wrong' does not in fact have much to do with this procedural immunity. Its true meaning is that the king has no legal power to do wrong. His legal position, the powers and prerogatives which distinguish him from an ordinary subject, is given to him by the law, and the law gives him no authority to transgress...But the king had a personal as well as a political capacity, and in his personal capacity he was just as capable of acting illegally as was anyone else - and there were special temptations in his path. But the procedural obstacles were the same in either capacity. English law never succeeded in distinguishing effectively between the king's two capacities.[45]

As far as Dominica and Trinidad and Tobago are concerned, their constitutions provide exemptions for the exercise of the president's powers on advice and after consultation (as shown above) largely in keeping with the principle that 'the king can do no wrong'. Both constitutions also go further to protect the president in both his official and personal capacities. In Trinidad and Tobago, section 38 of the Constitution reads as follows:

> Subject to section 36, the President shall not be answerable to any court for the performance of the functions of his office or for any act done by him in the performance of those functions. [46]

There are also further exemptions in respect of civil and criminal proceedings contained in the same section. The Dominica Constitution has provisions on this subject that are somewhat similar to Trinidad and Tobago and they read as follows:

> Whilst any person holds office or is acting as President no criminal proceedings shall be instituted or continued against him in respect of anything done or omitted to be done by him either in his official capacity or in his private capacity and no civil proceedings shall be instituted or continued in respect of which relief is claimed against him in respect of anything done or omitted to be done in his private capacity.[47]

While this is, perhaps, not an unusual protection for any head of state to enjoy, the fact that political responsibility (exclusive of misbehaviour) does now exist and the fact that it is no longer accompanied by judicial exemption places the presidents of Dominica and of Trinidad and Tobago within the reach of the Constitution and the law in the exercise of their powers.

In the case of Dominica, the presidency is not cloaked in the Royal Prerogative as the country went from being an associated state to being an independent republic. On the other hand, Trinidad and Tobago has cloaked its presidency in the Royal Prerogative insofar as the transitional provisions in the republican constitution Act of Parliament are concerned. Section 6 of the Act reads as follows:

> Where under any existing law any prerogative or privilege is vested in Her Majesty the Queen or the Crown in respect of Trinidad and Tobago that prerogative or privilege shall, on the appointed day, vest in the State and, subject to the Constitution and any other law, the President shall have power to do all things necessary for the exercise thereof.[48]

It is quite clear that in making the transition from monarchical to republican status, Trinidad and Tobago opted to invest its presidency with the Royal Prerogative of the British Monarchy. This did not sever the link, but rather transferred it to the presidency to be exercised 'subject to the Constitution and any other law'.

Guyana also made provision for the continuance of the Royal Prerogative and royal privileges under the Republic Act, No. 9 of 1970, which was passed on February 20, 1970.[49] This particular issue had to be handled in this way so as to ensure the effective transition of the powers of the head of state from the monarchy to the presidency.

A New Exercise of Presidential Power: Consultation

The 1970 presidency that was created in Guyana did not include an exercise of powers after consultation, while the 1976 presidency in Trinidad and Tobago did. This was not a power that was previously exercised by either Her Majesty or Her governor general in relation to either country. It was a novel creation in Trinidad and Tobago in 1976 and was subsequently adopted by Dominica in 1978. Guyana also adopted it in 1980 within the confines of deliberate judgment, but its presidency is an executive one that is politically responsible for its actions.

The idea of consultation can be traced back to the recommendations of the 1971–74 Constitution Review Commission in Trinidad and Tobago under the chairmanship of Sir Hugh Wooding.[50] The endorsement of this proposal by the government of Trinidad and Tobago saw its introduction, in a substantive way, into the 1976 republican constitution. Its influence has spread since then, even into the monarchical constitutions of some former associated states that attained their independence from the UK after 1976, namely St Lucia[51] and Antigua and Barbuda.[52]

While there is evidence to show that consultation was mentioned in the 1973 independence constitution of the Bahamas,[53] its operation did not resemble what was later proposed and introduced in Trinidad and Tobago.

This new means of exercising state power has diluted the powers of the political directorate more so in Trinidad and Tobago than in Dominica owing to its widespread use in the former and its limited use in the latter. In Guyana, its use must be seen within the confines of the exercise of the deliberate judgment of the president who is elected directly by the people. This creates the dimension of political responsibility for the president and earns for him the right to exercise the largest portion of his powers in his own deliberate judgment.

Removal from Office

The removal of the president from office in all three republics is accomplished through Parliament with the assistance of the judiciary. The grounds of removal appear to be more widely defined in Dominica when compared to Trinidad and Tobago, while they are somewhat more narrowly defined in Guyana. The actual grounds as defined in the three constitutions are as follows:

Dominica (s. 24)

(a) wilful violation of the Constitution;

(b) behaviour that may bring the office of President into hatred, ridicule or contempt;

(c) behaviour that endangers the security of Dominica;

(d) inability to perform the functions of office because of physical or mental incapacity;

(e) circumstances that arise that would disqualify the President from being elected or appointed to the House of Assembly if he were not President;

(f) appointment to another office of emolument or engagement in another occupation for reward.

Trinidad and Tobago (s. 35)

(a) wilful violation of the Constitution;

(b) behaviour that may bring the office of President into hatred, ridicule or contempt;

(c) behaviour that endangers the security of Trinidad and Tobago;

(d) inability to perform the functions of office because of physical or mental incapacity.

Guyana (ss. 179, 180)

(a) inability to perform the functions of office because of physical or mental incapacity.

(b) violation of the Constitution;

(c) gross misconduct.

The procedure for removal differs markedly between Guyana, on the one hand, and Trinidad and Tobago and Dominica, on the other.

Dominica

In the case of Dominica, one-third of the members of the House of Assembly (elected representatives and nominated senators combined) must sign a motion that must be supported by a resolution of two-thirds of all the members of the House proposing the removal of the president from office with full particulars of the grounds of complaint being specified in the resolution.

A tribunal to investigate the complaint shall be appointed by the chief justice (who shall also be a member of the tribunal). There shall be two other judges appointed by the chief justice for this purpose, being as far as practicable the most senior judges of the Supreme Court. After investigation of the complaint, the tribunal will report on the facts to the House of Assembly.

The president shall only be removed from office if, after consideration of the report of the tribunal, at least two-thirds of all the members of the House of Assembly support a resolution declaring that the president shall be removed from office. During the period of investigation, the president shall be suspended from the performance of his duties. An acting president will be designated either by the president after consultation with the prime minister and the leader of the opposition or if no one is so designated, then an acting president will be elected in the same way as the substantive holder of the office of president is elected.

Trinidad and Tobago

In the case of Trinidad and Tobago, the procedure for the removal of the president from office begins with a motion signed by one-third of the members of the House of Representatives that states the full particulars of the grounds of removal being adopted by two-thirds of the total membership of the House of Representatives and the Senate assembled together.

This will be followed by an investigation of the complaint by a tribunal consisting of the chief justice and four other judges appointed by him, being as far as practicable the most senior judges. This tribunal will report on the facts to a joint sitting of both Houses of Parliament summoned by the Speaker of the House of Representatives. This joint sitting will consider the report of the tribunal and the president shall be removed from office if two-thirds of the total membership of the two Houses combined support a resolution for the removal of the president.

During the period of investigation, the president shall be suspended from the performance of his functions and the president of the Senate shall act temporarily as president.

Guyana

In Guyana, the procedure for the removal of the president is divided into two parts. One deals specifically with removal on the grounds of physical or mental incapacity, while the other deals with removal on the grounds of violation of the Constitution or gross misconduct.

The removal procedure for physical or mental incapacity is limited to being initiated by those members of the National Assembly whose names were on the same list as that of the president at the last election. A motion questioning the physical or mental capacity of the president to discharge the functions of the office and calling for an investigation must be supported by a majority of those members and must be carried in the National Assembly.

As a consequence of such a majority vote, the prime minister shall inform the chancellor of the judiciary who shall appoint a board consisting of three qualified medical practitioners in Guyana who shall investigate the matter and report to the chancellor. This report must state their opinion as to whether or not the president is incapable, by reason of infirmity of mind or body, of discharging the functions of his office.

If the board reports that the president is incapable of discharging the functions of the office of president for these reasons, then the chancellor must certify this in writing and the president shall be removed from office. During the period of such an investigation, the president shall be suspended from office and the prime minister shall act as president. If there is no prime minister or the prime minister is unable to perform these functions of the presidency, then those members of the National Assembly whose names were on the same list as that of the president at the last election shall choose a member of the cabinet (that person being an elected member of the National Assembly) to perform the functions of the office of president.

In cases where it is alleged that the president is guilty of a violation of the Constitution or of gross misconduct, the procedure for removal begins with notice of a motion being signed by more than half the elected members of the National Assembly being given to the Speaker. This motion must specify the particulars of the allegations and it must propose the establishment of a tribunal to investigate the allegations. When Parliament is then sitting or has been summoned to meet within five days, the motion must be considered within seven days of the notice. When Parliament is not sitting, the Speaker shall summon the National Assembly (notwithstanding the fact that it may be prorogued) to meet within twenty-one days of the notice to consider the motion.

There shall be no debate on the motion and the Speaker is required to put the motion to a vote which must be supported by two-thirds of the elected members of the National Assembly for an investigation to proceed. The chancellor shall appoint a tribunal consisting of a chairman and not less than two other members from among persons who have held office as judges or appellate judges in some part of the Commonwealth to investigate the matter.

The president has the right to appear before the tribunal during the investigation. If the tribunal reports to the National Assembly that any of the allegations have been substantiated, the National Assembly may resolve by a motion supported by not less than two-thirds of all the elected members that the president is guilty. If such a motion is approved, the president shall cease to hold office on the third day following the passage of such a motion.

Comparison

Both Trinidad and Tobago and Dominica appear to mirror each other in respect of the general idea about the removal process for their presidents. However, in Dominica both elected and nominated members combined may initiate the impeachment process, while in Trinidad and Tobago this is confined to elected members of the House of Representatives only.

The separation of the procedure in Guyana allows the parliamentary party of the president the opportunity to make a decision about the state of health of the president to the exclusion of the rest of the National Assembly. While on the issue of constitutional violation or gross misconduct, there is no debate on the motion to establish a tribunal for investigation of the president. The tribunal itself is not based on the principle of judicial seniority, unlike in Trinidad and Tobago and Dominica where it is, but rather is left entirely up to the chancellor to choose judges of any rank in assembling its composition.

The president is required to vacate office within three days of a successful vote for removal in the National Assembly. In Trinidad and Tobago and Dominica, removal is automatic upon passage of a motion confirming guilt on the part of the president.

Conclusion

The development of presidencies in the Commonwealth Caribbean and the directions in the exercise of presidential power in differing ways have emerged. The issue of political responsibility for the exercise of the powers of the presidency after consultation and the widening of the powers exercised in the deliberate judgment of the presidents of Guyana and of Trinidad and Tobago in relation to the office of governor general that preceded them must be noted. Up to the time of writing, Dominica has not engaged in any post-independence constitutional reform and therefore its presidency is a product of the transfer from associated statehood to independent status itself.

These developments must be seen in the context of the creation of a constitutional model that has deviated considerably from the Westminster model. As argued earlier, there has been the creation of a Whitehall model in the Commonwealth Caribbean which removes the myth that the constitutions of these Commonwealth Caribbean countries can be classified as being Westminster-model constitutions. The introduction of powers of consultation for the three presidencies discussed here and the widening of their powers of deliberate judgment and discretion support the view of the creation of a Whitehall model.

Notes

1. *Laws of Trinidad and Tobago*, Act No. 4 / 1976.
2. Ibid., The Schedule.
3. *The Guyana Independence Order 1966*, S.I. 1966 / No. 575.
4. By virtue of Resolution No. XXVI passed by the National Assembly on August 29, 1969, Guyana became a Republic on February 23, 1970 and the alterations to the Constitution originally set out in the Second Schedule to the Constitution (S.I. 1966 / No. 575) took effect in accordance with section 73(5)of that Constitution.
5. By virtue of *Act No. 2 of 1980* Guyana enacted a new Constitution of the Co-operative Republic of Guyana, repealed the Guyana Independence Act 1966, the Guyana Independence Order 1966, and the Constitution existing at that time. The new Constitution was contained in *Act No. 2 of 1980* as a Schedule.
6. *Laws of the United Kingdom* 15 & 16 Eliz. 2, c. 4.
7. Ibid., s.10.
8. *The Commonwealth of Dominica Constitution Order 1978*, S.I. 1978/No. 1027.
9. *The Dominica Termination of Association Order 1978*, S.I. 1978 / No. 1031.

10. *The Trinidad and Tobago (Constitution) Order in Council 1962*, S.I. 1962 / No. 1875, s. 19. Also The Guyana Independence Order 1966, s. 30.
11. *Laws of the United Kingdom 2013* c. 20.
12. The Perth Agreement was between 16 prime ministers from Commonwealth realms at the 22nd Commonwealth Heads of Government Meeting in Perth, Australia from October 28–30, 2011 which formed the basis of the legislative changes that were made in the United Kingdom in 2013.
13. *Laws of Guyana, Constitution of the Co-operative Republic of Guyana*, Cap. 1:01, Schedule, s. 177.
14. *Laws of Guyana, Constitution (Amendment) Act 2000*, Act No. 2 of 2000, s. 5.
15. *Laws of Guyana, Constitution of the Co-operative Republic of Guyana, Act No. 2 of 1980, Schedule*, s. 177(2).
16. *Laws of Guyana, Constitution of the Co-operative Republic of Guyana*, Cap. 1:01, Schedule, ss. 60, 61, 70, 90, 91 and 92.
17. *Guyana Elections Commission, Report on the 1997 Elections*, 88-89. Accessed at http://www.gecom.org.gy/reports.html on May 30, 2017.
18. *Caribbean Community Mission to Guyana, Herdmanston Accord, Signed in Guyana, January 17, 1998*. Accessed at http://www.gecom.org.gy/pdf_laws/ Herdmanston%20Accord.pdf on May 30, 2017.
19. *Esther Perreira vs The Chief Election Officer and Others. In the High Court of the Supreme Court of Judicature Petition Questioning An Election to the National Assembly under the National Assembly Validity of Elections Act Chapter 1:04. Elections holden on the 15th day of December, 1997.* Judgment by Madam Justice C.M.C. Singh, January 15, 2001, 4–5.
20. Ibid., 77.
21. *Esther Perreira vs The Chief Election Officer and Others. In the High Court of the Supreme Court of Judicature Petition Questioning An Election to the National Assembly under the National Assembly Validity of Elections Act Chapter 1:04. Elections holden on the 15th day of December, 1997.* Order by Madam Justice C.M.C. Singh, January 26, 2001 and entered February 2, 2001.
22. *Sunday Chronicle*, April 1, 2001, 10. The *Sunday Chronicle* is a newspaper published in Guyana.
23. Ibid., 12.
24. *Laws of Trinidad and Tobago, Ch. 1:01, Schedule*, s. 28.
25. Ibid., s. 30.
26. Ibid., s. 33.
27. *Laws of Trinidad and Tobago, Ch. 1:01*, s. 67(2).
28. *Trinidad and Tobago, Parliamentary Debates, House of Representatives, Hansard*, April 5, 2002, 28–33.
29. *Laws of Trinidad and Tobago, Ch. 1:01*, s. 33(3).
30. *The Commonwealth of Dominica Constitution Order 1978*, s. 19.
31. Ibid., s. 18.
32. Ibid., s. 21.
33. Ibid., s. 63(1).
34. *Laws of Guyana, Constitution of the Co-operative Republic of Guyana*, Cap. 1:01, Schedule, s. 111.
35. *Laws of Trinidad and Tobago, Ch. 1:01*, s. 80.
36. *Laws of Trinidad and Tobago Ch. 1:01*, s. 75 and *The Commonwealth of Dominica Constitution Order 1978*, s. 60.
37. *Report of the Constitution Commission, January 22, 1974, Trinidad and Tobago* (Trinidad: Trinidad and Tobago Printing and Packaging Ltd., 1974), para., 287.

38. *Trinidad and Tobago, Parliamentary Debates, House of Representatives, Hansard, Vol.18, Session 1974–75*, 387.
39. *Laws of Trinidad and Tobago, Ch. 1:01*, s. 80 (2).
40. *The Commonwealth of Dominica Constitution Order 1978*, s. 118(3).
41. *Attorney General v Dumas* [2017] UKPC 12.
42. Ibid., para. 34.
43. *In Re Application of the Attorney General for Leave to Apply for Judicial Review in re the Appointment of James Alva Bain as a Member of the Public Service Commission*, High Court Action No. 3260 of 1987.
44. *Laws of Guyana, Constitution of the Co-operative Republic of Guyana*, Cap. 1:01, Schedule, s. 106.
45. H.W.R. Wade, *Administrative Law* (Oxford: Oxford University Press, 1990), 809.
46. *Laws of Trinidad and Tobago, Ch. 1:01*, s. 38.
47. *The Commonwealth of Dominica Constitution Order 1978*, s. 27.
48. *Laws of Trinidad and Tobago*, Act No. 4/1976, s. 6.
49. *Laws of Guyana, The Republic Act No. 9 of 1970*, February 20, 1970.
50. See note 37 above.
51. *St Lucia Constitution Order 1978*, S.I. 1978/No. 1901.
52. *Antigua and Barbuda Constitution Order 1981*, S.I. 1981/No. 1106.
53. *The Bahamas Independence Order 1973*, S.I. 1973 / No. 1080.

6.
The Challenges of Constitutional Reform

Commonwealth Caribbean constitutions, with the exception of Guyana since 1980, have all been based on a Westminster–Whitehall foundation. That foundation was laid out of an evolutionary process that started with the Old Representative System, the Crown Colony System, the New Representative System, post-Second World War Representative and Responsible Government, and either independence or associated statehood and then independence, as the case may be.

The systems of government that are based on the Westminster–Whitehall model are indeed indigenous because they have evolved in the region to the point of independence. There are difficulties associated with trying to change the model precisely because the Westminster–Whitehall model can be regarded as the indigenous system of government for the Commonwealth Caribbean due to its evolution as opposed to its importation.

Perhaps the best example of why there appears to be a conundrum in deciding whether countries in the Commonwealth Caribbean region are going to reform a constitution that was imported into its culture and society or one that is considered indigenous can best be captured by the following statement made by Dr Eric Williams on July 19, 1955 at a public meeting in Woodford Square, Port of Spain, Trinidad, before he had entered electoral politics:

> The Colonial Office does not need to examine its second hand colonial constitutions. It has a constitution at hand which it can apply immediately to Trinidad and Tobago. That is the British Constitution.[1]

At the same meeting he also said:

> Ladies and Gentlemen, I suggest to you that the time has come when the British Constitution, suitably modified, can be applied to Trinidad and Tobago. After all, if the British Constitution is good enough for Great Britain, it should be good enough for Trinidad and Tobago.[2]

Williams's advocacy of the British Constitution in a suitably modified format was his way of saying that the British constitutional formula was one that should be adopted because there was no indigenous system of government.

Williams's entire stewardship as chief minister, premier and prime minister of Trinidad and Tobago represented a defence of the British Constitution suitably modified and when the greatest opportunity of all presented itself for constitution reform in 1971 when his People's National Movement (PNM) won all 36 seats in the House of Representatives at the general election, he adopted the approach of engaging in a further suitable modification of the existing constitution which was already a suitably modified version of the British Constitution itself.

Williams's manner of thinking can be contrasted with his colleague premier in Jamaica, Norman Manley, who said in the Jamaican House of Representatives in January 1962:

> Let us not make the mistake of describing as colonial, institutions which are part and parcel of the heritage of this country. If we have any confidence in our own individuality and our own personality we would absorb these things and incorporate them into our being and turn them to our own use as part of the heritage we are not ashamed of.[3]

Manley was not speaking about importing the British Constitution and converting it into local usage in the way that Williams had advocated, but rather he was urging that the existing institutions of the colonial era, which evolved as part of Jamaica's development, should not be regarded as colonial, but rather as indigenous.

These institutions were installed as part of the colonial evolution. Yet, Norman Manley was describing it as a 'mistake' to regard these institutions as being 'colonial'. He preferred to bless them as being part of the 'heritage' of Jamaica.

The primary reason for the juxtaposition of these two views as expressed by two leaders, who were part of the independence movement in the late 1950s and early 1960s, will provide a better understanding of the difficulties that have been experienced with the prospect of making any meaningful constitutional reform in the post-independence era.

Are constitutions being reformed that have been imported into Commonwealth Caribbean societies or are the independence constitutions already indigenous to these societies? For Williams, the argument was that if it was good enough for Great Britain, it would be good enough for Trinidad and Tobago. For Manley, it was not colonial, but rather part of the heritage of Jamaica. Were they both talking about the same thing given the colonial heritage of the former British West Indies that has become the Commonwealth Caribbean?

In that context, why would there be the need to change something that is regarded as indigenous or that has been adapted to suit regional needs? The fundamental argument for change, therefore, has to be the desire to seek greater functional efficiency to include the common mantras of constitutional reform commonly known as 'good governance', 'transparency', and 'accountability'.

However, as far as the fundamental foundation is concerned, the region appears to be wedded to the Westminster–Whitehall model of governance and any alteration may only get as far as the creation of a hybrid by importing features that are genuinely alien to the regional heritage of the British Constitution suitably modified or domestically evolved colonial institutions that are part of the regional heritage.

For example, Grenada has had its own constitutional challenges between 1979 and 1983, and after the demise of the People's Revolutionary Government, there was a return to the foundations of the Westminster–Whitehall tradition that had stared totalitarian rule directly in the eye and totalitarianism blinked first.

The Washington Hybrid

The geographical location of the Commonwealth Caribbean exposes these countries to the Washington model as an alternative to the Westminster–Whitehall model. However, while there appears to be a collective fear of moving too far from the Westminster–Whitehall moorings, there is a desire to import certain aspects of the Washington model.

Since 1962 when the first two countries of the Commonwealth Caribbean attained their independence, there has been a growing desire to import some of the features of the Washington model in order to curb the excesses of power enjoyed by those who hold office under the Westminster–Whitehall model.

There has been particular concern in the region that prime ministers are able to exercise tremendous power because the adaptations from the British system in which there is a House of Commons of more than 600 members and a political culture that can function on the basis of an unwritten constitution either were not comfortably imported or have evolved differently in political systems where the size of the parliaments may vary from 63 elected members in Jamaica to 11 in St Kitts-Nevis.

The existence of royalty and nobility as part of the British system of government and the role that they play in the political culture as restraints on excessive uses or abuses of power do not have their equivalents in Commonwealth Caribbean traditions. The political trust that accompanies the role of the sovereign in British politics is difficult to emulate elsewhere.

In the absence of that trust, there is a growing desire to self-regulate the office of prime minister in the region by talking about term limits and fixed dates for elections. It does require some navigation of the parliamentary and presidential systems in order to insert these features to create the hybrid.

St Vincent and the Grenadines

In St Vincent and the Grenadines, the power of dissolution was circumscribed in the Constitution Bill 2009 insofar as there was to be no tendering of prime ministerial advice for four years and nine months after Parliament held its first sitting. Within the remaining three months, the prime minister would have been free to advise a dissolution.[4] These provisions never came into effect because the referendum that was held on November 25, 2009 to validate the bill was unsuccessful. The intent of these provisions were to institute a virtual fixed term for the Parliament after a general election by prohibiting an exercise of prime ministerial authority to advise the proposed president in that Constitution Bill to dissolve Parliament only after a period of four years and nine months had elapsed. Provision was also made for the eventuality of a successful motion of no confidence which could have resulted in an early general election prior to the end of the period of four years and nine months.

In recognition of the retention of a parliamentary system concurrent with a desire to provide some stability to the term of office of any government that was elected at a general election, the intention was to guarantee a term of office that would enter into its fifth year. However, in parliamentary systems, there is always the possibility that issues of no confidence in a government may arise and so provision must be made for that.

In the circumstances, provision was made for the calling of a general election prior to the elapse of four years and nine months if a successful motion of no confidence had been passed against the government.

Such provisions were designed to guarantee a reasonable amount of certainty for a term of office as well as to permit a changing of governments if the representatives in the Parliament were to form that opinion. This would then subject the government to seeking a fresh mandate from the electorate or provide a mandate for some other government.

Jamaica

Another Washington-type hybrid was commenced in Jamaica during the life of the Parliament that was dissolved in December 2011. The then government had brought to Parliament a bill that sought to introduce term limits for the office of prime minister.

The long title of the bill was: 'An Act to Amend the Constitution of Jamaica to Preclude Appointment to the Office of Prime Minister of a Person Who Has Previously Held That Office for a Specified Period'.

The intention of the bill was to amend section 70 of the Jamaican Constitution which reads as follows:

> 70.-(1) Whenever the Governor-General has occasion to appoint a Prime Minister he, acting in his discretion, shall appoint the member of the House of Representatives who, in his judgment, is best able to command the confidence of a majority of the members of that House and shall, acting in accordance with the advice of the Prime Minister, appoint from among the members of the two Houses such number of other Ministers as the Prime Minister may advise.[5]

The amendment proposed to insert a subsection (1A) and (1B) after subsection (1) that was to read as follows:

> (1A) A person shall not be appointed to the office of Prime Minister if he has held that office for periods (whether consecutive or not) which when added together total more than nine years.

> (1B) A person appointed to the office of Prime Minister shall not be required to vacate office by reason only that, while in office, the period of his holding office when added together with any previous periods of his holding office total more than nine years.[6]

The Memorandum of Objects and Reasons attached to the bill by the then minister of justice, Dorothy Lightbourne, indicated that the government *has taken a decision to amend the Constitution, in order to limit the period of time for which a person may hold office as Prime Minister to periods (whether consecutive or not) which when added together do not exceed nine years, however, an incumbent Prime Minister shall not be required to vacate his office by reason only of the fact that after his appointment he exceeds the nine year limit.*[7]

It is clear from this statement that the then Jamaican government was proposing to address the issue of term limits for the prime minister on the basis of time elapsed as opposed to the number of terms served. In parliamentary systems in the Commonwealth Caribbean, a term of office can be as little as one day to as much as five years and three months. In this way, the proposed legislation was attempting to get around the stricter concept of the time elapsed for a term that is used in the Washington model by adopting a formula that sought to permit someone to have the flexibility to hold office for a possible period of up to 14 years depending upon the dates of their appointment and re-appointment.

This would have constituted an adaptation of the Washington model concept of the two-term limit into a Westminster–Whitehall model Constitution such as Jamaica. Former Minister Lightbourne went on to state in the Memorandum of Objects and Reasons for the bill as follows:

> This constitutional limitation is considered desirable in order to strengthen democracy by encouraging the infusion of new leadership at the highest level of Government. Similar time limitation has been imposed in relation to heads of state or Governments in Commonwealth countries such as Dominica, Nigeria and South Africa and in other countries such as the United States of America, Mexico and Chile.[8]

These forays into the domain of restricting prime ministerial power represent responses that have echoes in the wider society. The bill never went through the legislative process to full enactment and lapsed. The Parliament was dissolved in December 2011 and a general election was held that resulted in a government of a different political party being elected. That government took office in January 2012.

Trinidad and Tobago

In August 2014, the then government of Trinidad and Tobago brought to the Parliament the Constitution (Amendment) Bill 2014. One of the aims and objects of the bill was to introduce term limits for the office of prime minister. The bill was debated in the House of Representatives and in the Senate. Amendments were made to the bill in the Senate and it was returned to the House for the Senate amendments to be considered.

Those amendments were never considered as the Parliament was dissolved on June 17, 2015 and accordingly the bill lapsed. In the ensuing general election, there was a change of government and the proposal was not revived by the new government.

The bill had proposed to amend section 76(1) of the Constitution which reads as follows:

> Where there is occasion for the appointment of a Prime Minister, the President shall appoint as Prime Minister –
>
> a. a member of the House of Representatives who is the Leader in that House of the party which commands the support of the majority of members of that House; or
>
> b. where it appears to him that that party does not have an undisputed leader in that House or that no party commands the support of such a majority, the member of the House of Representatives who, in his judgment, is most likely to command the support of the majority of members of that House;
>
> and who is willing to accept the office of Prime Minister.[9]

It sought to insert the following clauses after section 76(1):

> (1A) No person shall hold the office of Prime Minister for more than ten years and six months, whether or not such service is continuous or has been interrupted, and on attaining that length of service the Prime Minister shall vacate his office.
>
> (1B) In calculating the length of service of a Prime Minister, no account shall be taken of any time spent serving as acting Prime Minister without having been appointed Prime Minister.
>
> (1C) Where, after the first poll of a general election, one or more supplementary polls are, or are to be, held in accordance with section 73(4), the President shall not appoint the Prime Minister before the results of all the supplementary polls have been declared, but the current Prime Minister and Ministers shall remain in office until they are required to vacate office in accordance with section 77(2)(a) and (3)(a), respectively.[10]

The explanatory note to the bill that was piloted by then prime minister Kamla Persad-Bissessar stated:

> With respect to term limits for the office of Prime Minister, the Bill would, by clause 8, amend the Constitution to limit service as Prime Minister to no more than ten years and six months, whether such service is continuous or has been interrupted. A Prime Minister would therefore be required to vacate his office upon attaining that length of service. No account would, however, be taken of any time spent serving as acting Prime Minister for the purposes of calculating length of service. Further, no one would be appointed as Prime Minister who has served ten years or more in that office, whether or not such service is continuous or has been interrupted.[11]

The bill had the benefit of debate in both the House of Representatives and the Senate in August 2014. It was approved by a vote of 23 in favour, 14 against, and one abstention in the House of Representatives, and 18 in favour and 12 against in the Senate. The Senate did record amendments to the bill which were to be returned to the House of Representatives for ratification. That process was never completed and the bill lapsed upon the dissolution of Parliament on June 17, 2015.

Guyana

The only country in the Commonwealth Caribbean that has introduced term limits for its Head of Government up to the time of writing is Guyana. By virtue of Act No. 17 of 2000, section 90 of the Constitution of Guyana that provides: 'A person elected as President after the year 2000 is eligible for re-election only once.'[12]

The first presidential candidate in a Guyanese general election to be affected by this was former president, Bharrat Jagdeo, who was unable to have his name placed on the ballot in the 2011 general elections in Guyana because he had been re-elected as president in 2006.

In confirming his pride at being the first president of Guyana to demit office by virtue of the presidential term limit provisions of the Constitution, President Jagdeo on September 21, 2011 told the United Nations General Assembly:

> Mr President, This is the last time that I will address this great chamber as the President of my country. Before the end of this year, 1 will be proud to be the first President of Guyana to demit office under the constitutional term limits I signed into law in the early days of my Presidency.[13]

In 2015, a legal challenge was commenced against the constitutionality of the presidential term limit in Guyana. At the time of writing, the matter was being appealed to the Caribbean Court of Justice.

Term Limits and Fixed Dates for Elections

There has been debate about regulating the term of office of the heads of government in the Commonwealth Caribbean as well as attempting to curtail the ability of prime ministers to advise early dissolutions of Parliament based on actual legislative attempts that have been made.

The Westminster–Whitehall model in the Commonwealth Caribbean does not operate on the basis of British conventions that apply to the office of the prime minister, particularly where incumbency in hung Parliaments are concerned.

According to Geoffrey Marshall:

> For one thing it may be that future General Elections will not produce a Parliament in which any one party has an overall majority. That would not necessarily place the Queen in any immediate difficulty since after a General Election the existing Prime Minister, even if in a minority, is entitled to remain in office and to meet the House of Commons. [14]

In the United Kingdom (UK), the inconclusive will of the electorate rests on the premise that every prime minister is entitled to have his/her fate determined when they go to Parliament for the first sitting of the House after a general election. In practice, common sense prevails and a prime minister whose party has lost a general election normally resigns, thereby making it necessary for a new prime minister to be appointed to fill the vacancy. However, in the case of a hung Parliament there appears to be no doubt that a prime minister is entitled to stay in office and to meet the next Parliament if he or she wishes to do so.

This is supported by Vernon Bogdanor who wrote:

> The British system of government does not require the prime minister to resign immediately after an election. Rather, an incumbent prime minister is entitled to remain in office if he or she so wishes until he or she loses the confidence of the Commons. [15]

Bogdanor, however, goes on to point out that no UK prime minister in the twentieth century ever chose to meet the next Parliament when their party had the second largest number of seats in a hung Parliament. [16]

The evidence here supports the right of the prime minister to stay in office after a general election and suggests that the monarch must allow a prime minister the opportunity to meet the next Parliament if the prime minister so wishes. This view reinforces the dominance of the incumbency theory over the right of the monarch to revoke a prime ministerial appointment and refers an inconclusive electoral outcome to the elected members of Parliament for resolution.

Both views are supported by Rodney Brazier:

> A Prime Minister who had failed to obtain a majority at a general election would be following precedents if he were to resign immediately (Baldwin 1929), or if he were to stay to see if he could form a coalition (Heath 1974), or if he were to wait and meet Parliament (Baldwin 1923–24). He is in theory entitled to remain in office until defeated on a vote of confidence. [17]

Brazier reinforces the views expressed above on the incumbency theory by citing specific examples in which there is a certain degree of consistency regardless of the circumstances. In each case, the prime minister was entitled to stay in office and meet the next Parliament. It would appear that a tie between two major parties would only serve to strengthen the view of the incumbency theory, since the incumbent government would not be in a disadvantageous position as regards the number of MPs who support the prime minister.

These views are reinforced by former prime minister, Harold Wilson. In discussing the aftermath of the February 1974 general election where there was a hung Parliament, Wilson said:

> There were suggestions that, as the Conservatives had fewer seats than Labour, and were having difficulty in securing allies, the Labour leader should have been invited to try. This would have been contrary to precedent. A Prime Minister was there – at Downing Street. If and when he resigned that would create a new situation. Alternatively, were he to face Parliament without allies, and be defeated, then he would resign. As things were, there was no vacancy to fill.[18]

Wilson was only offered the opportunity to try and form a minority government after Edward Heath had resigned. Heath's decision to resign was clearly based on his inability to secure a coalition with the Liberal Party and was not based on any automatic decision to resign. He certainly tried to sustain his government in power and if the Liberals were willing to join him in a coalition, it is apparent that he would have chosen to face the next Parliament.

Clearly, every British prime minister is entitled to meet the next Parliament after a general election if he or she does not resign. Any decision to resign would be based on a political calculation by the incumbent prime minister that he or she would be unable to command the support of a majority after the outcome of a general election. This convention was confirmed after the British general election of May 2010 when Prime Minister Gordon Brown chose to resign after remaining in office for a few days following the election owing to the fact that there was a hung Parliament and it was not immediately clear whether the Labour Party or the Conservative Party would be able to form a coalition with the Liberal-Democratic Party. His decision to eventually resign was clearly motivated by the fact that he subsequently recognized that he would have been unable to form a government once the Conservative Party and the Liberal-Democratic Party arrived at a consensus for the formation of a coalition government with majority support in the House of Commons.

Indeed, this convention of resignation after an unsuccessful general election result emerged in the nineteenth century, and the constitutional scholar, A.V. Dicey, commented on it in the introduction to the eighth edition of his famous work, *Law of the Constitution*:

> In 1868 a Conservative Ministry in office suffered an undoubted defeat at a general election. Mr. Disraeli at once resigned office without waiting for even the meeting of Parliament. The same course was pursued by Mr. Gladstone, then Prime Minister, in 1874, and again, in his turn, by Disraeli (then Lord Beaconsfield) in 1880, and by Gladstone in 1886. These resignations, following as they each did on the result of a general election, distinctly reversed the leading precedent set by Peel in 1834. The Conservative Ministry of which he was the head, though admittedly defeated in the general election, did not resign until they suffered actual defeat in the newly-elected House of Commons.[19]

This convention was applied by Stanley Baldwin in December 1923 when his party was 50 seats short of an overall majority and he decided to meet the next Parliament where his fate was sealed in January 1924 on an amendment to the Address from the Throne.[20]

Prior to that, it was Lord Salisbury in 1885 who decided to meet Parliament as the leader of the second largest party, and he had his fate determined for him there.[21]

Given these considerations and experience that pertain to the British system of government, the issue of term limits for the prime minister must be considered separate and apart from that because there appears to be no embedded constitutional right for any Commonwealth Caribbean prime minister to face Parliament without an appointment being made by the governor general or the president before a prime minister can face Parliament.

This was clearly confirmed in Trinidad and Tobago on December 24, 2001 when President A.N.R. Robinson revoked the appointment of then Prime Minister Basdeo Panday and appointed the then Leader of the Opposition Patrick Manning as prime minister in a situation in which both parties led by both men had won 18 seats each in a 36-member House of Representatives.

The reason for this is that in the Commonwealth Caribbean, there are written constitutions that regulate the manner in which the prime minister is to be appointed. The flexibility enjoyed under the British system of government in permitting a prime minister to meet the next Parliament is as a direct result of the existence of an unwritten constitution which has no parallel in the Commonwealth Caribbean.

The imposition of term limits on the president of Guyana has no correlation with the British system of government. Guyana's model of government is a presidential one which is also different from the Westminster–Whitehall model that operates in those Commonwealth Caribbean countries with written constitutions based on parliamentary systems.

The importation of the American presidential technique of limiting the terms of office of the prime minister was directly considered by the Constitution Review Commission under the chairmanship of the Right Honourable Sir Hugh Wooding in Trinidad and Tobago during the period 1971–74. The Wooding Constitution Commission took a hostile view of term limits for the prime minister in paragraph 284 of its 1974 Report as follows:

> We considered and rejected the suggestion that a limit should be placed on the number of terms which any person may serve as Prime Minister. Essentially at any general election voters choose the party which they wish to form the government. It seems to us unthinkable to impose any restrictions on the number of successive terms which any party could win. Once that is conceded, it would seem to be wrong in principle to place a restriction on the party's choice of leadership. This could have a significant effect on their chances of winning the elections. Compelling them to change their leader may, in effect, reduce their chances of success. We do not think that any useful purpose can be served from a study of the experience of the United States of America and some Latin American countries where the choice of President is essentially the choice of a person, not of a governing party. In these systems the office of President stands by itself separate and apart from Congress which may be controlled by a party other than that to which the President belongs.[22]

The Wooding Commission was linking the personality of the prime minister to the electoral fortunes of the governing party. By doing so, the Commission felt that any consideration of introducing a hybrid by using the Washington model as the example ought to take into account the fact that the US president is elected independent of the Congress and the political outcomes could yield a president of one party and a Congress of another.

The parliamentary model only works when the executive can dominate Parliament. A presidential model can function with different parties controlling the executive branch and the legislative branch of government or one party may control both with the concurrence of the electorate.

The key factor here is that both the fixed dates for elections and the proposal for term limits are features of presidential models of government and are not features of parliamentary systems.

The proposal for term limits for the prime minister is fashioned after the Twenty-Second Amendment to the United States Constitution that was ratified in 1951. The Amendment read as follows:

> **Section 1.** No person shall be elected to the office of the President more than twice, and no person who has held the office of President, or acted as President, for more than two years of a term to which some other person was elected President shall be elected to the office of the President more than once. But this article shall not apply to any person holding the office of President when this article was proposed by the Congress, and shall not prevent any person who may be holding the office of President, or acting as President, during the term within which this article becomes operative from holding the office of President or acting as President during the remainder of such term.

> **Section 2.** This article shall be inoperative unless it shall have been ratified as an amendment to the Constitution by the legislatures of three-fourths of the several States within seven years from the date of its submission to the States by the Congress.[23]

The amendment did not apply to the person holding office at the time of its approval, but would apply to future holders of the office of president. This amendment came into effect while President Harry Truman was in office; however, he did not seek to be elected for another term after the New Hampshire primary in 1952.

The problem with term limits in Commonwealth Caribbean parliamentary systems is that a term cannot be fixed because of the power of dissolution which is available to a prime minister to terminate the life of a Parliament or a motion of no confidence which is available to the elected House to terminate the term of office of a prime minister and can bring about a premature end to a five-year term of office.

The importation of fixed dates for elections and term limits for the prime minister would have to be carefully assessed for implementation without introducing an element of instability if it were to be considered. A term limit usually weakens a president in the latter part of the second term because it is known that the president is not eligible to run for office again. Any public popularity is overcome by the fact that the Constitution, and not the people, will end the term of office of the president. The same reality will apply to the prime minister who will get to the latter part of their final terms as their political influence would be greatly diminished owing to their imminent departure.

In Commonwealth Caribbean parliamentary systems, the appointment of the prime minister is not determined by the people, but rather by the head of state based on constitutional guidelines. In these circumstances, under a system of term limits the governor general or the president will determine the term of office for the prime minister. In Guyana, no such consideration arose in 2011 when President Jagdeo did not seek re-election for another term because of the constitutional prohibition on the Guyanese presidency.

The Caribbean Court of Justice

Any attempt to reform Commonwealth Caribbean constitutions must come up against the fact that something indigenous is being reformed which is not alien. When Sir Shridath Ramphal raised the question in the Eleventh Sir Archibald Nedd Memorial Lecture in Grenada in 2011[24] of whether or not the West Indies were still at the doorstep of colonialism by not embracing the Caribbean Court of Justice (CCJ) as its final court of appeal, he was actually hitting on the central artery of the very existence of the region.

The title of his lecture was, 'Is The West Indies West Indian?' In the lecture, he referred to the Caribbean Court of Justice and his disappointment that the court had not been more widely accepted in the following way:

> In 2001, twelve CARICOM countries decided they would abolish appeals to the Privy Council and establish their own Caribbean Court of Justice serving all the countries of the Caribbean Community with both original jurisdiction in regional integration matters and appellate jurisdiction as the final court of appeal for individual CARICOM countries. As of now, only Guyana (which had abolished appeals to the Privy Council on independence, believing it to be a natural incident of 'sovereignty'), Barbados and now Belize – have conferred on the CCJ that appellate jurisdiction. It is instructive that in Guyana's case, in adopting the CCJ as its final court of appeal, it dispensed with its own national final Court of Appeal, subordinating its own sovereignty to the logic of a Community Court of Appeal – a Caribbean Community of which it is a part with all the other member states of CARICOM, with whom one would expect the same logic to prevail.
>
> Constitutional amendment is required for the abolition of appeals to the Privy Council. In practical terms, this means bipartisan political support

for the CCJ. In Jamaica and Trinidad and Tobago (where the Court has its much sought after location) that political consensus does not exist – because the political party now in office in each of those two major regional jurisdictions has turned its back on its regional court. In St. Vincent and the Grenadines, a referendum last year rejected the transference of appeals to the CCJ. [25]

Why is there political uncertainty? The then People's Partnership Government in Trinidad and Tobago indicated in its 2010 election manifesto that it intended to put the matter to the population in a referendum. The people of St Vincent and the Grenadines in a referendum voted against it, together with other constitution reform measures.

The government of Belize was able to implement it because it had the requisite majority in its House of Representatives to make the change.

Dominica joined the CCJ in its appellate jurisdiction in March 2015 thereby replacing the Privy Council with it as its final court of appeal. This has brought the number of CARICOM countries with the CCJ as their final court of appeal to four.

The CCJ represents a real test of regional unity and constitutional reform. None of that will happen meaningfully if it is imposed mechanically. The best preservative will be the organic test of referenda endorsed by governments and oppositions in the region on agreed terms and conditions worked out through dialogue and debate, compromise, and consensus.

However, there is a deeper reason why the pace of change from the Privy Council to the CCJ has been so slow. The primary argument advanced by proponents of the CCJ for its replacement of the Privy Council has been the argument of completing the cycle of independence in the region.

According to Sheldon MacDonald writing in the *Fordham International Law Journal*:

> On the other hand, the CCJ will also sit at the apex of the judiciary of those Member States that have chosen to adhere to its Appellate Jurisdiction in substitution for the Judicial Committee of Her Majesty's Privy Council in England. The tribunal in this instance will be applying the Constitution, statutes and the common law of the country from which it hears matters as the court of final instance. The Commonwealth Caribbean Member states of the Community have decided on this step in order to complete the cycle of independence by patriating the highest judicial function.[26]

This argument about completing the cycle of independence has been widely adopted by proponents of the CCJ as a primary argument in making their case for the CCJ to replace the Privy Council as the final court of appeal for the region. If the constitutional systems of government in the Commonwealth Caribbean are indigenous by virtue of their evolution, what is there to be patriated?

The existence of a court system with UK judges serving as the final arbiters of the process has been part of the evolution of constitutional systems in the Commonwealth Caribbean that was formerly the British West Indies in the colonial era. If the argument about patriation is about changing the personnel who will preside over the cases themselves, then that argument may very well enter into a more questionable domain related to the strong personal bonds between the regional judiciary and the British honours system.

Writing in the *Sunday Guardian* in Trinidad and Tobago on April 27, 2014, the author said as follows:

> The editorial also raised the issue of Sir Dennis Byron, the current Chief Justice of the CCJ, continuing to hold on to his knighthood while calling on countries in the region to complete their independence process by severing ties with the Privy Council of which he accepted membership in 2004. In April 2012 Sir Dennis Byron held an engagement meeting in Trinidad at which he said that Caricom countries should 'complete their independence and sovereignty by claiming the rights to completely manage our judicial affairs.'

> The argument that was being advanced by Sir Dennis on that occasion was based on an anti-colonial premise, however, the Web site of the CCJ has the following information about the former chief justice of the CCJ, Michael de la Bastide: 'Mr Justice de la Bastide demitted office as Chief Justice on July 18, 2002. He was sworn in as a member of the Privy Council by Her Majesty Queen Elizabeth II on July 27, 2004 and as President of the Caribbean Court of Justice on August 18, 2004.'

> The CCJ Web site says the following about its current Chief Justice, Sir Dennis Byron: 'In 2000 Mr Justice Byron was knighted by Queen Elizabeth II and he was appointed a member of the Privy Council in 2004.'

> These postings on the official Web site of the CCJ confirm the point that what we are dealing with is a major contradiction about why the court should be offered to the people of the Caribbean as an authentic final court of appeal so that the countries of our region can 'complete their independence and sovereignty by claiming the rights to completely manage our judicial affairs.'

> Why was it necessary for the first President of the CCJ to be 'sworn in as a member of the Privy Council by Her Majesty Queen Elizabeth II' mere weeks before his assumption of duty as President and Chief Justice of the

CCJ? The fact that the second President and Chief Justice of the CCJ, Sir Dennis Byron, is also a member of Her Majesty's Privy Council and was knighted in 2000 must also be noted.

The CCJ has to answer why it is necessary for its President and Chief Justice to be made a member of Her Majesty's Privy Council. This question has been raised before and there continues to be a stony silence from the CCJ on the subject. A lot of this has to do with the fact that the knighthood is indeed the gold standard of West Indian accomplishment in public affairs. Its desirability is widespread and the prestige that it conveys comes from the very source that is being criticised, namely the British colonial connection.[27]

This is the great contradiction about the CCJ and its slow acceptance in the region. The primary argument here, which can also answer Sir Shridath Ramphal about whether the West Indies is West Indian, is that the knighthood and the membership of Her Majesty's Privy Council are deeply cherished accolades of West Indian political and judicial elites.

The following is a list of Members of Her Majesty's Privy Council from the Commonwealth Caribbean as at the end of January 2015:

1.   Mr Owen Arthur

2.   Mr Michael de la Bastide

3.   Sir Nicholas Brathwaite

4.   Sir Dennis Byron

5.   Mr Perry Christie

6.   Dr Denzil Douglas

7.   Sir Manuel Esquivel

8.   Mr Hubert Ingraham

9.   Sir James Mitchell

10. Dr Keith Mitchell

11. Mr Said Musa

12. Mr P.J. Patterson

13. Sir Lloyd Erskine Sandiford

14. Mr Edward Seaga

15. Sir Kennedy Simmonds

16. Mr Freundel Stuart

17. Sir Edward Zacca [28]

This list represents the core elements of the Commonwealth Caribbean political and judicial elite. They have all accepted the role of being a Privy Counsellor to Her Majesty Queen Elizabeth II, and they have all taken the requisite oath to assume membership. That oath is indeed a demanding one and reads as follows:

> You do swear by Almighty God to be a true and faithful Servant unto the Queen's Majesty as one of Her Majesty's Privy Council. You will not know or understand of any manner or thing to be attempted, done or spoken against Her Majesty's Person, Honour, Crown or Dignity Royal, but you will let and withstand the same to the uttermost of your power, and either cause it to be revealed to Her Majesty Herself, or to such of Her Privy Council as shall advertise Her Majesty of the same. You will in all things to be moved, treated and debated in Council, faithfully and truly declare your Mind and Opinion, according to your Heart and Conscience; and you will keep secret all Matters committed and revealed unto you, or that shall be treated of secretly in Council. And if any of the said Treaties or Councils shall touch any of the Counsellors, you will not reveal it unto him, but will keep the same until such time as, by the Consent of Her Majesty, or of the Council, Publication shall be made thereof. You will to your uttermost bear Faith and Allegiance unto the Queen's Majesty; and will assist and defend all Jurisdictions, Pre-eminences and Authorities granted to Her Majesty and annexed to the Crown by Acts of Parliament, or otherwise, against all Foreign Princes, Persons, Prelates, States or Potentates. And generally in all things you will do as a Faithful and true Servant ought to do to Her Majesty. So help you God.[29]

This oath of a Privy Counsellor has revealed the nature of the duty of personal loyalty to Her Majesty that must be undertaken by anyone who takes that oath. The fact that the first and second chief justices and presidents of the CCJ have taken such an oath is a matter of great contradiction in promoting the CCJ as a regional court that will 'complete the cycle of our independence'. Why would anyone think that the cycle of independence has not been completed because of the inability to remove the Privy Council as the final court of appeal and replace it with a so-called indigenous institution when the Privy Council is about as indigenous a court as any in the region given its long historical ties and the desire of CCJ jurists to join its ranks as Privy Counsellors at the service of Her Majesty Queen Elizabeth II.

How does one interpret that part of the oath of a Privy Counsellor that says: *You will to your uttermost bear Faith and Allegiance unto the Queen's Majesty; and will assist and defend all Jurisdictions, Pre-eminences and*

Authorities granted to Her Majesty and annexed to the Crown by Acts of Parliament, or otherwise, against all Foreign Princes, Persons, Prelates, States or Potentates. And generally in all things you will do as a Faithful and true Servant ought to do to Her Majesty.

It will be difficult for anyone who has taken that oath to speak out publicly about any interpretation of the oath itself because of the personal burden of secrecy imposed upon such a person. However, as a region coming to terms with the narrative of the CCJ to complete the cycle of independence by severing links to the Privy Council, it is something about which there is good reason to pause and consider.

Indeed, the question has been asked whether it is possible that a Privy Counsellor can resign their membership of the Privy Council.

According to Rogers, 'Being able to resign was a new development and it is still questionable whether this is constitutionally correct.'[30]

The CCJ narrative is to criticize the British colonial connection and to ask the region to let it go, yet its premier jurists cling firmly to that connection and cannot tell the region why.

The issue of retaining knighthoods and the connection with the Judicial Committee of the Privy Council has a long history in the Commonwealth Caribbean. On August 1, 1976, Trinidad and Tobago became a republic in the Commonwealth. At the opening of the new law term that year on October 4, the then Chief Justice Sir Isaac Hyatali made remarks at the opening ceremony about the Privy Council connection and the retention of his knighthood despite the fact that Trinidad and Tobago had become a republic.

In a restricted dispatch to Myles Preston at the Caribbean Department of the Foreign and Commonwealth Office in London from J.R. Paterson, the British High Commissioner in Port of Spain reported as follows:

1. When the Chief Justice, Sir Isaac Hyatali, made his address at the opening of the Law Term on 4 October he included some ideas about the Privy Council, recalling proposals he had made in 1973 to the effect that the Judicial Committee should include distinguished Caribbean, and other Commonwealth judges, and that it should sit from time to time in the Caribbean. I attach the extract from his speech.

2. The High Commissioner afterwards asked the Chief Justice whether he, the High Commissioner, should take official cognizance of what the Chief Justice had said. Hyatali said he did not want this and intimated that the idea needed further thinking about in Trinidad and other Caribbean countries first.

3. This idea may well come to nothing; such information as we have had indicates that it might be unpopular with barristers here; it will of course present grave difficulties for the Judicial Committee itself. However, we should perhaps be prepared to receive a more formal demarche on this subject in due course.

4. One other intriguing side-light of the official opening was that Sir Isaac Hyatali said that he had no intention of relinquishing his Knighthood; (it had been understood here that following the advent of the republic all officials would drop their British titles). Hyatali gave as his reasons –

    a. The fact that Trinidad and Tobago is still a member of the Commonwealth, of which Her Majesty is Head;

    b. that the Privy Council continues to be the official Court of Appeal for the Republic and

    c. that there was every likelihood of frequent communication between himself and Her Majesty's judges and the Lord High Chancellor.[31]

It was clear that Sir Isaac Hyatali, the first chief justice of Trinidad and Tobago as a republic, was determined to retain personal usage of the titular aspect of his knighthood and his reasons were linked to his official duties which he felt were important enough for his identity.

The issue of Trinidad and Tobago acceding to a Caribbean Court of Appeal was raised in a confidential dispatch from High Commissioner Paterson to J.C.E. Hyde in the Commonwealth Coordination Department in the Foreign and Commonwealth Office on December 2, 1976 as follows:

> As you are no doubt aware, the current attention Trinidadians are paying to the continuing access to the Privy Council, provided by their new constitution, has been brought about largely because of certain local comment, probably representing a small minority view, on the apparent incongruity of such access under their new republican status. We will certainly be non-committal, but there are as yet no signs that anyone has even made a first move towards the establishment of the 'Caribbean Court of Appeal'. From here it looks therefore as though recourse to the Privy Council will prove to be a much longer term arrangement than some Trinidadians would like to admit.[32]

The prophecy in this dispatch has certainly come to pass as Trinidad and Tobago, despite becoming a republic in 1976, has not acceded to the appellate jurisdiction of the CCJ and has retained the Judicial Committee of the Privy Council as its final court of appeal up to the time of writing.

As regards the issue of the Judicial Committee of the Privy Council holding sittings in the Commonwealth Caribbean, this has happened in The Bahamas in 2006, 2007, 2009, and 2017, up to the time of writing, at the request of the government of The Bahamas.

On the subject of Commonwealth Caribbean membership of the Judicial Committee of Her Majesty's Privy Council, there has been considerable internal debate within the British civil service about this over the years.

In a dispatch from J.C.E. Hyde of the Commonwealth Coordination Department in the Foreign and Commonwealth Office to J.R. Paterson, Acting British High Commissioner in Port of Spain dated November 24, 1976, the following was stated:

> Commonwealth Judges were first appointed to the Privy Council in 1962. It came about as the result of a proposal in 1960 (though the idea had been canvassed at various times since the early 1900s) by the then Minister of Justice for Ceylon that there be a Commonwealth Court of Appeal. Following discussion at the Commonwealth Prime Ministers' Meeting in 1960, a United Kingdom Official Committee was set up to examine the proposal (as far as we are aware, Britain was the only country to do this), and they found that it was unlikely to be generally acceptable throughout the Commonwealth as well as presenting considerable difficulties. However, they suggested two alternatives for increasing the Commonwealth aspect of the Judicial Committee:
>
> a.   the strengthening of the Judicial Committee by appointment of members from other Commonwealth countries possessing the necessary high qualifications who could come and sit for a few months at frequent intervals;
>
> b.   sittings of the Judicial Committee in Commonwealth countries outside Britain.
>
> With regard to (a), The Queen approved the conferment of Privy Counsellorships on all the Members of the High Court of Australia and of the Court of Appeal of New Zealand, and from time to time of individual distinguished Judges from other Commonwealth countries. The first appointments included, apart from the Australians and New Zealanders, the Chief Justice of Nigeria, and the Chief Justice of the Federation of Rhodesia and Nyasaland, both of whom were considered to be of the desired standard. Correspondence at the time (1962) shows that, 'the Lord Chancellor at present knows of no Judge of any of the Caribbean Benches who measures up to the requisite standard. If any such Judges do emerge, it is the firm intention that

they should be gathered into a scheme which is directed to forming a Commonwealth pool of first class Judicial talent'. In fact in 1966, Sir Hugh Wooding, Chief Justice of Trinidad was appointed, and served with distinction on the Judicial Committee. But, other than these three Judges I have mentioned, no other appointments have in fact been made from countries other than Australia and New Zealand. The reasons for this are partly constitutional, and partly because of the lack of suitable candidates. I enclose copies of a letter by Sir James Mc Petrie dated 15 January 1968 which explains the difficulties of appointments from countries (in that case Malaysia) who retain in some form the appeal to the Privy Council, but which are not part of Her Majesty's dominions, together with a further note written by Mr. Duggan of this department of 4 September 1969 regarding proposed appointments from Singapore. From these you will see that the question of future appointments with respect to Trinidad would present difficulties.[33]

It is obvious that Sir Isaac Hyatali had touched an issue that had a long history of internal consideration and debate within the British Civil Service when he spoke about Commonwealth Caribbean judges being appointed to the Judicial Committee of the Privy Council in October 1976. What emerges here is that the only judge from the Commonwealth Caribbean who was deemed to have met the Privy Council standards in the 1960s was Sir Hugh Wooding. From the list of Privy Counsellors cited above[34], it is apparent that a few more judges have been deemed in more recent times to have met the Privy Council standard and their nationality and eligibility circumstances were deemed acceptable for appointment by Her Majesty Queen Elizabeth II.

In a minute dated September 4, 1969, prepared by a Mr Duggan of the Foreign and Commonwealth Office for a Mr Underwood, the following is recorded:

This is not however a purely legal matter and there are important political factors involved which have to be taken into account in making any recommendation to Her Majesty on appointment. These are as follows:

a.   To sit on the Judicial Committee of the Privy Council a judge has to be appointed a Privy Counsellor and all appointments to the Privy Council are made on the advice of the Prime Minister of the United Kingdom to Her Majesty.

b.   The Privy Council is 'The Queen's Inner Council', its nature and the functions of the Privy Counsellors as a private body of advisers to Her

Majesty make all appointments a matter for The Queen personally. The oath sworn on appointment is a reflection of this.

c. Appointments have been held to be incompatible with citizenship of any country of which Her Majesty is not Head of State, i.e. of a country which is a republic within the Commonwealth. It has also been the practice to defer the offer of appointment to citizens of Commonwealth countries known to be contemplating the adoption of republican status.

d. For judicial appointments, the judicial standing of the individual concerned is of the essence: such judicial appointments are in this sense distinct and separate from those of Commonwealth Prime Ministers and other distinguished persons. The judge concerned is required to have held high judicial office in his own country and to be well regarded abroad.[35]

These criteria are most instructive for a deeper understanding of how the system of appointing judges to the Privy Council bench actually works. The roles of the sitting prime minister of the UK and that of Her Majesty Queen Elizabeth II have been vital to the sustenance of the process over the years. Such appointments are not considered on the basis of purely legal criteria, but also political criteria as well.

The correspondence by Sir James Mc Petrie dated January 15, 1968 is most instructive, particularly paragraph 7 which reads:

7. In considering any proposal to broaden the basis of appointments to the Judicial Committee one must, of course, keep in mind the necessity of maintaining a high professional standard in the Committee. This aspect of the matter was mentioned both in relation to a Commonwealth Court of Appeal and a broader-based Judicial Committee in the Report of the Committee of Officials which sat under Coldstream's chairmanship in 1960–61. One must also recognise that such a proposal could raise questions of a political nature. The following occur to me –

(a) What would be the attitude of, say, New Zealand, the Australian States or Malta to a proposal that Judges from countries in Asia (and perhaps eventually from Africa) might sit to hear their appeals?

(b) Would it be possible to select new members of the Judicial Committee from overseas countries basically on merit and without undue regard to whether the selections preserved some sort of territorial balance? Mr. David Marshall assumes that the appointment of a Singapore Judge would necessitate the appointment of one from Malaysia and he may be right; but if a Judge were appointed from each of these two countries it might be difficult to overlook the claims of Ceylon. The Caribbean is already represented in the person of Sir Hugh Wooding from Trinidad; but I do not think that any of the African countries that use the Judicial Committee could provide a Judge of the requisite calibre. Sierra Leone might be an exception but the rest find it difficult, or impossible, to produce even a Puisne Judge from their own resources.[36]

Given the content of these dispatches, it is apparent that the replacement of the Judicial Committee of the Privy Council by the CCJ is not an easy task in the Commonwealth Caribbean having regard to the standards that have been set for the Privy Council's operation together with the complicit involvement of Commonwealth Caribbean judges in their membership of the Privy Council.

The creation of that tradition has only been emboldened by the involvement of Michael de la Bastide and Sir Denis Byron, as latter day appointees to Her Majesty's Privy Council, insofar as they have sworn an oath to Her Majesty Queen Elizabeth II and they are simultaneously trying to convince a Commonwealth Caribbean population of the virtues of the CCJ despite their divided loyalties.

The 1976 comment by the British High Commissioner J.R. Paterson that 'the Privy Council will prove to be a much longer term arrangement' has indeed turned out to be prophetic on a wider scale more than four decades later.

The Persistence of the Westminster–Whitehall Model

The fundamental premise of the Westminster–Whitehall tradition is that it has operated in the Commonwealth Caribbean with great success because of the fact that it evolved together with the advance of all of the countries that attained their independence so that there was no revolution or any war of independence. The process was one of peaceful transition from the colonial era into independence.

Concomitant with that, the acceptance and preservation of the British honours system inclusive of membership of Her Majesty's Privy Council and the retention of Her Majesty Queen Elizabeth II as the Head of State of nine out of the 12 independent countries of the Commonwealth Caribbean is testimony to the incorporation of these symbols into the constitutional architecture without controversy.

The main deviations from this standard operating procedure were to be found, firstly, in Guyana where Forbes Burnham used his left-leaning ideological slant to insist on breaking with the monarchical parliamentary system in two phases (1970 and 1980) after Guyana became independent in 1966.

Secondly, Dr Eric Williams led constitutional reform for Trinidad and Tobago that moved it from a parliamentary monarchy in 1962 to a parliamentary republic in 1976.

Thirdly, the People's Revolutionary Government that overthrew Prime Minister Sir Eric Gairy in Grenada in 1979 left the governor general, Sir Paul Scoon, untouched in his office. After they were removed from power in 1983, there was a gradual return to a functioning parliamentary system and the reinstatement of the Judicial Committee of the Privy Council by 1991, after it had been suspended in 1979.

Perhaps, one of the more compelling reasons to resist any constitutional reform can be gleaned from a parliamentarian from Trinidad and Tobago who was arguing against the Constitution (Amendment) Bill 2014 that was being debated in the House of Representatives in August 2014. In arguing against a change from the first-past-the-post electoral system to a second ballot runoff system as a variant of the first-past-the-post model, then Opposition MP Colm Imbert said:

> And the countries that have it like France, they have a presidential system, Mr. Speaker, they follow the Napoleonic Code. Their laws are not based on English common law. It is a completely different system. [Interruption] Yes, the entire court system, the judicial system, the administration of justice, they are based on that Napoleonic Code, completely different to our English common law system.[37]

This line of argument may actually have highlighted what the issue with constitutional reform is all about. The systems are all indigenous and have evolved over centuries of British colonial rule. The independence constitutions were established with the full concurrence of Commonwealth Caribbean political elites, on all sides of the political divide, across the region. The common denominator was the desire to maintain, as far as possible, the connection to English common law.

All constitutions in the region have differing levels of consensus that are required for their amendment. Consensus will be required for the attainment of special majorities for bills seeking to amend Commonwealth Caribbean constitutions in their legislatures as well as in the referenda that some countries will require. Compromise is the tool that will bring this consensus.

How many opposition parties are willing to compromise with governments in the region to make this happen? Or, is the issue much deeper than that insofar as retaining the essential systemic components is concerned, while the incidental changes are contemplated?

For example, how many of today's opposition parties in the CARICOM region support the switch from the Privy Council to the CCJ? To what extent do the people of the region support the idea? If there is a change of government in some countries of the region, will there be advocacy for the CCJ?

In other words, will the court become a part of the regional landscape on an organic or a mechanical basis? If the court is not endorsed across the political aisles in the current majoritarian democratic systems and fails to gain acceptance through the use of referenda where such requirements exist, then what message can the region take from that?

In Grenada, on November 24, 2016, there was a constitutional referendum on seven amendments to the Grenada Constitution. All seven amendments were roundly defeated as follows:

Question	For	Against	Turnout
1. Caribbean Court of Justice and other Justice-related matters.	9,369	12,635	32.53%
2. Elections and Boundaries Commission	8,944	13,239	32.53%
3. Ensuring the appointment of Leader of the Opposition	6,116	15,556	32.51%
4. Fixed date for Elections	7,089	14,536	32.52%
5. Name of State	9,694	12,485	32.54%
6. Rights and Freedoms	5,067	16,388	32.51%
7. Term of Office of Prime Minister	5,396	15,301	32.48%[38]

It is obvious that the electorate made a very powerful statement in Grenada by (i) their low turnout at the referendum; and, (ii) their overwhelming rejection of all seven proposed amendments that were put to them.

This serves to confirm the point that there is a tremendous desire to retain the Westminster–Whitehall model in the Commonwealth Caribbean if these results are linked to the referendum results in St Vincent and the Grenadines in 2009 when the draft constitution was rejected by the electorate on November 25, 2009.

In St Vincent and the Grenadines, the result of the referendum was:

NO	YES	TURNOUT
29,167	22,646	53.48% [39]

Constitution reform in the Commonwealth Caribbean does not enjoy the level of public support that many leaders, political elites, and commentators would like to think. The quantitative evidence from St Vincent and the Grenadines (2009) and Grenada (2016) is compelling. There is no energy from the mass populations of the countries of the region for constitutional change. This has really been driven by political elites who have an interest in the subject matter and are yet to convince Commonwealth Caribbean electorates that this is a matter for their attention.

Perhaps, it all goes back to what Norman Manley said in January 1962:

> Let us not make the mistake of describing as colonial, institutions which are part and parcel of the heritage of this country. If we have any confidence in our own individuality and our own personality we would absorb these things and incorporate them into our being and turn them to our own use as part of the heritage we are not ashamed of.[40]

Notes

1. Eric Williams, *Constitution Reform in Trinidad and Tobago*. Public Affairs Pamphlet No. 2 (Port of Spain, Trinidad: Teachers' Educational and Cultural Association, 1955), 30.
2. Ibid.
3. *Proceedings of the Jamaican House of Representatives 1961–62*, January 24, 1962, 766.
4. *The St Vincent and the Grenadines Constitution Bill 2009*, Schedule, s. 92(5).
5. *The Jamaica (Constitution) Order in Council 1962, S.I. 1962 No. 1550, Second Schedule*, s. 70.
6. *Parliament of Jamaica*, The Constitution (Amendment) Bill No. 2, 2010.
7. Ibid.
8. Ibid.
9. *Laws of Trinidad of Trinidad and Tobago, Ch. 1:01, Schedule*, s. 76(1).
10. *Parliament of Trinidad and Tobago*, The Constitution (Amendment) Bill 2014.
11. Ibid.
12. *Laws of Guyana, Constitution of the Co-operative Republic of Guyana*, Cap. 1:01, Schedule, s. 90(2).
13. *Address by His Excellency Mr Bharrat Jagdeo President of the Republic of GUYANA to the Sixty-Sixth Session of the United Nations General Assembly*, September 21, 2011, New York.
14. Geoffrey Marshall, *Constitutional Conventions* (Oxford: Clarendon Press, 1993), 32–33.
15. Vernon Bogdanor, *The Monarchy and the Constitution* (Oxford: Clarendon Press, 1997), 148.
16. Ibid.
17. Rodney Brazier, *Constitutional Practice*. 3rd ed. (Oxford: Oxford University Press, 1999), 39.

18. Harold Wilson, *The Governance of Britain* (London: Weidenfield & Nicholson/ Michael Joseph, 1979), 25–26.
19. A.V. Dicey, *Law of the Constitution*. 8th ed. (London: Macmillan & Co.), xlix.
20. For an account of these events see Bogdanor, 148 and 152. Also see Brazier, 33–34.
21. See Bogdanor, 148.
22. Report of the Constitution Commission (Trinidad: Trinidad and Tobago Printing and Packaging Co., 1974), para. 284.
23. *Twenty-Second Amendment to the United States Constitution*, 1951.
24. Sir Shridath Ramphal, 'Is the West Indies West Indian?' (The Eleventh Sir Archibald Nedd Memorial Lecture, Grenada, January 28, 2011).
25. Ibid., Part II.
26. Sheldon A. Mc Donald, 'The Caribbean Court of Justice: Enhancing the Law of International Organizations,' *Fordham International Law Journal* 27, issue 4 (2003): 929–1016.
27. Hamid Ghany, 'The Colonial Mindset and the Caribbean Court of Justice,' *Sunday Guardian*, April 27, 2014. The Sunday Guardian is a newspaper published in Trinidad and Tobago.
28. David Rogers, *By Royal Appointment* (London: Biteback Publishing Co., 2015), 325–32.
29. Ibid., 2–3.
30. Ibid., 10.
31. *UK National Archives, FCO 68/695*, J.R. Paterson to M. Preston, October 7, 1976.
32. Ibid., J.R. Paterson to J.C.E. Hyde, December 2, 1976.
33. Ibid., J.C.E. Hyde to J.R. Paterson, November 24, 1976.
34. See note 28 above.
35. *UK National Archives, FCO 68/695*. Copy of minute dated September 4, 1969 by Mr Duggan CCD to Mr Underwood.
36. Ibid. Copy of letter by Sir James McPetrie dated January 15, 1968.
37. *Parliamentary Debates, Hansard, House of Representatives*, August 11, 2014, 336.
38. *Parliamentary Elections Office* at peogrenada.org accessed on June 5, 2017.
39. SVG Government – Referendum results 2009 at https://en.wikipedia.org/wiki/ Vincentian_constitutional_referendum,_2009. Accessed June 5, 2017.
40. See note 3 above.

Bibliography

Books

Alexis, Francis. *Changing Caribbean Constitutions*. 2nd ed. Barbados: Carib Research & Publications, Inc., 2015.

Barnett, Lloyd. *The Constitutional Law of Jamaica*. Oxford: Oxford University Press, 1977.

Birch, Anthony. *The British System of Government*. 4th ed. London: George Allen and Unwin, 1980.

Bogdanor, Vernon. *The Monarchy and the Constitution*. Oxford: Clarendon Press, 1997.

Brazier, Rodney. *Constitutional Practice*. 3rd ed. Oxford: Oxford University Press, 1999.

Burns, Alan. *Parliament as an Export*. London: George Allen and Unwin, 1966.

Chamberlain, Mary. *Empire and Nation-building in the Caribbean: Barbados 1937–66*. Manchester: Manchester University Press, 2010.

Dale, William. *The Modern Commonwealth*. London: Butterworths, 1983.

Dicey, A.V. *Introduction to the Study of the Law of the Constitution*. 8th ed. London: Macmillan and Co. Ltd, 1927.

Haniff, Yusuff. *Speeches by Errol Barrow*. London: Hansib Publishing Ltd, 1987.

Harris, Carolyn. *Magna Carta and its Gifts to Canada*. Toronto: Dundurn Publishers, 2015.

Marshall, Geoffrey. *Constitutional Conventions*. Oxford: Clarendon Press, 1984.

———. *Constitutional Conventions*. Oxford: Clarendon Press, 1993.

Melton, James, and Robert Hazell, eds. *Magna Carta and its Modern Legacy*. Cambridge and New York: Cambridge University Press, 2015.

Nwabueze, B.O. *Constitutionalism in the Emergent States*. London: C. Hurst & Co., 1973.

Phillips, Fred. *Commonwealth Caribbean Constitutional Law*. London and Sydney: Cavendish Publishing Ltd, 2002.

Poser, Norman. *Lord Mansfield: Justice in the Age of Reason*. Montreal and Kingston: Mc Gill-Queen's University Press, 2013.

Robertson, Charles Grant, ed. *Select Statutes Cases and Documents*. London: Methuen & Co. Ltd, 1935.

Roberts-Wray, Kenneth. *Commonwealth and Colonial Law*. London: Stevens and Sons, 1966.

Robinson, Tracy. 'Our Inherent Constitution,' in *Transitions in Caribbean Law*, ed. David S. Berry and Tracy Robinson, 273. Kingston: The Caribbean Law Publishing Company, 2013.

Rogers, David. *By Royal Appointment*. London: Biteback Publishing Co., 2015.

de Smith, S.A. *The New Commonwealth and its Constitutions*. London: Stevens and Sons, 1964.

Sutton, Paul. *Forged from the Love of Liberty*. Trinidad: Longman Caribbean, 1981.

Wade, H.W.R. *Administrative Law*. Oxford: Oxford University Press, 1990.

Walvin, James. *The Zong : A Massacre, the Law and the End of Slavery*. New Haven and London: Yale University Press, 2011.

Williams, Eric. *Capitalism and Slavery*. London: Andre Deutsch, 1964.

———. *From Columbus to Castro: The History of the Caribbean 1492–1969*. First Vintage Books Edition, 1984. London: Andre Deutsch Ltd, 1970.

Wilson, Harold. *The Governance of Britain*. London: Weidenfield & Nicholson/Michael Joseph, 1979.

Journal Articles

Ghany, Hamid. 'The Evolution of the Power of Dissolution: The Ambiguity of Codifying Westminster Conventions in the Commonwealth Caribbean.' *The Journal of Legislative Studies* 5, issue 1 (1999): 54–76.

Madden, A.F. '"Not for Export": The Westminster Model of Government and British Colonial Practice.' *Journal of Imperial and Commonwealth History*, 8, issue 1 (1979).

McDonald, Sheldon A. 'The Caribbean Court of Justice: Enhancing the Law of International Organizations.' *Fordham International Law Journal* 27, issue 4 (2003): 929–1016.

Rathbone, Mark. 'The Human Rights Act: A Magna Carta for the Twenty-first Century?' *Political Studies Association Essay* (May 2014): 1–2.

Wolf-Phillips, L.A. 'A Long Look at the British Constitution.' *Parliamentary Affairs* 37, issue 4 (1984): 385–402.

Cases

Attorney General v Dumas [2017] UKPC 12.

Bribery Commissioner v Ranasinghe [1965] AC 172.

Campbell v Hall (1774) 1 Cowp. 204, 98 ER 1045.

Coard v Attorney General [2007] UKPC 7.

Esther Perreira vs The Chief Election Officer and Others. In the High Court of the Supreme Court of Judicature Petition Questioning An Election to the National Assembly under the National Assembly Validity of Elections Act Chapter 1:04. Elections holden on the 15th day of December, 1997. Judgment by Madam Justice C.M.C. Singh, January 15, 2001.

Esther Perreira vs The Chief Election Officer and Others. In the High Court of the Supreme Court of Judicature Petition Questioning An Election to the National Assembly under the National Assembly Validity of Elections Act Chapter 1:04. Elections holden on the 15th day of December, 1997. Order by Madam Justice C.M.C. Singh, January 26, 2001 and entered February 2, 2001.

Gregson v Gilbert (1783) *3 Doug. KB 232.*

In Re Application of the Attorney General for leave to apply for judicial review in re the appointment of James Alva Bain as a member of the Public Service Commission, High Court Action No.3260 of 1987.

Mitchell & Others v DPP and Another [1985] 3 WLR 724 (P.C.).

Somerset v Stewart (1772) 98 ER 499

Official Publications

Address by His Excellency Mr Bharrat Jagdeo President of the Republic of GUYANA to the Sixty-Sixth Session of the United Nations General Assembly, September 21, 2011, New York.

Belize Constitution (Fourth Amendment) Act, 2001, Act No. 39 of 2001.

Belize Constitution (Sixth Amendment) Act, 2010, Act No. 13 of 2008.

British Guiana: Report of the Constitutional Commission 1950–51 and Dispatch from the Secretary of State for the Colonies to the Governor of British Guiana dated October 6, 1951, Colonial No. 280, 1951. London: H.M.S.O., 1951.

Canadian Bill of Rights S.C. 1960, c. 44.

Canadian Charter of Rights and Freedoms, Part I of the Constitution Act, 1982, being Schedule B to the Canada Act 1982 (UK), 1982, c 11.

Caribbean Community Mission to Guyana, Herdmanston Accord, Signed in Guyana , January 17, 1998. Accessed at http://www.gecom.org.gy/pdf_laws/Herdmanston%20Accord.pdf on May 30, 2017.

Ceylon (Constitution) Order-in-Council 1946 S.R.& O.1946, 2248.

Ceylon: Report of the Commission on Constitutional Reform, Cmnd. 6677/1945. London: H.M.S.O., 1945.

The Colonial Office List for 1922. London: Waterlow and Sons Ltd.

Conference on the Closer Association of the British West Indian Colonies 1947, Cmnd. 7291/1948, Part One: Report. London, H.M.S.O., 1948.

Conference on the Closer Association of the British West Indian Colonies 1947, Cmnd. 7291/1948, Part Two: Proceedings. London, H.M.S.O., 1948.

Conference on the Reform of the Second Chamber, Cmnd.9038/1918. London: H.M.S.O., 1918.

Constitutional Proposals for Antigua, St. Kitts/Nevis/Anguilla, Dominica, St Lucia, St Vincent and Grenada, Cmnd. 2865/1965. London: H.M.S.O., 1966.

Constitution of Guyana 1980, Act No. 2/1980, Schedule.

Council of Europe, *The European Convention on Human Rights.* Strasbourg: Directorate of Information, 1952.

The Definitive Treaty of Peace and Friendship between his Britannick Majesty, the Most Christian King, and the King of Spain. Concluded at Paris the 10th day of February, 1763. To which the King of Portugal acceded on the same day (Articles VIII and IX). Located in the Lillian Goldman Law Library at Yale University in the Avalon Project and accessed on November 14, 2015 at http://avalon.law.yale.edu/18th_century/paris763.asp

Laws of Grenada, Act No. 1 of 1985.

Guyana Elections Commission, Report on the 1997 Elections. Accessed at http://www.gecom.org.gy/reports.html on May 30, 2017.

Laws of Guyana, Act No. 2 of 1980.

Laws of Guyana, Constitution of the Co-operative Republic of Guyana, Cap. 1:01.

Laws of Guyana, Constitution (Amendment) Act 2000, Act No. 2 of 2000.

Laws of Guyana, The Constitution Amendment (No. 3) Act No. 14 of 2000.

Laws of Jamaica: The Charter of Fundamental Rights and Freedoms (Constitutional Amendment) Act, 2011 (Act No. 12 of 2011).

Laws of Trinidad and Tobago, Act No.4 / 1976.

Laws of Trinidad and Tobago, Ch. 1:01, Schedule.

Laws of the United Kingdom 1 Geo. 1, St. 2, c. 38.

Laws of the United Kingdom 6 Geo. 3, c. 12.

Laws of the United Kingdom 28 & 29 Vict. c. 63.

Laws of the United Kingdom 39 & 40 Vict., c. 59.

Laws of the United Kingdom 1 & 2 Geo. 5, c. 13.

Laws of the United Kingdom 22 Geo. 5, c. 4

Laws of the United Kingdom 25 & 26 Geo. 5, c. 42.

Laws of the United Kingdom 1 Edw.8 & 1 Geo.6, c.38.

Laws of the United Kingdom 12, 13 & 14 Geo. 6, c. 103.

Laws of the United Kingdom 4 & 5 Eliz. 2, c. 63.

Laws of the United Kingdom 6 & 7 Eliz. 2, c. 21.

Laws of the United Kingdom 10 & 11 Eliz. 2, c. 54.

Laws of the United Kingdom 15 & 16 Eliz. 2, c. 4.

Laws of the United Kingdom 1998 c. 42.

Laws of the United Kingdom 1999 c. 34.

Laws of the United Kingdom 2005, c. 4.

Laws of the United Kingdom 2011, c. 14.

Malta Letters Patent S.R. & O. 1936, 3681.

Parliamentary Debates, Lords, 1961–62, Vol. 242, 859.

Parliamentary Elections Office at peogrenada.org accessed on June 5, 2017.

Parliament of Jamaica, The Constitution (Amendment) Bill No. 2, 2010.

Parliament of Trinidad and Tobago, The Constitution (Amendment) Bill 2014.

Proceedings of the Jamaican House of Representatives 1961–62, January 24, 1962.

Report by the Hon. Major E.F.L Wood, MP (Parliamentary Under Secretary of State for the Colonies) on his Visit to the West Indies and British Guiana, December 1921– February 1922, Cmnd. 1679/1922. London: H.M.S.O. 1922.

Report of the Barbados Constitutional Conference 1966, Cmnd. 3058/1966. London: H.M.S.O., 1966.

Report of the Chief Electoral Officer 1961, Referendum 1961. Kingston: Electoral Office, October 17, 1961.

Report of the Constitution Commission, 22nd January, 1974, Trinidad and Tobago. Trinidad: Trinidad and Tobago Printing and Packaging Ltd., 1974.

Report of the East Caribbean Federation Conference, 1962, Cmnd. 1746/1962. London: H.M.S.O., 1962.

The Report of the Jamaica Independence Conference 1962, Cmnd. 1638/1962. London: H.M.S.O., 1962.

Report of the Windward Islands Constitutional Conference 1966, Cmnd. 3021/1966. London, H.M.S.O., 1966.

The St Vincent and the Grenadines Constitution Bill 2009.

SVG Government – Referendum results 2009 at https://en.wikipedia.org/wiki/ Vincentian_constitutional_referendum,_2009. Accessed June 5, 2017.

Trinidad and Tobago Legislative Council, Report of the Constitution Reform Committee 1955, Council Paper No.16 /1956.

Trinidad and Tobago Legislative Council, Report from the Select Committee on a New Constitution for Trinidad and Tobago Council Paper No.11 / 1959.

Trinidad and Tobago, Meeting of Commentators on the Draft Constitution at the Queen's Hall, April 25–27, 1962.

Trinidad and Tobago Official Report, Debates of the Legislative Council, Vol. 9, 1958–59, 131.

Trinidad and Tobago, Parliamentary Debates, House of Representatives, Hansard, Vol.18, Session 1974–75.

Trinidad and Tobago, Parliamentary Debates, House of Representatives, Hansard, April 5, 2002.

Trinidad and Tobago, Parliamentary Debates, House of Representatives, Hansard, August 11, 2014.

Twenty-Second Amendment to the United States Constitution, 1951.

United Nations General Assembly, *Universal Declaration of Human Rights,* December 1948.

United Kingdom Hansard, House of Commons Debates February 6, 1962, Vol. 653 c. 230.

United Kingdom Hansard, House of Commons Debates June 30, 1966, Vol. 730 c. 2168.

United Kingdom Hansard, House of Commons Debates July 7, 1966, Vol. 731 c. 92W.

United Kingdom Hansard, House of Commons Debates October 28, 1966, Vol. 734 c. 1653.

United Kingdom National Archives CO 1031 / 1301, No. 198 Intel, Confidential, November 8, 1956.

United Kingdom National Archives, CO 1031/3278, Mordecai to Secretary of State for the Colonies, Immediate, Secret and Personal, Personal No. 196, September 20, 1961.

United Kingdom National Archives, CO 1031/3278, Mordecai to Secretary of State for the Colonies, Emergency, Secret and Personal, Personal No. 197, September 21, 1961.

United Kingdom National Archives, CO 1031/3278, Macleod to Macmillan, Secret, P.M. [61] 73, September 22, 1961.

United Kingdom National Archives, CO 1031/3278, Administrator, Antigua to Secretary of State for the Colonies, Immediate, Secret and Personal, Personal No. 19, September 25, 1961.

United Kingdom National Archives, CO 1031/3278, Hailes to Maudling, P.M. 12/016, October 17, 1961.

United Kingdom National Archives, CO 1031/3278, Maudling to Hailes, Confidential, No. 992, October 24, 1961.

United Kingdom National Archives, CO 1031/3278, Secret and Personal, Note by Dr. A. Lewis, November 9, 1961.

United Kingdom National Archives, British Cabinet Conclusions, CC(62) 11th Conclusions, February 6, 1962.

United Kingdom National Archives, CO 1031 / 3226, Explanatory Memorandum by the Constitutional Adviser to the Cabinet on the Draft Independence Constitution for Trinidad and Tobago, April 16, 1962.

United Kingdom National Archives, PREM 13/1326, Letter from Douglas Williams to M.H.M. Reid, June 29, 1966.

United Kingdom National Archives, PREM 13/1326, Handwritten note by M.H.M. Reid addressed to the Prime Minister on the Letter from Douglas Williams to M.H.M. Reid, June 29, 1966.

United Kingdom National Archives, PREM 13/1326, Confidential Memorandum by the Colonial Secretary attached to the Letter from Douglas Williams to M.H.M. Reid, June 29, 1966.

United Kingdom National Archives, PREM 13/1326, Internal Confidential Note from A.M. Palliser to Prime Minister Harold Wilson, July 1, 1966.

United Kingdom National Archives, PREM 13/1326, Handwritten note by Harold Wilson addressed to A.M. Palliser on the Internal Confidential Note from A.M. Palliser to Harold Wilson, July 1, 1966.

United Kingdom National Archives, PREM 13/1326, Confidential memorandum from A.M. Palliser to A.P.H.T. Cumming-Bruce dated July 1, 1966.

United Kingdom National Archives, PREM 13/1326, A.M. Palliser to A.P.H.T. Cumming-Bruce, July 4, 1966.

United Kingdom National Archives, PREM 13/1326, A.H. Poynton to Michael Adeane, July 26, 1966.

United Kingdom National Archives, PREM 13/1326, Michael Adeane to A.H. Poynton, July 27, 1966.

United Kingdom National Archives, FCO 68/695, J.R. Paterson to M. Preston, October 7, 1976.

United Kingdom National Archives, FCO 68/695, J.C.E. Hyde to J.R. Paterson, November 24, 1976.

United Kingdom National Archives, FCO 68/695, J.R. Paterson to J.C.E. Hyde, December 2, 1976.

United Kingdom National Archives, FCO 68/695, Copy of minute dated September 4, 1969 by Mr Duggan CCD to Mr Underwood.

United Kingdom National Archives, FCO 68/695, Copy of letter by Sir James McPetrie dated January 15, 1968.

Orders-in-Council

The Antigua and Barbuda Constitution Order 1981, S.I. 1981/No. 1106.

The Bahamas Independence Order 1973, S.I. 1973/No. 1080.

Barbados Independence Order 1966, S.I. 1966/No. 1455.

Belize Independence Order 1981, S.I. 1981/No. 1107.

The Commonwealth of Dominica Constitution Order 1978, S.I. 1978/No. 1027.

The Dominica Termination of Association Order 1978, S.I. 1978/No. 1031.

Grenada Constitution Order 1973, S.I. 1973/No. 2155.

The Guyana Independence Order 1966, S.I. 1966/No.575.

The Jamaica (Constitution) Order-in-Council 1944 (S.I. 1944/No. 1215).

The Jamaica (Constitution) Order in Council 1959 (S.I. 1959/No. 862).

Jamaica (Constitution) Order in Council 1962, S.I. 1962/No. 1550.

St Kitts-Nevis Constitution Order 1983, S.I. 1983/No. 881.

The St Lucia Constitution Order 1978, S.I. 1978/No.1901.

St Vincent Constitution Order 1979, S.I. 1979/No. 916.

Trinidad and Tobago (Constitution) Order in Council 1950, S.I. 1950/No. 510.

Trinidad and Tobago (Constitution) (Amendment) Order in Council 1956, S.I. 1956/No. 835.

The Trinidad and Tobago (Constitution) Order in Council 1961, S.I. 1961, No. 1192.

The Trinidad and Tobago (Constitution) Order in Council 1962, S.I. 1962 / No. 1875.

The West Indies (Federation) Order in Council 1957, S.I. 1957/No. 1364.

Monographs

People's National Movement. *Election Manifesto: General Elections 1961*. Port-of-Spain: P.N.M. Publishing Co. Ltd., 1961.

Newspapers

Ghany, Hamid. 'The Colonial Mindset and the Caribbean Court of Justice.' *Sunday Guardian*, April 27, 2014. The *Sunday Guardian* is a newspaper published in Trinidad and Tobago.

Sunday Chronicle. April 1, 2001. The *Sunday Chronicle* is a newspaper published in Guyana.

The *Times*. December 19, 1923. The *Times* is a newspaper published in the United Kingdom.

The *Times*. May 11, 1974. The *Times* is a newspaper published in the United Kingdom.

Pamphlets

Williams, Eric. *Constitution Reform in Trinidad and Tobago*. Public Affairs Pamphlet No. 2. Port-of-Spain: Teachers' Educational and Cultural Association, 1955.

Public Lectures

Ramphal, Shridath. 'Is the West Indies West Indian?' The Eleventh Sir Archibald Nedd Memorial Lecture, Grenada, January 28, 2011.

Theses

Ghany, Hamid A. 'Constitution-making in the Commonwealth Caribbean with special Reference to Trinidad and Tobago'. PhD Thesis, London University, 1987.

Index